Hip Hop's Hostile Gospel

Studies in Critical Research on Religion

Haymarket Books is proud to be working with Brill Academic Publishers (www.brill.nl) to republish the *Studies in Critical Research on Religion* book series in paperback editions. This peer-reviewed book series offers insights into our current reality by exploring the content and consequences of power relationships under capitalism, and by considering the spaces of opposition and resistance to these changes that have been defining our new age. Our full catalog of *SCRR* volumes can be viewed at https://www.haymarketbooks.org/series_collections/6-studies-in-critical-research-in-religion.

Series Editor
Warren S. Goldstein, Center for Critical Research on Religion (U.S.A.)

Editorial Board
Christopher Craig Brittain, University of Toronto (Canada)
Heather Eaton, Saint Paul University (Canada)
Titus Hjelm, University College London (U.K.)
Darlene Juschka, University of Regina (Canada)
Lauren Langman, Loyola University Chicago (U.S.A.)
George Lundskow, Grand Valley State University (U.S.A.)
Kenneth G. MacKendrick, University of Manitoba (Canada)
Andrew M. McKinnon, University of Aberdeen (U.K.)
Sara Pike, California State University, Chico (U.S.A)
Dana Sawchuk, Wilfrid Laurier University (Canada)

Advisory Board
William Arnal, University of Regina (Canada)
Roland Boer, University of Newcastle (Australia)
Jonathan Boyarin, Cornell University (U.S.A.)
Jay Geller, Vanderbilt University (U.S.A.)
Marsha Hewitt, University of Toronto (Canada)
Michael Löwy, Centre National de la Recherche Scientifique (France)
Eduardo Mendieta, Penn State University (U.S.A.)
Rudolf J. Siebert, Western Michigan University (U.S.A.)
Rhys H. Williams, Loyola University Chicago (U.S.A.)

Hip Hop's Hostile Gospel

A Post-Soul Theological Exploration

Daniel White Hodge

Haymarket Books
Chicago, IL

First published in 2016 by Brill Academic Publishers, The Netherlands.
© 2016 Koninklijke Brill NV, Leiden, The Netherlands

Published in paperback in 2018 by
Haymarket Books
P.O. Box 180165
Chicago, IL 60618
773-583-7884
www.haymarketbooks.org

ISBN: 978-1-60846-845-4

Trade distribution:
In the U.S. through Consortium Book Sales, www.cbsd.com
In the UK, Turnaround Publisher Services, www.turnaround-uk.com
In Canada, Publishers Group Canada, www.pgcbooks.ca
All other countries, Ingram Publisher Services International, intlsales@perseusbooks.com

Cover design by Jamie Kerry of Belle Étoile Studios.

This book was published with the generous support of Lannan Foundation and the Wallace Action Fund.

Library of Congress Cataloging-in-Publication Data is available.

Contents

Series Editor Preface   VII
Preface   VIII
Acknowledgements   XIII

Introduction: Hip Hop's Complexity & Theological Intricacy   1
    The Quest for God in Hip Hop   4
    The Study of Hip Hop Culture   9
    Hip Hop's Theology: An Oxymoron?   13
    The Hostility of A Gospel   22
    The Research & Background   26
        Chapters   28

1   Context, Societal Change, & the Construct of Hip Hop Culture   30
    The Social Conditions of the 'Hood   32
    The Post-soul Emergence   40
        Soul & Post-soul Variations   41
    Hip Hop & Postmodernism   47
        4 Key Elements of Hip Hop & Postmodernism   50
    Chapter Summary   52

2   God in the Cypher: Theological Narratives in Hip Hop   53
    Theological Inferences   57
        A Tribe Called Quest   57
        Digable Planets   62
        Nas   68
        Bone Thugs-N-Harmony   73
        Kanye West   77
        Ice Cube   82
        Kendrick Lamar   86
        Lauryn Hill   90
    Chapter Summary   94

3   Hip Hop's Totemic Prophet: Tupac Amaru Shakur   95
    Tupac & the Post-soul Context   99
    Locating Tupac's Gospel   108
    Toward a Theology of Tupac the Post-soul Prophet   113
    Chapter Summary   114

4 **Violence, Death, & Suffering in Hip Hop Context**   116
    Violence in Context   122
    Processing Pain & Violence   128
    Contemplating Violence in Context   131
    Transmediated Violence & A "Just God"   142
    Chapter Summary   147

5 **No Jesus in the Wild: Race, & The Jesuz Figure**   149
    The Hip Hop Community & The Jesus Figure   160
        The Outlawz & Black Jesuz   166
    Toward Sensationalized Images of the Hip Hop Jesus   172
    Chapter Summary   174

6 **Conclusions: What is Theology & Spirituality in Hip Hop?**   175
    Five Central Typologies of Hip Hop's Theological Sensibilities   186
    Hip Hop's Post-Soul Centrality   193
        The Neo-Secular Sacred within Hip Hop   196
    Further Research in Hip Hop & Spirituality   199

Appendix 1: *The Source* **Magazine's Top 100 Rap Albums**   203

Appendix 2: Top 25 List Generated from Interviewees of Hip Hop Theologically Influenced Artists   206

Bibliography   207
Index   220

Series Editor Preface

There has been a long-standing tension between theology and the social scientific study of religion. Daniel White Hodge in his book on *The Hostile Gospel* successfully bridges this gap. He provides us with a post-soul critical theology that is more palatable to those on the secular side. His work is based on interviews with both Hip Hop artists and Hip Hop community members, including an analysis of the theological and social content of the artists' lyrics. The Gospel of Hip Hop is rightfully hostile; it expresses the anger, rage and frustration of those living in the deteriorated social conditions of the Ghetto. In its place, it provides us with an image of a bad-ass dope smokin', drinkin' and cussin' Black Jesuz who is counter-hegemonic and has the potential to resonate with all of us.

> *Warren S. Goldstein, Ph.D.*
> Center for Critical Research on Religion
> *www.criticaltheoryofreligion.org*

Preface

Exploratory in nature, this study takes into account the Christological, theological, and ecclesiological ruminations of a selected group of Hip Hop and rap song lyrics, interviews, and interviews from those defined as Hip Hoppers. The aim of this examination is to ascertain what a Hip Hop theology of community might entail, how it may look, and what it could feel like. The central premise are questions: does a Hip Hop 'theology' even fit? Is there an actual motif which Hip Hoppers are espousing within the supernatural realm? The reader should keep these questions in mind while reading this work, as the result of the exploration of the material is revealed.

This study concerns itself with just over 8,500 songs. Its timespan is between 1987–2011, and it contains interviews from those in the Hip Hop community. It uses Spencer's theomusicological methodology as a framework of analysis. This book attempts to explore the socio-theological messages of Hip Hop culture within an urban post-industrial framework. It examines how new theological models and paradigms, formed from Black Theological perspectives (James Cone, J. Cameron Carter, and Anthony Pinn), emerge within Hip Hop culture and society in the wake of political, racial, and socioeconomic inequality. It uses a critical approach to examine how Hip Hop developed its theology in the womb of suffering, inequality, and social injustice, to provide some type of cohesion. In addition, this work seeks to investigate the various theological features and facets of Hip Hop culture. These features and facets exist in Hip Hop's lyrics, videos, cultural norms, historical foundations, and the context in which the song, the album, and the artist reside and create works, in response to political, racial, and socioeconomic inequality. This is done as a means to study Hip Hop and to enhance the growing body of scholarship in Hip Hop Studies. Further, this study serves as an initial discussion of the Christological and eschatological ruminations within Hip Hop, as I will explore in later chapters. It also delves into a discussion of how Hip Hoppers view the nature of the divine, the nature of humanity and how the two interact, and thus how a Hip Hop theology is formulated within the culture.

A mixed methods approach was adopted in this study. First, the following data sources are used to determine the context in which the albums were created: demographic and cultural data from the U.S. Bureau of the Census, and select interviews from members within the Hip Hop community (30 were conducted).

The second of the mixed methods approach is that this study is a theomusicological study using the methodological approaches established by Jon

Michael Spencer (1991b, 1992b, 1995, 1997).[1] Theomusicology is defined as "…a musicological method for theologizing about the sacred, the secular, and the profane, principally incorporating thought and method borrowed from anthropology, sociology, psychology, and philosophy" (Spencer 1991b, 3). It is, as Cheryl Kirk-Duggan and Marlon Hall state, "Music as spiritual practice…[to] hear the challenges and evils in the church and the world as the music reveals" (2011, 77). What distinguishes theomusicology from other methods and disciplines such as ethnomusicology[2] is:

> Its analysis stands on the presupposition that the religious symbols, myths, and canon of the culture being studied are the theomusicologist's authoritative/normative sources. For instance, while the Western music therapist would interpret the healing of the biblical patriarch Saul under the assuagement of David's lyre as a psychophysiological phenomena, the theomusicologist would *first* take into account the religious belief of the culture for whom the event had meaning. The theomusicological method is therefore one that allows for scientific analysis, but primarily within the limits of what is normative in the ethics, religion, or mythology of the community of believers being studied
>
> SPENCER 1991b, 3–4

Therefore the theomusicologist is concerned with multi-level data within the context of the people they study, and subsequently analyzes the material within the proper time, culture, and context in which it was created. The three approaches of theomusicology are:

1. The Sacred: not only those elements within a society that are set apart and forbidden for ritual, but those elements within the given society and culture that are aspiring toward both a pious stance, and search for deity.

---

1 Created initially as a discipline, theomusicology is a methodological inquiry as it seeks to understand the theological inferences within the studied culture's music. This method has been used by scholars to examine other areas of music and popular culture such as issues of sexuality and promiscuity (McRobbie 1995; Epstein 2001); understanding poetry in context (Faulkner 2007); understanding the basic elements of Hip Hop spirituality (Spencer 1992a); examining the sacred and profane within Black music (Costen 1991); and examining it as a methodology in practice (Reed 1991).
2 There is no universal or singular definition of Ethnomusicology, as William Darity states; several words come to mind for ethnomusicology such as sound, music, performance, context, and culture. For some, it is the study of music in culture, or, more broadly, the study in context (2008, 20–22).

2. The Secular: those items which are designated by a given society and culture who have little to no connection with a form of deity.
3. The Profane: those areas in a society labeled or given the designation of being outside the given morals, codes, ethics, and values established as "good" and/or "right" by the society and culture being studied.[3]

This trinary approach best discloses the nature of the religion within the Hip Hop community. Theomusicology rises above simple lyrical analysis and the imagining of what the artists might be attempting to say, and goes into the complex arena of where the sacred, the secular, and the profane intersect. This means that songs which express an explicit sexuality might, in fact, be connecting to a spiritual realm. Theomusicology broadens the discussion of religion within Hip Hop contexts and asks the question "What is the Hip Hop community saying in the context in which the music, the art, the album, and the artist were created?" The following is also used in this study in order to provide a clearer picture of Hip Hop's theological construction:[4]

- Cultural context
- Political climate
- Artists' upbringing and background
- Album cover and art
- Cultural era
- Religious landscape
- Geographic location

In their article "Theomusicology and Christian Education: Spirituality and The Ethics of Control in the Rap of MC Hammer," N. Lynne Westfield and Harold Dean Trulear state:

> Theomusicology treats black music in a holistic manner and secularity as a context for the sacred and profane rather than as the antithesis of the sacred ... As such, theomusicology is a tool for us to move beyond the simplistic notions of 'good' and 'bad' that are uncritically used to characterize black secular music and especially rap music, and to help us

---

3 In addition to these three definitions, this book will explore the use of these definitions of the sacred, secular, and the profane. Sacred: those things that are divine or could be construed as divine; the secular: that which is devoid of a God or lacks in spirituality; and the profane: that which is nefarious, oblique, and at times, contrary to 'good.'
4 Spencer asserts that these areas are crucial in the understanding of the theological message (1990, 1991b) at the time the song was created.

> develop an understanding of the meaning system under construction by African American youths.
>
> TRULEAR and WESTFIELD 1994, 219–220

Similarly, this book examines theology and spiritual pursuits beyond moralism established by dominant structures, and asks complex questions about God (or Gods) and the performativity within religious domains.

Within theomusicology, there are three analytical approaches that this project will utilize: descriptive, normative, and predictive (Spencer 1990, 1991b). *Descriptive theomusicology* is a non-judgmental approach to the culture, music, and people being studied and allows the space for the researcher to take in the bulk of data for what it is, rather than placing a judgment label on it (e.g. perceived sexual behaviors, 'bad language'). It also examines the creators of the music and the consumers within the context of it. In this project, Chapters One and Two will be part of the descriptive analysis.

Normative theomusicology continues the analysis previously listed while comparing the tenets of canonical authority that the culture being studied describes as a norm and the broader standardized canon. In other words, normative theomusicology examines the sacred texts that a culture—in this case Hip Hop—determines as canonical and compares that with what, say, the "Bible" is discussing. Normative theomusicology allows this project to delve into a canonical space that Hip Hop may or may not be espousing. Chapters Three, Four, and Five will be a part of this analysis.

Lastly, *predictive theomusicology* is an analysis of the future state of affairs to which music speaks or directs a society and/or culture (Spencer 1991b, 4). Attempting to avoid condemnatory polemic statements, this book will offer this analysis in Chapter 6, the conclusion, and begin to assert what a Hip Hop theology might in fact look like. Predictive theomusicology is important as it establishes what the culture may actually be saying about God, or the lack of a God. As Spencer states:

> Analogously, the theomusicologist recognizes that human beings not only exist *in time*—in the present that is shaped by the past and perceptions of the future—but that during ritual they are caught in another, numinous time: in black religious ritual, because time stands still, and in African religious ritual, because time progresses counterclockwise to the time of the ancestors. Hence, while musicology historically examines music created *at one time*, and ethnomusicology anthropologically investigates music contemporary ethnic cultures produce in *present time*, theomusicology theologically studies music produced in the *diety's time*—the 'wholly informed, the pure mood' (1991b, 6).

Here, Spencer discusses the prominence of such a study, and within a space that is constantly changing, such as Hip Hop, the predictive analysis is vital. Spencer is also correct in asserting that theomusicology provides a more balanced approach to understanding the theological messages within music. As a culture and society such as Hip Hop grows, it is important to engage in a predictive nature and allow its members to speak of the direction in which it may possibly be headed.

Conversely, lyrical analysis limits the scope of this study and does not produce a complete picture of what Hip Hop is communicating religiously. I must interject here that from a rhetorician's perspective, word/lyric is imperative, and needed for study. However, to place meaning on a lyric, something the song never intended to say, is problematic on many levels. I seek to establish the "why": why an artist would construct an album like Nas' "God's Son," or Remy Ma's articulation of a female version of Jesus, and the social conditions which aided in creating those works. Rhetoricians, I would imagine, are interested in this too. Moreover, lyrical analysis requires an ethnographic dimension to it in order to grasp clearly what the artist was trying to implement in that song. And while a multitude of lyrics will be examined in this book, the analysis uses theomusicology and its trinary approach, while taking into account the context and environment in which the song/album was created.[5]

This study, therefore, investigates Hip Hop from a theological and spiritual standpoint. While the ever growing field of Hip Hop studies begins to explore religion in Hip Hop, the present work seeks to address this and develop new theologies/theories that fit both an urban and Hip Hop context. While the formal discipline of theology in the United States focuses on Christianity,[6] and this book takes a Judeo Christian approach, it will also look at the influence of Islam, Five Percenters and Rastafarian religions on Hip Hop. This book seeks to add to the study of Theology in the U.S., thus the book will return to a discussion of whether or not a post-Christian Theology has been formulated by Hip Hop culture.

---

5 It must be noted that this methodology, while it is robust and will provide greater insight, will not fully produce a shift in what we understand theology to be.
6 Arguably, within the U.S. the study of God, theology, has been mostly relegated to the study of the Christian God (e.g. Miller 2013b; Pinn 2002; Reed 2003). Most universities offering degree programs in Theology go to great lengths to describe the Christian religion and pay little to no attention to other religious interpretations of God. Some Hip Hop artists found their first critique of the God language as a critique of the Christian religious expression of God talk. Others have used the medium of Hip Hop to further explain misinformation and other reflections of theology (Nation of Islam, Five Percenters, etc.).

Acknowledgements

No book is written in solitude, at least from a macro process perspective. This book is the product of six years' worth of editing, re-writing, author changes, and more editing. During that time, I underwent a stay in the basement of my in-laws' home as a result of unemployment; a situation where my daughter was ill and needed hospital care; a mental crisis; bankruptcy; and a move half way across the country. When I first began this research, I had anticipated a finish date of August 2011. But, as 'luck'—or whatever existential label you wish to give it—would have it, that journey was a starting point and this book took on several versions, and at one point I had a co-author who then had to leave the project. What a time, indeed! Getting this book to completion felt like finishing another very long and arduous dissertation, a second one in which I could not see the finish line for quite some time. Yet, the finish line is no less sweet and very much welcomed!

The state of Hip Hop Studies is at an exponential growth period. Emerging voices such as Christopher Emdin, Julius Bailey, and Fanon Wilkins have given the field of Hip Hop a much broader and solid foundation with works focusing on pedagogy, communication studies, and even using Hip Hop to teach in s.t.e.m. Yet, while the field of Hip Hop Studies has grown, a silent but equally powerful voice has begun to emerge in a sub-field called Hip Hop and Religion. Scholars such as Monica Miller, Anthony Pinn, Christopher Driscoll, Ebony Utley, Andre Johnson, Travis Harris, Christina Zanfagna, and Biko Gray have shaped a discipline that, at the beginning of this book's journey, would have been almost laughable in some academic circles. But not anymore. Over the past five years, six major volumes have been completed with even more on the near horizon. These volumes take the study of Hip Hop in new directions by focusing on the religious and spiritual aspects of a culture that is still emerging, with complexities and nuances which only scholarship can purge forth. I humbly submit my volume into this canon and diverse conversation. Tricia Rose's landmark text in Hip Hop Studies cited a new direction for the investigation into Hip Hop; the sub-field of Hip Hop and Religion promises to do the same thing.

And so, with that, I wish to start by thanking my mom, Beki Virgen. Without her decisive and difficult decision to move from a racist and bigoted West Texas rural town, my voice might have never been heard. What she did as a single mother is still phenomenal to me and I cannot thank her enough for the sacrifice she made to make sure I did not end up a statistic, or even worse, in a mediocre state of life. Thank you mom! I owe you a lot! To my grandmother,

Dede, God rest her soul. She provided the stability for me in life to do the things I needed to do to succeed. With a seventh grade education, she was one of the wisest woman I have known; patience and love garnished her temperance and she always showed nothing but support for my endeavors—even when those endeavors were not always the wisest for me. Thank you Dede! You are so missed and I wish we could still talk about God, life, and just laugh about some old Mexican jokes just one more time. Godspeed on your new journey!

I must thank North Park Universities Center For Youth Ministry Studies and the Biblical Theological &Youth Ministry department. Without the creative space, conversation, debate, and helpful funding, I imagine this book would still be in the draft stages. I would also like to thank my two supervisors: my former supervisor, Joe Jones, who continually encouraged me to pursue "things" outside the "box;" and my current supervisor, Michael Emerson, whose vast knowledge of demography, sociology, and religion have helped me shape some of the arguments here.

Thank you to my American Academy of Religion (AAR) community. AAR has been an oasis to me for many years and has provided the space for dialog, growth, and acceptance of ideas that did not fit into my evangelical circles. AAR and its acceptance of our group, Critical Approaches to Hip Hop & Religion (CAHHR), was a formative place not just for me, but to many new and soon-to come voices in the sub-field of Hip Hop and Religion. CAHHR has been a place where the ideas contained in this book have been shaped, argued, and engaged with. I am so grateful that we have an official environment in which to wrestle with our ideas, thoughts, debates, and theories concerning Hip Hop and Religion.

A special thank you to Alberto who designed the book cover and for your continued artistic eye. Keep on with the fight!

To my team at *The Journal Of Hip Hop Studies* (JHHS). Created and formed in 2012, JHHS is the backbone to the field of Hip Hop studies and offers both seasoned and emerging scholars a place to write, specifically about Hip Hop. Interdisciplinary by nature, JHHS is an exciting new journal and I thank all who have helped shape it and have helped in the formation of this book.

To my near and dear Hip Hop religious heads: Monica Miller, Chris Driscoll, Travis Harris, Anthony Pinn, Craig Detweiler, Ebony Utley, Christina Zanfagna, Efrem Smith, Phil Jackson, Soong-Chan Rah, Ralph Watkins, Jude Tiersma Watson, Roberta King, De'Anna Monique, Andre Johnson, Benji Rolsky, Marcus Simmons, Kamasi Hill, Roy Whitaker, Regina Bradley, Julius Dion Bailey, Earle Fisher, Diego Hunter, Josef Soret, Tom Beaudoin, Joseph Boston, Marcia Dawkins, and Matt Sheedy. Thank you to all of you for your thoughts, energy,

ACKNOWLEDGEMENTS

prayers, insights, and scholarship! I hope this book makes you proud of all our work.

Thank you to Deshonna Collier-Goubil, who, on an earlier version of this manuscript, provided content, voice, and direction. Thank you to my editor, Warren Goldstein, who had the vision and much patience to see this project through.

Last, but in no way or form the least, I would like to thank my daughter, Mahalia Joy White Hodge, whose daddy had to finish edits or write another chapter when she wanted to go out to the park, or play Star Wars. Thank you kiddo, for your patience, love, and continued questioning spirit! Keep it up, you'll need every ounce of it in life. Daddy loves you and is so proud of you for who you are now, and for what you will become! Thanks also to my wife, who has stuck with me through thick and thin, literally. Emily White Hodge, you are a blessing and light unto my life and path. Without your dogged determination—which I will admit I do not always appreciate in its fullness—I would have not gotten this far in life, nor would I have seen a new vision for my own life and writing. Thank you for being patient while I wrestled through another chapter, thank you for your insight when I was stuck, and thank you for your love that you have given so much of, over our marriage. I could not have done this project without you! This book is dedicated to our new season, our new path, and the struggle this book represents of an era in life. Much love!

Introduction: Hip Hop's Complexity & Theological Intricacy

> If you got religion, show some sign.
> GENEVA SMITHERMAN

∴

> Hip Hop is the last true folk art.
> MOS DEF

∴

> Only God can judge me, so I'm gone. Either love me or leave me alone.
> JAY Z

∴

Hip Hop is larger than the radio, commercialized artists, and record industry branding. It is a culture, a people, a movement, a growing community of people that live, breathe, eat, love, hate, and work just as anyone else does. Hip Hop cannot be easily understood or defined. It is complex and full of narratives that would blow away even the strongest anthropologist.[1] Hip Hop, in the words of KRS-One, is "something that is being lived" (2003).

I was five years old when I first recognized the power of Hip Hop. I had never heard lyrics, music, and prose that sounded like that. I never realized that an artist could be that direct and open with their artistic style. Moreover, I was made to feel that my own identity was validated in the music and that it was "okay" to be me. Living in a rural town in the center of Texas, one might think

---

1 Hip Hop studies is a growing field and therefore this research and this book is an exploratory study of the culture. Much more research needs to be done on the socio-sexual tendencies of Hip Hop, how male dominance in the church has affected Hip Hop's view of God, how the LGBTQ community engages God and rap, how global rap artists like the Iron Sheik (from Iraq) deconstruct neo-colonialism, and how atheism is dealt with within a Hip Hop construct.

that Hip Hop had no reach, but it did. I was able to witness the culture develop from a small group of grassroots artists in the Bronx. By the time I moved to the Bay Area in California, I saw the depth of the Hip Hop community, affectionately referred to as Bay Area Rap. These artists, who emerged onto the public scene, gave a voice to the oppression, anger, and frustration felt by many living in the post-industrial urban environment[2] during the crack era.[3] For many, Hip Hop became a discourse vehicle which echoed the concerns, anger, hate, love, pain, hope, vision, anxiety, desire, and joy which had gone unheard in the media. Hip Hop was, as Chuck D once said, "our CNN." It was the voice of a generation. That voice provided a place at the social table to create space for the turmoil being lived out across the America's ghettos (Moss 2007).

Through Hip Hop, one was able to realize the reprehensible common experience happening in the urban centers, and that one was not alone in that experience; it was a narrative that needed explaining and needed to be told. It was a narrative which would lay the ground for postmodern and post-soul[4] resistance for decades to come.[5] Hip Hop was, and still is, a way to construct thought, question authority, and express anger, frustration, hate, revolutionary worldviews, and rebellious spirits.

Additionally, Hip Hop created a space for people like myself to find a way in life. My life, especially during the crack era of the 1980s, was increasingly filled with messages such as be a "good" student and "turn the other cheek," but in my school there were White racist classmates who tried to beat me up every day during recess and after school. Doing well in school and getting good grades was difficult because my teachers lowered my grades unfairly. The idea that Blacks cannot score higher than their White peers was a reality. Thus,

---

2 This phrase was first raised by Nelson George (2004) to describe the acute forms of discrimination, oppression, and societal ailments experienced by those living in the inner city during the 1980s. This will be discussed later in Chapters 1 and 2.

3 This was the period between the years 1979–1991 for most of the U.S.'s urban areas. It was the height of the crack cocaine epidemic in the inner city (Boyd 2002; Floyd 1995; George 1990, 1992, 1998, 2004; Hassan 1996; Hodge 2009, 2010, Kitwana 2003; Oliver 2006; Ruskin 2009).

4 This term will be further defined in Chapter 2; it is used to describe the period and era which followed the soul era. Both of these terms, originated by Nelson George (1992), are contextualized for what postmodernism is for Black, Latino, Urban, and Hip Hop contexts and which includes such societal shifts as the Civil Rights Movement, The Migrant Farm Workers Movement, and the Black Power Movement—to name a few—which helped shape postmodern elements of current societal mores (See George 2004; Hodge 2009).

5 The civil unrest in Libya, Egypt, and Paris had Hip Hop as its core voice and used U.S. artists such as KRS-One, The Roots, Tupac Shakur, Lauryn Hill, and N.W.A. (among many others) as templates for social revolutions.

"doing good" meant surviving, often in a physical sense. So, Hip Hop created, and continues to create, a voice to push back on these types of double messages. It is a vehicle in which those who are questioning authority, challenging dominant narratives of normality, the disenfranchised and voiceless, can still find solace in a community of other likeminded people. It is a space in which communities can yell and be angry while eliciting violent images through song and lyrical prose. Hip Hop is a basic connection to that which looks, feels, talks, smells, laughs, cries, and moves, like *you*—the community of those living in oppressed or disenfranchised conditions.

Music, in its rawest form, is powerful. Ethnomusicologists Mark Slobin and Jeff Todd Titon contend that "...every human society has music. Music is universal; but its meaning is not" (Slobin and Titon 1984, 1). Therefore it is imperative that we study Hip Hop's musical meaning and expression in rap to better understand its theological message. Music speaks, but the context in which it was created—the socio-political, the socio-geographical, the socio-theological, and the time period—speaks as the artist crafts music from within that space (Costen 1991; Spencer 1991b). Thus, the context and culture in which music is born is a crucial part of its meaning, social nuance, rhythmic construction, and lyrical pathway. When music is able to transcend culture in a way that creates meaning for people, then there are aspects such as transcendental meaning, spiritual identity, and theological construction that are worth investigating. In other words, when you consider the societal and living conditions of urban enclaves within the United States, their history of development, the exclusion of Blacks from society for centuries, the ongoing issue of police brutality, and the rise of the prison industrial complex, it can be overwhelming and debilitating. Yet, Hip Hop culture does not back down. It delves into these issues while creating a space of identity and relevance for its listeners. One must foster an understanding of the cultural conditions, context, geographical location, political atmosphere, social events, cultural background, and theological conditions in which a Hip Hop artist chooses to write their song. This allows for a clearer and much more rigorous understanding of to whom and "what" the music is speaking.

Music has always been about expressing time and space within a current context and current setting (Spencer 1991b, 3–5). Music sets moods, creates atmospheres, and can transport you to another time and dimension. Its very rhythm can take you to the same place or taste that you experienced when you first heard that particular song. Music is just that powerful.

Therefore, it should be no surprise that rap is such a powerful medium for so many people. As Murray Forman has noted, "Hip-hop has evolved into one of North America's most influential youth oriented forces. It provides a sustained articulation of the social partitioning of race and the diverse experiences of being young and black or Latino in North America" (Forman 2002, 3). When DJ Jazzy Jeff and The Fresh Prince won the first rap Grammy in 1989, the entire music industry was changed and it marked the dawn of a new era for both Hip Hop and America. Hip Hop and rap remain a powerful social and musical might in the shaping of American pop culture.

The Quest for God in Hip Hop

The contextualized persona of God is not novel. Civilizations have continually attempted to make God, or the gods, more accessible and to have "human like" characteristics (Glock and Stark 1965; Johnstone 2009; Yinger 1957). This apotheosis approach is a fundamental attempt to create meaning and context for a supernatural world, particularly in oppressive conditions (c.f. Southern 1983; Cone 1990). A sense of life, meaning, context, identity, and space are key elements to understanding how religion fits into a person's life (Corrigan and Hudson 2010). Moreover, these areas represent pathways for societies to create a spiritual journey and experience with God.[6] It was what the original thirteen colonies—albeit in a colonizing manner—were reaching for in their attempts to contextualize God in the "new promised land" (Corrigan & Hudson 2010, 35–40). Further, religion in society is typically an effort to make some type of meaning and create space for God and the self (Yinger 1957; Johnstone 2009). Narratives about God and higher powers, allegorical rhetoric, and the language of a "Gospel" (Wilder 1999) are all crucial elements when a spiritual journey is being forged. Further, within the narrative dialogue about God, good, evil, sacred, profane, and questions of purpose, a deeper meaning of God can be had when the space is given to explore these areas. Therefore, the process of finding meaning is crucial in the socialization process of an individual into any given society.[7]

---

6 This would also connect with Stark and Glock's (1968) observations of religious movements' five dimensions: belief, practice, experience, knowledge, and consequences.

7 These socialization processes also carry with them certain tags such as class, according to Rodney Stark and William Bainbridge (1985). Power has a way of wielding its force into the way people find religion and do religion; Stark and Bainbridge assert that "...we must realize that this [understanding religion] can be influenced greatly by power" (p. 11). Moreover, they contend that power means the ability to gain rewards and it stands to reason that the powerful will tend to monopolize the rewards available from religion (p.11). This is an area in which I am most interested—especially in the telling of sacred narrative (e.g. whose sacred narrative is told, who are the "devils" within that narrative, and who are the "saints"?) This is something with which I will discuss in Chapter 4.

As important as these processes of socialization and religion are, hegemonic power structures weave their way in and create obscured narratives, allegorical notions, and skewed philosophies of what is right and wrong. In this sense, those who possess the most power, access, and resources are the ones who control the narratives, sacred texts, images of the deity, and morality/immorality, thereby generating a religious supremacy.[8] It typically works to oppress and subvert the voice of those who would dare to create a parallel contextual narrative. Hip Hop, at its core, rejects this hegemonic mantra. In the urban post-industrial living conditions, White conservative, heterosexual, upper class Christianity is severely impotent. The version of God within this theology does not work for everyone—even though numerous attempts are made to make it work—and areas such as suffering, pain, racism, sexism, classism, and death tend to be deficient. Therefore, Hip Hop creates a new way for God to be attained. Murdered rapper and now Hip Hop Saint (Dyson 2001; Hodge 2009) Tupac Amaru Shakur argues this:

> I feel like I'm doing God's work. Because, these ghetto kids ain't God's children? And I don't see no missionaries coming through there. So I'm doing God's work. While Reverend Jackson do his shit up in the middle class and he go to the White house and have dinner and pray over the president, I'm up in the 'hood doing my work with my folks.[9]

Here, Tupac asserts there is already a discrepancy between the classes and who is given "God" and who is not. Tupac takes it upon himself to create a space for those who do not fit the dominant vision of piety to come to God in their own way.

In that same sense, Spice 1 begins to question how a God can allow such violence:

> But now the street is a place
> you could be swallowed by death

---

8   This supremacy often involves race, gender, and class. Thereby, White, male, upper middle class Christian heterosexuals are typically the most favorable of "Christian" models which is what scholars such as Marcella Althaus-Reid (2000, 2004), Carter Heyward (1999), James Cone (1997a, 1997b), and the social activist and public intellectual Frantz Fanon (1968) vehemently argue against. Instead, they attempt to create not only parallel narratives, but sub-narratives which contextualize God and create stories which do not get heard in the public sphere.
9   Taken from an interview done on BET roughly around the mid-1990s.

> Brothas takin each other's lives
> And goin to REST IN PEACE
> I wonder if heaven got a ghetto
> My cousin died last year
> And I still can't let go
> I walk the streets of my city of my neighborhood
> Seein dope fiends livin off can goods[10]

We see a hermeneutic here which questions the existence of a heaven in the midst of such pain and suffering. Yet, the heaven that Spice 1 has constructed has been that from the dominant culture, therefore he wonders how this type of lifestyle even fits in the worldview of a God who seems to bless those who are "good." He further raps about the racial implications of all this:

> From across the seas comes cocaine
> But you never seen a black man fly the plane
> Look at the news: a young black death
> Was it drug related, take a guess
> I flash when I look in the mirror black
> Cause my reflection is a 9 millimeter Gat
> I think about genocide
> And have thoughts of my homies who died
> Everybody backstabbin
> But I ain't the one to talk I'm into gafflin
> Death gives a shit about your color
> But yet I see mo dead young brothas

Thus, we can therefore envision the possibility of beginning to see the implications of a theology that becomes a discourse, and rhetoric to re-imagine authority—specifically White hegemonic authority—and suggest a reworking of what theology is and does; more specifically, what it is and what it does for those oppressed, and those who are not part of the dominant structure.

Hip Hop culture, thus, creates an innovative and more creative space for those in disenfranchised spaces to rework their theological and religious ideologies. Theology and religion have, traditionally and historically, been a space and place in which to theorize for those in power, authority, and dominant positions. But Hip Hop, part of a post-soul and postmodern ethos, is a form

---

10   *Spice 1* (1992) "Welcome to the Ghetto."

in which original and more inspired ways of "finding God" can be sought. In other words, Hip Hop culture is a religious and theological meaning-making center for those who still want to seek a God, but do not trust or care for the traditional spaces in which to do that.

Charles Long (1987, 444) writes, "Religion is thus understood to be pervasive not only in religious institutions, but in all the dimensions of cultural life." Phenomenologist of religion Gerardus Van der Leeuw puts this in a more laconic and succinct way when he argues that "ultimately, all culture is religious" (1963, 679). If this then is true, Hip Hop culture, and its artists (M.C.'s, graffiti, dance, art), can provide a pervasive contextualized form of religious and theological discourse with the abstractness and direct content of their work. Hip Hop is attempting to reformulate theology and how culture in general is attempting to create a more relevant and less dogmatic view of a God or Gods.[11] Hip Hop culture and community is endeavoring to reconstitute a theological and religious narrative that is more relative and customizable to its community using the elements that Long and Van der Leeuw are already stating.

With this in mind, Robin Sylvan poses the question of inquiry that fuels much of this scholarship into Hip Hop and religion, because "What happens, however, when the encounter with the numinous, the religious experience, can no longer find adequate expression in the traditional religious institutions provided by the culture?" (2002, 5). Thus, this quest for God in Hip Hop culture is not without its social and cultural pursuits through and in the vernacular of religious discourse—as noted in the lyrics by Spice 1 and Tupac. Artists such as these are attempting to work through pain, suffering, and violence in completely different ways than, say, Marin Luther King or Billy Graham. While both of these cultural and social figures are vastly different, their social acceptance, and "keep hope alive" ethos are very similar; "I have a dream" and "The good news of Jesus" both create meta-narratives of hope. Yet, what does one do when there is no hope? What does one say to the relentless drum of inequality, racism, police brutality, and generational disconnect? "Hope" in that sense will look very different; it will appear in the vernacular of rap artists

---

11 This is not without its own argument. Is all of Hip Hop religious? Is Hip Hop, in turn, a religion in and of itself as someone like KRS-One would argue? How does one deal with the direct and acute nihilism, sexism, misogyny, and pure capitalism within the genre and culture? As such, one might argue again that religion and "church" are filled with those items already; Hip Hop merely makes use of them. But does that make them "okay?" Does that make something like sexism any less potent? These are areas needing further exploration as we look into the religious and theological dimensions of and within Hip Hop.

who present a more realistic attempt at finding God in times of trouble and woe. For a religion to "work" and be relevant for the people at hand, religion—socially shared and organized ways of thinking, feeling, and acting which concern ultimate meanings about the existence of the supernatural or "beyond" (Cunningham and Kelsay 2010, 5)—must also concern itself with both the social and cultural frameworks which construct the religious experience for the said "culture," and the situations in which those people find themselves (e.g. poverty, homelessness, depression). Thus, Hip Hop culture, for the purpose of this book, engages the issues and problems within its culture to create alternate theological and spiritual structures which are applicable and contextual for the culture and people in it. Hip Hop helps in creating its own discourse for theological pursuit for many of its users and listeners and while the artists, who at times invoke theological and spiritual discourses, may not always consciously be intending to do just that, the meaning created within the community is thereby spiritual and theological.[12]

Therefore, for this study, the relevant and proper questions to begin asking are:[13]

- How do we, as scholars and religionists, begin to explore how Hip Hop culture expresses its theology and spiritualty (if any) in a culture which is hostile towards it and its messages? Is there such a thing? Is there a Hip Hop theology?
- What does the rhetoric of Hip Hop say about hegemonic religious structures (theological and religious institutions); including those that are within its community (e.g. The Black Christian Church)?
- When looking at how society in the U.S. interprets and engages with God (Hempton 2008; Washington 1986; Wuthnow 1988) what happens when the popular and dominant theological highway runs out and a new path begins to be forged by the Hip Hop community?

This particular study will keep these questions in mind throughout the book. The goal here is to explore what I will argue is the theological nature of Hip Hop

---

12 This is based on interviews and the analysis of data in this research. Yet, this raises the question: are the artists who produce this music wrestling with these issues of poverty, God, and religion for the sake of the people or for the sake of capital and the selling of records? After all, sex, violence, and drama sells. We will deal with this question later in the book, but it needs to be posed here early on.

13 These questions are what drove the investigation into Hip Hop culture and thereby, the following chapters of the book are the results of what I found, and with which I interacted.

and how those natures develop, are constructed, and in what context they are established.

The Study of Hip Hop Culture

The study of Hip Hop spans, now, over two decades. Scholars such as Tricia Rose, Michael Eric Dyson, Cornel West, Anthony Pinn, Jeff Chang, Nelson George, Bakari Kitwana, and Murray Forman, among others, were some of the first scholars to give Hip Hop academic "feet" and legitimacy. Rose's work *Black Noise: Rap Music and Black Culture in Contemporary America* discussed the context and cultural attributes of Hip Hop culture and gave insight into the contextual elements of the culture and musical genre. Dan Charnas is the author of one of the most exhaustive books on how Hip Hop developed into a commercial, trans-global, multi-billion dollar entity and gives direct insight into how Hip Hop "lost its soul and went corporate" over the last thirty five years. He gives a powerful historical account of the culture from a socio-economic posit (Charnas 2010).

Using Black popular culture as a backdrop, much of the scholarship engages the historical and socio-political areas of Hip Hop. Jeff Chang and Nelson George give accurate social portraits of the historical settings which gave rise to Hip Hop. They lay out Hip Hop's historical ontology and argue for the legitimacy of Hip Hop within the American pop culture scene.[14] While Kitwana (2005) describes what the Hip Hop generation is, he is also responsible for a cultural study on the attraction of Hip Hop to White adolescents. Yvonne Bynoe (2004) has continued this conversation and asserted both the political leadership within Hip Hop and the growing need for it within the young Black community.

These works give a solid foundation to the field of Hip Hop studies and legitimize it in academia.[15] Hip Hop studies, as coined by scholars such as Mark Anthony Neal and Michael Eric Dyson by the mid-2000s, is a field which

---

14 The mid to late 1990s gave rise to a multitude of scholarship focused around Hip Hop culture. Scholars such as (Potter 1995; Dyson 1996; Boyd 1997; Neal 1997) all gave treatment to the multi-levels of Hip Hop within communication, cultural, and African American studies. These works were critical in understanding Hip Hop beyond its historical aspects.

15 This of course is arguable, but in the last decade of Hip Hop scholarship, most academic professional associations have started a section or group on Hip Hop studies. This, along with the growth of doctoral candidates doing their dissertations on or around a Hip Hop issue, is grounds to suggest that Hip Hop has, in fact, grown from just a sub-cultural study.

encompasses sociology, anthropology, communication studies,[16] religious studies, cultural studies, critical race theory, missiological studies, and psychology. It is a multi-disciplinary area of study—much like the culture of Hip Hop. In its early phases, Dyson, West, and Pinn began the conversation of the socio-religious[17] within Hip Hop and the dimensions of the quest for meaning in the lyrics of artists.

These studies, while groundbreaking in the right context, tended to focus largely on the lyrical features of artists and did not engage the broader social, religious, political, and cultural contexts. In 1991 Jon Michael Spencer published a special edition of *Black Sacred Music: A Journal of Theomusicology* titled "The Emergency of Black And The Emergency of Rap." In this issue, the elements of Hip Hop's socio-religious context were examined. This pioneering work began to explore what protest and prophecy was like in Hip Hop. William Perkins wrote an essay on the Islamic rudiments within Hip Hop,[18] and Angela Spence Nelson argued for the theological scope of Hip Hop within rap artists Kool Moe Dee and Public Enemy. This work broke new ground on the religious arenas of Hip Hop. Then, in 1996, Michael Eric Dyson forged new pathways at the height of the Golden Era of Hip Hop with his book *Between God & Gangster Rap: Bearing Witness to Black Popular Culture* which took elements of the Black religious experience and applied them to Hip Hop culture. An avant-garde work, Dyson would also follow up with his work on Tupac (see Chapter 3). Anthony Pinn in 1995 digs even deeper with his work on suffering, pain, and evil within the Black theology in *Why, Lord? Suffering and Evil in Black Theology*. This book also created fresh arguments around what it meant to be Black, to suffer, and still desire some type of response from God. Pinn broke from the Black Christian angle so many scholars had taken. He peered deep into the

---

16 A little known work published by Russell Potter (1995) examines the rhetorical aspects of Hip Hop culture from the point of view of communications. *Spectacular Vernaculars: Hip-Hop and the Politics of Postmodernism* was the first to argue that Hip Hop vernacular might in fact be part of the postmodern language.

17 By socio-religious, I mean the conflation and connection between the religious and the sociological. In other words, the interaction between what is religious, spiritual, and the faith sensibilities of a particular group, culture, people, musical genre, and/or space (geographic). This can also embody the social constructs, social developments, and social conditions within that which is religious and spiritual.

18 During this time, known as the "Golden Era" of Hip Hop (between 1987–1996), a strong Muslim element existed within Hip Hop. Ice Cube was known to be part of the Nation of Islam and rap groups such as X-Clan and Gang Starr were associated with the Zulu Nation—connected to the Islamic roots.

issue of suffering within the Black community and challenged typical notions of Judeo-Christian suffering: how a 'good' God could allow suffering for a specific group of people. Within this work Pinn peers into what suffering looks like within a Hip Hop context by arguing for "nitty-gritty hermeneutics"—a hermeneutic for life that goes beyond a 'just pray about it' worldview. This is the essence of Hip Hop. Pinn continued by publishing an edited volume in 2003, *Noise And Spirit: The Religious and Spiritual Sensibilities of Rap Music*, which was also pioneering as it exclusively explored theological and spiritual spaces within Hip Hop. This work was foundational for the study of religion in the Hip Hop context. It challenged the notions that the study of religion was limited to popularized music such as Rock & Roll, Jazz, and Metal. Works which explored music and religion (Betts 2004b; Sylvan 2002), often overlooked Hip Hop as a field of study, or, worse, footnoted it as a "emerging culture" and disregarded it altogether (Sullivan 1997; Stapert 2000; Seay 1986; Leonard 1987; Gilmour 2009).[19]

This type of "disregard" is typical for the arts and media of ethnic minorities. Hip Hop's bravado, hard hitting social messages, and Black male power is often seen as a threat to hegemonic systems of domination; thus, it is either labeled as "evil," "immoral," "racist," and/or "violence" when, in comparison, White male artists such as Insane Clown Posse, are able to sing about death, killing others, and morbid fantasies of sex and "sin" and receive nowhere near the negative press that rap artists receive.[20] Therefore, Pinn's work was foundational in establishing links between rap and religion, the spiritual and the profane, and a quest for a contextual deity in Hip Hop contexts.

Related approaches to Hip Hop and religion have also been emerging within the last decade. Christian perspectives on Hip Hop such as Efrem Smith and Phil Jackson's work *The Hip Hop Church: Connecting with The Movement Shaping Our Culture*, gives deference to Black youth and Hip Hop engagement from a Christian context. Smith and Jackson explore what a "Hip Hop church" may look like for a new approach to "church." Alex Gee and John Teter created a "Bible study" text exploring the lyrics and theological stances within Tupac

---

19   While these texts offer good insight into religious quests within generalized and "popular" music, they do not give treatment to the Hip Hop context and tend to not mention Black music's religious experience and discourses.

20   Note that groups such as The 2Live Crew received negative press regarding their lyrics and sexualized messages which went all the way to the Supreme Court. Problematic yes, but White male rock and metal groups such as Poison received none of the same treatment despite, in videos, engaging openly in sexualized imagery very similar to that of The 2Live Crew.

Shakur and Lauryn Hill's work *Jesus and The Hip Hop Prophets: Spiritual Insights from Lauryn Hill and Tupac Shakur*. These works are crucial, although niche, and focused largely on "evangelistic tools," for the study of Hip Hop and religion.[21]

Christina Zanfagna, an ethnomusicologist, contended to investigate Hip Hop by understanding the people's responses, reactions, and worldviews within the culture of Hip Hop under an ethnomusicological background. Zanfagna writes,

> ...my study seeks to redefine the parameters of "spirituality"—that is, what is considered spiritual—it is not my intention to give a hard fast definition of hip-hop's spirituality or even define what kind of God figure hip-hop music might point to, for such theological preoccupations would obscure the flexible, adaptive, ecumenical nature of hip-hop's anatomy of belief and the spiritual experience it produces (2006, 2).

Here Zanfagna, also evoking the importance of a theomusicological study, begins to explore the profane nature within Hip Hop culture and pushes deeper than lyrical analysis within the culture. Zanfagna argues that the profane aspects of Hip Hop—connecting them back to Black musical genres such as blues and jazz—actually offer theological insight once you move past the seemingly sinful facade (2006, 3–4).

Recent works by Monica Miller (2012), Ebony Utley (2012), Andre Johnson (2013), Emmitt Price (2011), Ralph Watkins (2011), and myself, Hodge (2010, 2012) offer a broader yet specific look into the dimensions of Hip Hop religion. These works are more focused and critical in their approach to religion.

Miller offers a strong critique of Hip Hop's religious areas while challenging the notions that Hip Hop's religion is Christian centered. Miller explores Hip Hop's religion and pushes us to look beyond what Russell McCutcheon calls a "private affair" in religion when the narrative becomes a tradition and experience that is universalized in the world, and argues that we should not limit the religious narrative to just a singular phenomenon (2013b, 15–16).

---

21 Pertaining specifically to Christian rap and Hip Hop theology, one book and two scholarly articles stand out which delve deeper into the religion and Hip Hop: Garth Kasimu Baker-Fletcher's "African American Christian Rap: Facing 'Truth' and Resisting It" (2003), and Cheryl Renee Gooch's "Rappin For the Lord: The Uses of Gospel Rap and Contemporary Music in Black Religious Communities" (1996). Felicia M. Miyakawa's book "Five Percenter Rap: God Hop's Music, Message, and Black Muslim Mission" gives a comprehensive overview of the relationship between Hip Hop and this Islamic sect.

Miller also challenges the study of Hip Hop and religion by naming works which approach it from Hegemonic studies, mainly within Christian contexts which limit the study of Hip Hop and religion broadly (2013b, 81–85). Miller plainly questions whether the religious is actually religious, or whether it is hyper-imposed by creative authors wanting to find something that is not there. These are tough, yet necessary questions for us as Hip Hop scholars to wrestle with. I will discuss more on this perspective later.

Johnson's reader provides a construction of what Hip Hop's spirituality looks like and creates a dialog between religious expressions and the space in which they were created. These essays provide a two part focus on theoretical and methodical approaches—which, as the field of Hip Hop Studies develops, is a much needed conversation. How might one conduct extensive and longitudinal research specifically focused on the religious expressions? The second section examines Hip Hop and religion—what are the aspects of and dimensions within the religious in Hip Hop? Johnson provides a much needed resource for Hip Hop Studies by making a reader engage with its religious spaces.

Ebony Utley describes the "Gangsta's God" as a rhetorician's study into the socio-spirituality in Hip Hop. Utley covers the racial implications of Biggie's "Jesus Piece" (a gold and diamond encrusted medallion of a personified White Jesus) within Hip Hop. Hip Hoppers, in general, tend to criticize White images of deity, yet connect with it in the social market place of capital and social status (2012, 64–67).

Watkins is creating a romantic view of Hip Hop and its theological and spiritual dimensions, while this could be viewed negatively and prematurely given the newness of the emerging field of religion and Hip Hop. Watkins addresses such issues as Hip Hop's spiritual connection to the Blues (2011, 39–65), theological truth in story, and the spiritual discourse within narratives of oppression (2011, Chapters 5–7). Watkins' work provides a needed framework in understanding the "how" of Hip Hop's theological capacities.

Works such as these have broadened the study of Hip Hop and religion and have thereby expanded Hip Hop Studies. It is within these studies that this volume picks up the conversation. Theologically speaking, how does Hip Hop construct a theological discourse and how was that theology formed?

Hip Hop's Theology: An Oxymoron?

Hip Hop is a powerful cultural phenomenon which has dominated the popular culture scene for over twenty years. Gordon Lynch (2005) argues that Hip Hop culture has permeated almost every facet of American mainstream culture. Bakari Kitwana (2004) suggests that there needs to be a critical examination of the culture in order to better understand the current trends and styles within youth culture. Marketing executives will try to sell just about anything using rap music. As scholar of communication Ebony Utley has suggested elsewhere, when Jay Z made it to Oprah, Hip Hop had truly arrived. Further, Robin Sylvan has argued that "music is one of the most powerful tools for conveying religious meaning known to humankind. Music and religion are intimately linked in almost every culture and in almost every historical period" (2002, 4). Rap is that music, and Hip Hop is the culture in which it is housed. Historically, the last forty years have had many societal shifts.

Within almost any type of cultural genre in the West, the search for God or a type of God is inevitable (Durkheim 1965, 21–23). Hip Hop is no different. First, I will define theology and how it will be used in this book. Theology, in its basic sense, is the study of God[22]—the study of how God[23] interacts, intercedes, speaks, lives, thinks, wants, and is. In the West, God is a supernatural creator who shaped the Universe and intercedes, albeit limited or on a daily basis, in the lives of humans for the betterment of society and as part of a journey towards a space defined as "heaven."[24] Therefore, by that definition we will see how God (or gods as seen in some Zulu spiritual circles)[25] is constructed and is developed in Hip Hop and within a post-industrial urban context. This does not and will not assume that every person associated with Hip Hop culture is seeing a God-like meaning. Nor does it presume that MCs[26]—often thought of as God figures—are to be left out of the spiritual equation. In fact, it is the

---

22 It is important to note here that theology as a formal academic discipline focuses on the study of God in the Christian religion. While I will discuss Hip Hop's inclusion and expression of different religions, the main discussion of a Hip Hop theology will make references to the Christian religion and Christian religious expression.

23 Interrogating God is something reserved for another study. However, for this study, God will be, in a simplistic sense, a supernatural persona. Yet, it could be argued, from a gendered perspective, that God is not just a "He" in the masculine sense, but also embraces a feminine side. This is something which arose in the interviews about understanding God's "female" side. Most Hip Hoppers however, as I will argue later in the book, see God in a masculine form. This does present problems for a more egalitarian approach to God and theology.

24 While there are numerous versions of this story, for the purposes of this book and research, I will primarily refer to an Abrahamic God rooted in the three main faiths which stem from this ideological theology: Islam, Christianity, and Jewish belief systems.

25 Taken from Zulu beliefs and spiritual practices (Nation 2010).

26 "Master of Ceremonies," "Microphone Commander," or "Mic Controller."

opposite. Most of the lyrics are from MCs creating a spiritual discourse. To take this a step further, I will argue that Hip Hoppers reflect on divine action in the Hip Hop community. Hip Hop theology shows that God "shows up" in the most unusual of places and the most interesting locations—more often than not, in the intersection of the sacred and the profane.[27] We will look at those unusual places and those interesting places with both a theological and hermeneutical lens. In other words, violence, sexuality, "sin," and the nuancing of the secular will all be taken into consideration, using an ethnomusicological method. Therefore, Hip Hop theology is, in essence, the study of a Godhead (God, The Son or Daughter, & The Spirit)[28] in the Hip Hop post-industrial urban context/environment, to better understand the rich and complex manifestations of spirituality, divine interactions, God presence, and the revelation of a contextualized God from within the Hip Hop community, while being liberated from oppressive conditions.

The obscure part of Hip Hop is its theology—would anyone other than scholars consider it to be theological?—and this is therefore part of the focus of this book. What is it? Moreover, what kind of theology is it? Is Hip Hop rooted in religion? Or is Hip Hop truly misunderstood by those professing to be pious and theological? Those who only see rap music through the media's eyes or who do not have an understanding of cultural matters, tend to see loud music, rough sounding lyrics, deep bass, low riding pants, long white T-shirts, and ominous facial expressions in opposition to 'God's plan.' As I have interviewed those who claim to have an Evangelical Christian heritage,[29] Hip Hop is as much of an enigma to them as is, say, The New Age movement, or Muslims. Hip Hop continues to appear 'worldly' and 'secular' in all of its dimensions. Yet, artists such as Kanye West, in "The College Dropout" album, argue that God

---

27   This ideology of God at the center of theology is a changing conversation in the field of religious study. Anthony Pinn discusses this well in his book *The End of God Talk: An African American Humanist Theology* (Pinn 2012). Thus, in this book, while it is not the main focus, it deserves to be noted. This is not to assume that there are other forms of finding spirituality. For example, assuming that God would be at the center of a theological conversation is very different to assuming that a community or people are at the center of that theological conversation. MCs also facilitate much spiritual meaning and, in that sense, become a type of God for that space. These are all areas that need further study and research.

28   In some manner, this might be seen as a Christian Hip Hop theology. I would make the case that while Christian theology does provide this type of sensibility, but, in say, for example, Zulu theologies, there is room for a three-person Godhead.

29   Typically those affiliated with a conservative and literal view of the Christian Bible and the appeal of 'missions' to 'non-Christians.'

loves the hustlers, pimps, killers, prostitutes, and people that society would otherwise not deal with. Tupac questions whether there is a heaven for real Niggaz. Tupac changed the letter "S" to "Z" to indicate a deeper meaning of the word suggesting a "class" or lower socio-economic status rather than the more racialized term "nigger." In this sense, Tupac has contextualized a word that was once meant for negativity.[30] Big Syke asks if the church can even handle Hip Hoppers, while KRS-One has suggested that Hip Hoppers need to start their own church. The underlying assumption here is that God loves the Hip Hoppers.

While Hip Hop is not without its problems, as seen constantly in media outlets, and while some elements of it even deal with the occult,[31] it does not deserve the ridicule and scorn to which many in the public eye—including those in academia—have subjected it. More importantly, it does not deserve the alienation that many religious institutions (Christians, Jews, some Muslims) have also imposed upon it. What is even worse is when some Christian churches—who in all fairness believe that they are doing "right" by Hip Hop—give up one Sunday every quarter to the youth and believe that this "reaches out" to the community. This is just a fallacy and does not promote a true conversation and dialogue with the Hip Hop community which is what this study is attempting to explore along with an exploration of Hip Hop's theological paradigms.

Part of the reason why religion and theology in Hip Hop might appear so vague to outsiders and other scholars is that its roots, history, and religious backgrounds have both multiple and complex sources. We are dealing with a culture, Hip Hop, which originates in poor Black and Brown communities with a myriad of religious, spiritual, and faith backgrounds.[32] Many of those traditions, in turn, seep into the norms of Hip Hop—for example, the social employing of Christological symbolism is a regular custom for some rappers. Kanye, DMX, Tupac, and even Kendrick Lamar have a stated fascination with the deity, yet claim no specific denomination or church affiliation. This presents many problems for scholars and lay people attempting to deconstruct

---

30 Robin Kelly (1994, 207–212) agrees, and further suggests that the term can permeate skin color as well.
31 Not to place a negative judgment on this, but this is based on interactions with those who have stated they are dealing with the occult and "dark magic" while rapping.
32 If studied, the core of Hip Hop's cultural mores can be traced back to 5th and 6th century West Africa with connections to the Griot and core cultural attributes, which are: consciousness, self-awareness, community, spirituality, unity, love of God & self (Hine; Hine, and Harrold 2010, Chapters 1–2).

Hip Hop within a standard hermeneutical lens.[33] Hip Hop cannot be easily defined. Nor can Hip Hop be boxed into a five step process in order to "reach" into the culture; it is just too complex. This book sets out in an exploratory fashion to discover Hip Hop's complexity within its spirituality.

One aspect of Hip Hop's complex theology is that it engages the realness of life as it comes at you—in real time. Christina Zanfagna states:

> Mainstream hip-hop percolates with unlikely and multifaceted religious inclinations. Despite its inconsistent relationship to organized religion and its infamous mug of weed smoking, drug pushing, gun slinging, and curse spewing, rap music is not without moral or spiritual content. On the flip side, religious music continues to draw upon popular music idioms—a smart mission strategy to reach today's listeners. (2006, 1)

Therefore, Hip Hop begins to talk about a basic theology of life. This theological paradigm is not new (Cone 1990, 1992; Cone 1991; Dyson 2001; Pinn 2002, 2010; Pinn 1995, 2001). Good and evil are common subject matters for the expressions and life of urban popular culture (Hodge 2010, 22).[34] Likewise, a new type of spiritual rotundity is needed as society changes and people continue the wrestle with the problem of evil.

As descendants of Black musical traditions (Kirk-Duggan and Hall 2011, 89–115), we realize that there is more to the story of Hip Hop. Hip Hop begins

---

33 What I mean by this is that most Christian pastors are "classically" trained and have a modernistic way of approaching sacred scripture. Thus, the issue of salvation, for example, then becomes very mechanical, predictable, and "efficient." In other words, the pastor would rely on "traditional" methods of evangelism to reach a Hip Hop nation. This simply will not work with most in Hip Hop culture. Moreover, traditional ways of approaching the Bible will not work. You are dealing with a culture that loves who Jesus is, but despise the institutional aspect of religion. Most seminaries still train their pastors to be a part of the church (little C) while not truly understanding the community of Church (Big C, the biblical aspect of church which means that it goes beyond not only the four walls of the church, but also the programmatic aspect of church).

34 For example, artists such as Aretha Franklin, Curtis Mayfield, Stevie Wonder, and Ray Charles all provided a diverse spiritual message in their music. Ray Charles, in his time, was considered "profane" and "unholy" yet his music today is heard in many churches. Jon M. Spencer argues that there is much protest within Black Gospel music and that stories from the Bible were told through old Negro spirituals (1990). Moreover, in the time of slavery, music became the message for church and for life—as detestable it may have been; there was no delineation between sacred, profane, and secular. All were one. See Spencer (1990 3–34).

the complex theological discussion of how the profane, secular, and sacred all meet in one place. Moreover, within Black musical traditions, there is this ideology within the music that infuses and sees the sacred in the profane (Spencer 1992b; Zanfagna 2006). Spencer believes that the Black secular music of the masses, while still "sinful," secular, evil, and corrupt, is not completely unreligious and might actually present a spirituality and theology for everyday life (1991a, 9). Teresa Reed reminds us that "James Brown captures the soulful spontaneity of the Sanctified church and the animated exhortation of the Sanctified preacher" (2003, 15).

This is the theological paradox—or neo-spiritual movement depending on how one poses the phenomenon—not just for Hip Hop, but also for those seeking answers when their theological highway has run out.[35] Could "sin" actually produce a theological paradigm? Could the debauchery actually have a deep theological archetype? Could rappers like Scarface and Geto Boys, with all their violent discourse and the stark viciousness of the life in which they have lived, actually be creating a space for God to enter and create new meanings within that muddle? (I shall discuss this further in Chapter 4). These are areas which need more exploration. There is not a definitive word on this, but it does in fact require us, as scholars of religion, to investigate and not to dismiss the pursuit of God in awkward, strange, and even disreputable places. Or, could it be that we who study religion are more afraid than we care to admit about dealing with the real nature of the profane? These are not necessarily questions for the scholar of religion, but more an ecclesial commitment to justice in theological dialogue. Zanfagna tells us, "To accept this presupposes that popular culture could be a sacred place—an area in which one may encounter God even in the most unholy of places" (2006, 1). Hip Hop theology not only embraces the sacred, it dines, sleeps, laughs, cries, loves, hates, and lives with the profane. It is just a part of everyday life. If one is to understand Hip Hop truly, then a basic theological worldview of the profane must exist (Arnal 2013).

---

35 There is a growing case for those who live in oppressive conditions seeking a theology that "fits" within spaces in which normative theological inquires cease to exist. Issues such as violence confound theological inquiries which promote a peaceful message, but in the face of injustice as that in Ferguson, Missouri and Baltimore, Maryland, how does one respond when "peace" has failed? Could there be a theology of violence for Black and Brown youth who are brutally murdered by White police officers such as the case in New York city? Is David Walker's appeal much more relevant now, in 21st century America for the Black youth? Is Hip Hop part of that "appeal?"

This theological oxymoron—theology of the profane—is not a new concept.[36] If, for example, we investigate the time period in which Jesus lived, then we must look at the controversy Jesus created. We must look at the profane language Jesus used when describing the Pharisees and Sadducees, and we must also contend with the fact that there were multiple messianic narratives of Jesus (some of which do not align with the current Judeo Christian theological prototype).

Hip Hoppers can resonate with the eccentricities of many Bible characters: Noah, who was a drunk and cursed out his kids; David, who was not only promiscuous, but also sold his "boy" out in order to steal that same friend's wife (he placed Uriah on the front lines of the war just so that he could attain Uriah's wife Bathsheba in II Samuel 11); and women in the Bible such as Mary, Martha, and Apphia, who were left out of the New Testament canon yet provided rich first-hand knowledge of Jesus. These are narratives to which Hip Hoppers can relate, engage with, and connect to.

Hip Hop says, "Man, we're dealing with it all!" One of Tupac's greatest sins was that he called out his own "sin" which made others extremely uncomfortable. For example, Tupac confessed his very active sex life and "love" for female "beauty" at the same time he was receiving an NAACP[37] image award. Black leaders such as Jesse Jackson strongly criticized the NAACP for that decision, yet Jackson has been noted to have had several interactions with women other than his wife. Bill Cosby was also outspoken about Tupac's "womanizing" yet, as time has revealed, Cosby has had his own womanizing problems. Artists such as Tupac continue to be problematic for many religious zealots who hold fundamental views of religion. The million-dollar question is "How can the profane exist within God?"

Hip Hop can be, at least partially, based on Hip Hop scholar Anthony Pinn's five central themes[38] of African American humanism as "...a mode for religious

---

36 In fact, theologians and church heroes such as Martin Luther assert that God meets us first in the profane, or "shit" of life. Therefore, only those who enter the "shit" can encounter the God of Jesus Christ. Of course, Luther used much more "colorful" language than this. However, the point of strong language and its connection to a strong theological message is noted.

37 National Association for the Advancement of Colored People.

38 These themes are taken from Anthony Pinn's chapter "Rap's Humanist Sensibilities" (2003, 8–88). Pinn's themes are focused around African American religious traditions, but I use these five themes here to illustrate the connection with Hip Hop theology and culture.

orientation."³⁹ While these principles derive from an ideology which rejects the God idea, in particular, the notion that God will break into history, or could do so. The "controlled optimism" arises from waiting rather than getting help from God. Thus, in many regards, a portion of Hip Hoppers have taken a more gnostic position towards God. I however use these central themes as a critical position toward traditional modes of theological inquiry—that is, a more conservative fundamental approach to God in which God somehow "blesses" those who are "good" and as a result, a bounded set of theological parameters are established making the rules clear, normative, and standardized. So, in that sense, Hip Hop creates an alternate way to find God and since many Hip Hoppers, even though they may be living in conditions which could make them impatient in that "wait for God," are still on the journey to find a God that fits their circumstances. Thus, I have reframed Pinn's central themes for this current study. The central themes are:

1. Understanding of humanity as fully (and solely) accountable and responsible for the human condition and the correction of its plight, especially as it pertains to social justice.
2. Suspicion toward or rejection of supernatural explanation and claims, combined with an understanding of humanity as an evolving part of the natural environment as opposed to being a created being unable to change its path. This is one of the many reasons why traditional evangelistic tracks do not work on Hip Hoppers.
3. Appreciation for African American cultural production and a perception of traditional forms of Black religiosity as having cultural importance as opposed to any type of "cosmic" or "supernatural" authority that remains unnamed and vague.
4. Commitment to individual and societal transformation: this is a key aspect of all Hip Hop culture which reaches well into its theology.
5. Controlled optimism that recognizes both human potential and human destructive activities while leaving room for God, in that God would be able to intervene, at times, in the lives of humans.

I use Pinn's five elements here to provide a sort of theological premise in which to begin this conversation. These five elements are essential, in part, to

---

39 I am not arguing that Hip Hop is entirely humanistic. However, humanism is not without educational and theological positives. Part of Hip Hop's theology connects with Pinn's five themes; that is what this work is attempting to get at (2003, 87).

Hip Hop's theological mantra. These are building blocks for the structure of its theology and, in context, help create a type of meaning of God and also forces and necessitates an alternate approach and/or re-description of how we as scholars and academics think of theology.

The irreverent spirituality infused with a sacred element of God in Hip Hop music, has formed what Jon Michael Spencer calls theomusicology,[40] which is "...musicology as a theologically informed discipline" (Spencer 1990, vii). The fact that Hip Hop music is theologically rooted is no coincidence. Hip Hop is about liberation, authenticity, and freedom from the shackles of modernity. Spencer relates Black gospel music as being a liberating tone not only for Blacks but for anyone from an oppressed context. Hip Hop is a contemporary response for this generation of urban people including urban Whites (Spencer 1990, 35–39).

Artists such as DMX and Tupac argue that we can have a sacred relationship with Jesus, commune with Jesus, even grow in community without ever setting foot in a church. Tupac even asks the epistemological question, does heaven have a place for a "G?" For most people, even asking this question is profane. In addition, it raises another important question that states if you can reach Jesus without the 'church,' what good is the 'church'? Hip Hop puts that and many other questions like that at your front door. Hip Hop questions the institutional church while challenging the very moral fibers of pastors, reverends, deacons, and priests. Hence, this is one of the main reasons an artist like DMX can begin an album such as *Grand Champ* (2003) with illicit language regarding life, and end the album in a prayer "thanking God for making me righteous..."[41]

This neo-secular/sacred theology does three major things for Hip Hop:

1. It provides a basis for understanding life and not allowing simplistic answers to be used in order to explain pain, distress, suffering, anxieties, and evil acts.
2. It allows for everyday life, language, culture, and contexts to be given a fair examination. In other words, nothing is too "sacred" to talk about or deal with.
3. It gives room for rap music, as one of the vehicles for Hip Hop's message, to give critical insight, pose deep theological questions, reject the current hegemonic powers, and allow for change in its music.

---

40   I will further define this momentarily, as this is the main methodology used in this study.
41   "The Prayer v" in *Grand Champ* (2003).

These three concepts are central to many artists such as Common, Mos Def, Odd Thomas, Propaganda, and Tupac who use these three theological tenets in their music. This type of schema is nothing new. Noel Leo Erskine, in his chapter "Rap, Reggae, and Religion" states that "Rap theology...is intimately linked to notions of how society functions and who operates the levers of control" (2003, 78). Consequently, rappers then become the reporters (in some cases, the preacher if you will) of life—of both the sacred and the profane.

Erskine further states that, "In rap theology, God takes sides and identifies with rappers in their attempt to confront violence with counter violence. Their God is the God of the Old Testament..." (2003, 78). Rappers like Big Syke argue that God was both a killer and all-loving, but He will take the side of the marginalized to vindicate them and kill the oppressor.[42] While this may be a radical and even violent view for some, it should be kept in mind that for many years, God did operate in this realm. Read the Old Testament books of Joshua, Deuteronomy, Judges, and or Genesis and you will find this type of God. For many centuries scholars and lay people alike argued that there were two different Gods, one of the Old Testament and one of the New Testament (Funk 1993). So it stands to reason that artists such as GZA challenge the status quo and find alternate narratives which they can relate to—especially in violent living conditions.

The Hostility of A Gospel

It was the rap artist Talib Kweli who asserted that even a Gospel was hostile to begin with. In his song titled "Hostile Gospel," he begins by asserting that there are double standards and major issues which are being ignored in mainstream American society:

> Hip-Hop's the new WWF
> What do you rap or do you wrestle? Niggaz love to forget
> We got til it's gone, you think you on, you still hustling backwards
> Your topical norm a tropical storm, it's a fuckin disaster
> Back to the topic we on, it all started at Rawkus
> They couldn't find the words to describe me so they resort to the shortcuts
> Is he a backpacker? Is he a mad rapper?
> An entertainer or the author of the last chapter

---

42 Taken from Dyson's (2001) interview with Big Syke.

> We living in these times of love and cholera
> Synonymous with the apocalypse, look up the clouds is ominous
> We got maybe ten years left say meteorologists, shit
> We still waitin for the Congress to acknowledge this![43]

Here Kweli describes some of the current issues and the attitude of ignorance from dominant society. Kweli even argues that Hip Hop is the new "WWF." In other words, the commercialization of Hip Hop has created a type of hostility even from within the Hip Hop community which is then compounded with the fact that issues in the urban context continue to be ignored. The song goes on to say:

> In these tryin days and times
> All I need is to be free
> I can't do it on my own
> Lord can you deliver me?
> There are trials still to come
> It's salvation that I need
> So I'm reachin to the sky
> Lord can you deliver me?
> Deliver us...

The asking for deliverance is fundamental in the face of hostility and suffering. Kweli asks the higher power of God to deliver not only himself, but also the community (notice that the song ends with the word "us").

How does one deal with God in the face of such hostility? How, as rapper Tupac Shakur asks, does one act like an angel when surrounded by devils? Yet, in the same sense, the question can be asked: how can hostility be found in "good news?" The rapper and Hip Hopper living in the hostile urban context would rephrase and state that even in "good times" there are hostile elements to life; even in the midst of good days, there is still the chance of being killed; even with a loving God, shit still happens on a daily basis. Yet, can God, devoid of White dominant societal theology, deliver me in my messy and hostile context? Further, where can I find God in the hostility of life? Ralph Watkins tells us that, "the heaven-and-hell debate drives this song—the premise being that hell is right here on earth. Do you know hell? Do you know what hell feels like and looks like? Kweli says, 'if you ever walked through any ghetto then you

---

43 *Ear Drum* (2007), "Hostile Gospel, Pt 1."

know it well.' Living in the ghetto is hell" (2011, 109). This type of theology is rooted in the reality of the now, today, the pragmatic daily life existence—the ghetto reality.

In Part 2 of the song Hostile Gospel, Kweli asks for God's deliverance from this hostile context of economic, social, and theological inequality:

> Die on my feet before I live on my knees Lord
> Deliver me from point A to B like livery
> Nothin is free, you got to be a hero to save
> They got you working like a slave from the crib to the grave
> A minimum wage can barely keep a job for a home
> A car or a phone, forget about gettin a loan
> You starting to moan, your bank account is getting withdrawn
> It's pitiful how we becomin slaves to things that we own
> They en-slavin the brains with the whips and the chains
> End up in the coffin chasing the fortune, chasing the fame
> Slave to the rhythm, slave to the night, slave to the day
> They hop aboard the Underground Railroad and run away
> Pray for the day niggas don't get taken away
> For makin a way to stop their baby's stomach aching today
> I sip a whiskey straight, no chase
> It's hard to take a man away from the sin when it's inside of him
> Please[44]

Hip Hop theology is about engaging this hostility and tension head on. Watkins once again says, "The God of hip-hop is a God who is found inside those who follow this God [the God of justice, equality and freedom]" (2011: 110).

What makes this hostile is (1) the nefarious social and living conditions of the urban context (2) oppressive living and social conditions within urban areas that breed frustration and hostility within the Hip Hop community such that (3) Hip Hop creates a hostile form of theology which not only engages these issues, but also demands a voice at the theological table while it brings its frustration and hostility paired with a "good news" to get out of the current situation. Kweli might also suggest that his point is less sophisticated and more blunt—a Hip Hop mantra of being direct. The Christian Gospel is hostile to people.

Carter Heyward has a statement which captures the essence of this hostile Gospel in relation to Jesus Christ. Heyward states:

---

44 *Ear Drum* (2007), "Hostile Gospel, Pt 2."

Most Christians expect Jesus to be all good, completely good, perfect, "without sin," as the tradition has taught us. Either we overlook and ignore things that he did and said about which, if it were anyone but Jesus, we might complain (cursing and killing a fig tree?), we learn to rationalize away the biblical record (he didn't really do this), or we find positive ways of looking at what only appear to be negative images (he's not really belittling his mother at the wedding; he's just trying to stretch and re-image his friends' understandings of "family"). We cannot seem to bear the notion of a Jesus who didn't always do or say the right thing (1999, 144–145).

In other words, if one of the central figures of the Christian faith has hostility in their own life, is it not fair to say that Hip Hop can have this same mix with its approach to God?

To look at it in yet another way, the Gospel in its root meaning—aside from the Protestant meaning of the message of Jesus Christ—is 'good news.'[45] This good news is part of what Hip Hop is attempting to bring to its community and culture. This good news is not based in Christian values and theologies, but in a much broader view of social justice, social awareness, social consciousness, community mindedness, personal consciousness, and a journey to a God who can help and will provide shelter. Moreover, this gospel within the Hip Hop community is not always a sacred quest; the secular and profane are intertwined with weed, alcohol, sexuality, and 'living a good life/being successful.' These are all domains that seem to be anti-God and to appear 'sinful' in nature. Yet, Hip Hoppers say, we must also hold these areas in tension as part of the 'good news' for survival, and to rise above the current situation. There might actually be a spiritual presence within these domains which can uplift the person into a transcendental force; a spiritual presence in those domains which are often touted as sin, secular, and evil; a God in those spaces is good news for Hip Hoppers. If one is to examine truly the religious and theological meanings within a culture then we cannot ignore or overlook those areas labeled as "sinful" and "wicked" for in that sin and wickedness, Hip Hoppers are searching for a theology. As Spencer (1991) argues, Black secular music such as Hip Hop can masquerade as sinful, sexual, and sonically evil yet represent a spiritualty for the everyday (1991b, 9–10). Further, in some regards, this book (Chapters Three and Five) will demonstrate that certain artists such as Tupac offer a theological hermeneutic and ecclesiology that is "enough" for Hip Hoppers and the

---

45   Taken from an etymological study in the Oxford English dictionary database, 2013.

Hip Hop community theologically. In other words, Hip Hop actually becomes the "word" and "truth" through its artists and culture—an aspect KRS-One is also attempting to do in some respects (One 2009).

The Research & Background

This study draws from prominent Hip Hop albums from *The Source* magazine's top 100 rap songs (1998).[46] This song list, though dated, developed and emerged during what is now defined as Hip Hop's Golden Era (Watkins 2011; Kitwana 2003; George 1998) and is crucial because many of the contemporary artists also draw from this era of music. While *The Source* magazine may or may not be the most popular Hip Hop magazine, it is the oldest and longest running publication strictly devoted to rap music and culture. For the present study, songs from *The Source*'s list were categorized into several categories. This was done by taking a precursory look at the song titles and lyrics. Songs were categorized as either having a theological statement/critique (including all religions), songs having a socio-political critique, and neither. Songs that fell into both the theological and socio-political categories were then further analyzed using theomusicology.

To bring the study into the present and to utilize contemporary artists, the interviewees were asked in the interview process to divulge their top twenty list of artists who they considered to be theological, spiritual, agnostic, atheist, or prophetic in their messages and approach. From those lists a cumulative top twenty five list was created and, in turn, those artists and their albums were analyzed using theomusicology.[47]

Five recurring typologies arose in this analysis which helps form the conceptual framework of this book:[48]

1. Hip Hoppers create their own view of God, Jesus, and church in association with suffering, pain, and inequality.
2. The post-soul context helps to create a climate to question authority, rebel from current religious standards and worldviews, and to create a new path to God and church.
3. The felt need from the Hip Hop community aides in creating a spiritual avenue in order to make sense of suffering, pain, and inequality.
4. Human action is directed toward problem solving. In this case, Hip Hoppers create a way to problem solve through their music, poetry, and lyrics.

---

46 See Appendix 1 for the complete list of albums.
47 See Appendix 2 for the top 25 list of rappers.
48 These will be expanded on further in Chapter 6.

5. Distrust of current systems, institutions, and social structures is a part of the worldview of Hip Hoppers within a Post-soul context.

From this, six central characteristics were created from the theomusicological analysis, the artists' songs, and interviews:

1. Distrust of social institutions
2. Critique of religious and social structures
3. A New Ecclesiology and Eschatological aspiration
4. Suffering as a form of spiritual expression
5. Anger and rage for justice and equality
6. God suffers with us—the Christology of Hip Hop

These six central socio-memes were crucial in better understanding the hostility within the gospel message of Hip Hoppers and to grasp the post-soul message of God in correlation to suffering and marginalization.

This study is limited to rap songs distinguished as "good" or "the best" in the United States by readers of *The Source* magazine. While *The Source* magazine is longest running publication to date that strictly covers rap music and culture, the opinions of *The Source* magazine do not encompass the opinions of every member of the Hip Hop community. *The Source* magazine provides the only listing of "top rap albums" to date that include artists from a range of locations in the United States, and artists that may not be heard on mainstream radio. This study is further limited to those songs/artists whose song lyrics include theological and/or socio-political ruminations or critiques. Thirty interviews[49] were also used, employing a mixed methods approach, from individuals who labeled themselves as Hip Hoppers and from varying religious faiths (including Nation of Islam & Five Percenters of God & Earth).[50]

---

49 Please note that all of the names of the interviewees were changed to pseudonyms to protect the anonymity of those interviewed. This is also to gain the trust of the interviewees since many within the Hip Hop community feel a distrust towards any "outsiders" doing interviews. Some feel as though their names will be used against them. Therefore, during the interview process, I let all interviewees know that their real names would not be used in the study.

50 The discipline of Hip Hop studies has grown exponentially over the last decade. However, the study of Hip Hop and religion is a new and emerging area of study and scholars such as Monica Miller, Andre Johnson, Christina Zanfagna, and Ebony Utley have manuscripts which are currently being published in this field. They add a rich voice to the discussion of rap and religion. Further, The American Academy of Religion has recognized Hip Hop & Religion as an official group since 2011.

Lastly, this study is limited to North American rap music and its cultural context. This, as I will argue, constructs a template from which other countries and cultural contexts such as Europe, the Middle East, and Asia are able to build. This study intentionally adopts a broad scope of artists and contexts. One attains a broader and richer view of Hip Hop by examining the spectrum of events, contexts, artists, and cultural attributes over the last twenty-four years. This study will also build upon the notion that the reader understands the ten foundational elements of Hip Hop culture (DJing/Turntabalism, Breaking/Dance/B-Boying/Girling, Graffiti, Break Beats, Emceeing, Street Knowledge, Street Language, Street Fashion, Entrepreneurialism, and Knowledge of God and Self) and will proceed by keeping these in mind, but referencing them as crucial to the study of Hip Hop.

Chapters

The flow of this book illustrates and explores how Hip Hoppers (artists and the broader community) construct and develop a post-soul ideology and post-soul theology, which is formed in the social conditions of the urban and ghetto enclave. This is useful for those seeking to find a God outside of approved pathways and approved theodicies of suffering and violence. This book will present the results of the theomusicological study on Hip Hop culture I conducted between 1988 and 2012. Each chapter will observe the social conditions which made it ripe for Hip Hoppers to develop a theological mantra and *whether* any theological mantra exists in particular albums.

I find it necessary to describe, albeit not exhaustively, the social, cultural, political, theological, and varying geographic conditions in which this music was created. One must not overlook the various eras and societal shifts which gave rise to Hip Hop. Therefore, Chapter 1 discusses the major events and social conditions primarily for the Black community post World War II and its ensuing effect on the birth of Hip Hop culture during the 1960s.

Laying the groundwork and foundation for Hip Hop culture and the womb in which it was created, I then move into the theological messages within Hip Hop culture by examining the God in the cipher of Hip Hop in Chapter 2.

Moving to a more tighter inspection of Hip Hop, Chapter 3 looks specifically at one of Hip Hop's "prophets," Tupac Amaru Shakur. Throughout Hip Hop's history, very few other artists have attracted so much controversy, theological insight, and social awareness as he has done.

From here, we will be ready to engage with the issues surrounding violence, pain, and non-standard responses to disenfranchisement in Chapter 4. This chapter will provide an examination of how the Hip Hop community theologically wrestles with issues of violence.

Chapter 5 rounds out this discussion by looking at the racial significance of the Jesus figure in Hip Hop. In it, I will describe Hip Hop's theology of Jesuz. The letter "S" at the end of the name has been changed to "Z" to represent a savior for all and a messianic character for the oppressed and marginalized which is contextualized according to the Hip Hop community.

Chapter 6 will conclude this book by critically examining the data and whether Hip Hop has a religion, or whether elements of spirituality are socially constructed and created.

Though this work is primarily a theological investigation and exploration into Hip Hop's socio-theological nature, the ideas presented in this study can also serve as social indicators from the voices typically unheard in society for both the field of Hip Hop Studies and for the Hip Hop community. Thus, this project begins with a desire that this discussion would not only affect Hip Hop studies, but also affect society and post-industrial urban communities still living in dreaded social conditions—still seeking a God that would fit their current situation and still wondering whether heaven has a ghetto for them.

CHAPTER 1

Context, Societal Change, & the Construct of Hip Hop Culture

It seems like every time you come up, something happens to bring you back down.
   TUPAC AMARU SHAKUR

•••

Cause where I'm from if your soft your lost.
   KRS-One

•••

The 'hood dun took me under.
   MC EIHT

•••

Context is everything. In the Hip Hop community, geographical space, location, and locality are about representation, identity, meaning, and in some regards a spiritual awareness (Forman 2002). More importantly, in a context and region that has little to no social capital, area codes, street names, boroughs and city regions become a part of the social landscape which creates that person's being and quest for life (Fuller 2010; George 1992; Oliver 2006). Thus, for the Hip Hop community, space and place are critical in the development of not just the individual, but the community. To give a "shout out" and recognize a member in the community creates bonding and ties that show respect and admiration for a person and/or city region. To acknowledge one's roots and home is to establish a line that says "that is me; that is where I come from."

One young Hip Hopper who was interviewed, Miguel, told me that growing up as a young African American and Mexican American male in a rural southern town had its challenges. On the one hand, there was tremendous opportunity to simply be a child. Yet, on the other, there were powerful racial and class structures at work that were never seen but were felt on an almost daily basis. These invisible systems were put in place to control and circumvent a person from ever coming up, as Miguel recounted to me (Murray 1984). He told me that if a voice in the public sphere was not for the status quo, it was quickly shunned and put aside. Therefore, those who wished and dreamed to speak out did so in silence and behind closed doors; the risk of loss was too great. Miguel told me that religion was a centerpiece of his town and it aided in social control. It provided a way for those in power to utilize God as a means for control (e.g. sin, morals, salvation, heaven, hell). That is, God was an angry God who looked down on "back talkers," "hippies," and anyone who stood against "American values." Miguel was told that God and country were the same. He was educated to believe that the South had used slavery to nurture and develop Black people for the good of humanity. He was given a mantra that said that people who looked like him were inferior and only good for sports, manual labor, and the occasional sexual encounter out at the "back shed." These were the social conditions in which he festered daily. Miguel was not sure what to think of these conditions; they were, after all, constant and reinforced. Was God, in Tupac's words, just another White cop waiting to beat his ass in heaven? Was it that God was "for" White Christians and anyone who followed those theological creeds, and thereby "against" any other form of theological pursuit? He said he felt confused and unsure of who he was. It was not until he heard the musical style of rappers such as Run-DMC, KRS-One, and Public Enemy that he realized that the dominant group had lied to him. The possibility that God was "for him" was made clearer when he saw a representation who looked like him, talked like him, lived life like him, and called for social consciousness and self-awareness. His hope was realized. Miguel had moved from his rural town into a metropolitan city, hence, this transformation took place in a location and space he remembers well and is able to connect to. History now made sense and it made sense through the lens and scope of rappers.

Miguel's story is not unique; rappers Quest Love, Lil Wayne, Lauryn Hill, T.L.C, Beastie Boys, Common, Chill Rob G, KRS-One, and MC Lyte among many others, all recount a time and space when they were first introduced to Hip Hop and the social conditions in which they were living. When one examines the broad social context within which activities, political events, and religious movements were occurring, a broad picture is given as to how and in what conditions the music was created. Therefore, it is imperative that we take a moment to examine the social location, conditions, and historical context in which Hip Hop culture was created. Without it, history is lost and much of the foundation of this research would be lost.

This chapter explores the social conditions in which Hip Hop's theological mantras were incubating and thereby creating a foundation, on which this book is based: to explore and discuss Hip Hop's theological/spiritual tendencies. It chronicles major events from post-World War II, the late 1960s, and the early 1970s which helped shape much of Hip Hop's Golden era and begins to delineate the emergence of post-soul culture as Hip Hop created a new landscape in American popular culture. It will end by giving a brief overview of the soul and post-soul era's relation to postmodernism.[1]

The Social Conditions of the 'Hood

For a small period of time during an era of unprecedented momentum in American society, the years preceding World War II were among the most progressive years for ethnic minorities, and particularly for Black and Brown people (Murray 1984). Arguably the rise of the Black middle class came during the era between the mid-1950s to about 1965 when a middle class life was still available for many. In cities like Los Angeles, Detroit, Oakland, and Chicago, industrial companies such as Ford, General Motors, Firestone, Goodyear, and Sears Roebuck created jobs with good salaries, good benefits, and a livable wage. The work was hard, but it was consistent and steady. The quality of American life post-World War II was on the rise.[2] Even though there was a significant amount of acceptable racism, redlining, and zoning within many cities coupled with housing restrictions, many Black and Brown families were able to achieve middle class lifestyles by working for these industrial giants. Jobs were local and paid well enough so people could afford to purchase property and housing, a major component in achieving financial security in the U.S. (Bell 1976; Murray 1984; Thaker 2006).

For perhaps the first time in history, Black and Brown families were being integrated into society and could begin to see success with this pursuit of the

---

1 I want to state that this is not an exhaustive history of Hip Hop culture. For that, the following scholars take an in depth look into the historical connections of Hip Hop: Chang, Jeff. 2005. *Can't Stop Won't Stop: A History of the Hip Hop Generation*. New York: St. Martin's Press. George, Nelson. 1998. *Hip hop America*. New York: Viking. Kitwana, Bakari. 2003. *The Hip Hop Generation: Young Blacks and the Crisis in African-American Culture*. New York Basic Civitas. Rose, Tricia. 1994a. *Black Noise: Rap Music and Black Culture in Contemporary America*. Middletown CT.: Wesleyan University Press. My aim here is to establish major social phenomena in which Hip Hop was both created and is still rooted.
2 This did not, however, exclude extreme and salient racism toward Blacks & Latin Americans—it should be noted that lynchings and police brutality were a constant threat.

"American Dream" (Sides, 2003; Murray 1984; Peralta 2008). Families were able to have a typical nuclear (albeit heterosexual and patriarchal) family and create a path for intergenerational mobility.[3] By 1960, U.S. industrial development was in full swing and created thousands of jobs for families willing to relocate to cities such as New York, Chicago, and Los Angeles. In these cities, Blacks in particular were able to find a space and place to raise a family and develop their life. Further, even with housing restrictions, Blacks still found a way to secure housing,[4] attain loans, and create small savings within their communities which aided in the support of the family and gave people a sense of economic gain (David 1971; Hattery 2007; Lemelle 2003; Pinkney 2000).

Blacks transformed the communities in which they were living, which constructed what Stuart Hall (1998, 26–28) terms Black Popular Culture. Jazz, the blues, funk, rock and roll, and what would eventually evolve into Hip Hop was formed in these urban hubs in which Blacks were able to create their own sound, style, and lifestyle (Bennett 1993; Ward 1998).[5] In this sense, Brian Ward asserts that "although distinctive, black urban culture was crucially shaped by its relationship to a white-dominated mainstream culture which constantly affected both the material existence and the changing consciousness of black Americans" (1998, 58). Thus, a rich and complex culture was in formation and artists such as Fats Domino, Little Richard, Larry Williams, and Shirley and Lee crossed over to mainstream American culture to become early rock and roll hit makers and shapers of American popular culture (Ward 1998, 57). It would stand to reason that Blacks, in general, were beginning to "integrate" into American society and create a specific niche which still remains to this

---

3 Please note that this was not a utopian society. Jim and Jane Crow laws were in full effect in the Southern portions of the U.S. during this period of time (1940–1971). Housing restrictions rose exponentially on the West Coast which limited the areas where Black and Brown families were able to purchase homes, and prior to 1964, there were little to no laws which protected against almost any type of discrimination. What I intend to show here is that there was at least a pathway for Black and Brown families—typically one of the most undeservedly underrepresented groups next to Native Americans in U.S. history—to achieve middle class lifestyles.
4 Even within this housing boom for Blacks, many were often relegated to a small portion of cities referred to commonly as "the other side of the tracks." These housing restrictions, which did not disappear until the mid to late 60s, kept Blacks on "their side of town" and would eventually end up being the "ghettoes" once the industries left during the late 1960s and early 1970s (Sides 2003; Palen 1981).
5 An entire study and exhaustive look at the development of rhythm and blues is dealt with in Brian Ward's (1998) work *Just My Soul Responding: Rhythm and Blues, Black Consciousness, and Race Relations*.

day—although it is more commercialized and with less ownership by Blacks in contemporary U.S. pop culture.

What was unique about this time was that the affluent and working class Blacks lived side by side with each other due to segregation and housing restrictions. It was not uncommon to have a figure of high popularity and wealth like Ray Charles living next to a plumber like Dunker Lee. This created intergenerational connections and Black communities were much closer during this time. Older generations were essentially still connected to younger generations. Moreover, the common situation of contemporary Black families missing the father was not as big an issue for Blacks during this time. Even if a father was "missing" for whatever reason (killed in World War II, early death), many in the Black community adopted the African social mantra of "It takes a village to raise a child." Therefore, some families became blended and expanded during this era. One of the very few positive factors of segregation is that it kept all types of Black classes together and at times forced them to deal with many issues which had never quite been dealt with in this type of way (Bennett 1993).

The 1950s was a time when Blacks could be a "part of" the American system and create a future for their children (Wiese 2004). This was a crucial part of Black development and many Blacks flocked to the idea that they could own property and attain a livable wage. We have to bear in mind that at this point slavery had only been over for eighty five years,[6] and the effects of this atrocity was still an open wound for many Blacks. Therefore, the thought of being integrated into U.S. society with the real potential of attaining property and some manner of future generational stability seemed appealing to many Blacks.[7] The 1950s saw Blacks streaming into popular culture with musical artists such as Chuck Berry and Bo Diddley. In 1959 Berry Gordy founded Motown Records

---

6 Even though the Emancipation Proclamation was signed on September 22, 1862—going into effect three months later on January 1 1863, most Black historians and scholars would argue, as would I, that American slavery did not end until June 19, 1865 (Juneteenth).

7 This is not to discount or discredit the time period between 1870–1895 which several African American scholars have deemed as a time of "hope and vision" (Hine, Hine, & Harrold 2010). This period saw the exponential growth of African Americans into politics and the private sector. It was also a time when many African Americans were able to create a unique and contextual ethos in their communities, only to be cut short by policies, laws which excluded African Americans, and rogue groups such as the Red Shirts and Ku Klux Klan (see Franklin & Moss 2000). What makes the era we are discussing especially unique is the rate of growth for many African Americans into mainstream U.S. society through the arts, literature, music, and film.

which was the first record label to primarily feature Black artists.[8] This new "Black sound" helped to create a new era of Black popular culture and thereby aided in the social construction of identity for many Blacks—i.e. if one has the ability to see someone who looks like them in the public sphere, it gives them a type of hope and vision for their own life (Tatum 1999). This new sound would also influence and shape much of Hip Hop's musical discourse as well. Nelson George reminds us that Motown shaped and formed musical thoughts and expressions of later music moguls such as R. Kelly, D'Angelo, Sean Combs, and Russell Simmons (2007). Once Blacks were able to enjoy and purchase "Black music" as produced by Motown Records, the growth of a Black vision began and many Blacks began to see and interpret a future with possibilities, potentially ripe with reward.

After World War II, a booming automotive industry came into being and Blacks were a part of that industry (Wiese 2004). Major businesses and corporations like General Motors, Chrysler, Good Year, and Firestone made a home in what is now known as South Central Los Angeles.[9] These types of jobs employed thousands of people, many of whom were Black and Brown and benefited from the livable wages and benefits provided from such corporations (Peralta 2008). Josh Sides asserts that it was a moment of unprecedented Black prosperity and upward trajectory; people were on the rise, people were getting jobs, and were sending their kids to colleges. It was a moment of real optimism.[10]

It was during this time, that the Black church saw some of its largest growth and development. While the Black church was crucial and fundamental during slavery, for the most part it was small and underground. Yet, during this era,

---

8 There is a great deal of musical flurry occurring during this time. This project does not have enough time to deal adequately with the rise of blues, rock and roll, and Black Gospel music during this time. For a more in depth view see Floyd, Samuel A. 1995. *The Power of Black Music: Interpreting its History from Africa to the United States.* New York: Oxford University Press, and Grout, Donald Jay, and Claude V Palisca. 2001. *A History of Western Music.* 6th ed. New York: W.W. Norton & Company for a more descriptive account of this time period. See also Nelson, George. 2007. *Where Did Our Love Go? The Rise and Fall of the Motown Sound.* 2 ed, *Music in the American Life.* Chicago, Ill: University of Illinois Press for a study into the "Motown Sound" for Black popular culture.

9 This region of Los Angeles was not called this until the early 80s. Once those businesses had left, the middle class collapsed, those who had some semblance of wealth had left, and the lower class with no access to jobs was left creating a ghettoized part of Los Angeles. Other cities such as Oakland, Houston, Detroit, and Chicago also suffered the same fate in certain areas of the cities.

10 Interview taken from the documentary *Crips & Bloods: Made In America* (2008).

Black churches, as Eric Lincoln and Lawrence Mamiya state, became a central institution for Black Americans (1990, 7–10). The Black church was fundamental in providing spiritual formation and guidance for many, not just Blacks. Peter Paris tells us that "the black Christian tradition stands in opposition to the Western Christian tradition...The black Christian tradition has always been the source of inspiration for Black churches in their persistent attempts to reveal the fundamental depths of racism..." (1985, 11). Thus, the Black church was at the center of this shift in American society. Michael Battle reminds us that Black churches were crucial in the theological and social construction of Blacks during slavery (2006). Moreover, the Black church began to develop a type of theological construct which challenged White mainstream Christianity, even during slavery's harshest times (Battle 2006).

According to Battle, worship in the Black church aides in challenging the individual and group to engage in social action and form community (2006, 66–67). So, even in the presence of great injustice—housing restrictions, Jim and Jane Crow Laws—Blacks could, in the words of James Washington, "stubbornly trust in the promises of the Bible that God is a liberator" (1986, 8). Worship services, during this era, would be combinations of praise and a continued call to liberation and the restoration of the oppressed.[11] A great deal of the Civil Rights Movement took its theological cue from this type of ethos rooted in the Black church (Evans 1992).[12]

Three fundamental tenets emerged for Black families[13] during this era: community, family, and God. Community was about being together and creating

---

11   One must also note the construction of culture and societal norms as argued by Eric Lincoln and Lawrence Mamiya (1990, 2–7). This construction, popular during the post-World War II era for Blacks, has not resonated as much with the generation of Black youth during the late 1980s and early 1990s according to Lincoln and Mamiya. Part Three of this book will explore some of the reasons for this and what their findings mean for current Black youth.

12   In the same sense, it is important to note here that Black scholars such as Anthony Pinn pose a fundamental question of what does it mean to be Black and religious in the United States? What is the nature of Black religion? For an in depth examination to these questions, see *Terror and Triumph: The Nature Of Black Religion* (2003).

13   It is important to note that during the 1960s, two crucial works were released which shaped two fundamental ideologies for the Black family: first, Daniel Patrick Moynihan's work *The Moynihan Report* (1965), while providing insightful research and a snapshot of Black ghetto life, positioned Black families in what most African American scholars argue as pathological. This work shaped many studies, research projects, and public discourses regarding the Black family and created a negative framework in which Blacks were typically portrayed as socially lazy, genealogically deficient, and having low ethical standards. The other work, which challenged these notions, published in February 1966,

a space to worship, live, love, and grow. This meant that the younger generations, whether they approved of it or not, were closely connected to the Black church. Family meant staying together and creating a unit which was strong and solid—a foundation for future generations. Family was critical for Blacks who had lost so much of it during slavery. Moreover, the centerpiece of Black religious construct was the heterosexual patriarchal nuclear family. Lastly, God was an ever present force. Not just any God, but the Christian God. Even musical artists such as Aretha Franklin, Ray Charles, Diana Ross, and James Brown were closely connected to the Black church and would make reference to religious tones in their music (c.f. Southern 1983; Ward 1998). For better or for worse, it gave the younger generation a sense of hope, connection, and a vital outlook on life. There was a sense, among many younger Blacks, that there were clear social mores to succeed in life. College was at the top of this list, but God was always "first" in life. Upward mobility was thought to be possible and God was "helping us to move forward."[14] Therefore much of the younger generation of Blacks saw life through a Christian theological ideology; any waver in that was frowned upon and shunned in many Black circles. The Christian God was crucial and life was "not possible without him" for many Blacks. The fact that there was financial "prosperity" was more than enough proof that God was "doing something" for Black people; one simply needed to "keep the faith" and blessings would come.

These strict theological mores helped to create a social epistemology of meaning for many Blacks during this era. Even though artists such as Stevie Wonder, Donnie Hathaway, and even Lionel Richie, who became popular later during the 1970s, sang about a secular type of lifestyle, the Christian God was never too far away from their overall musical epistemology. For example, Marvin Gaye was one of the more pronounced artists who was born during this era making an impact during the late 1960s and early 1970s. He continually wove Christian Black theology into his music and created a social mantra of hope and love for many Blacks which was rooted in this era.

---

was Franklin E. Frazier and Nathan Glazer's book titled *The Negro Family in The United States*. This work acknowledges the poor social conditions that Moynihan had argued, but placed the Black family within the larger society. (One must also see Lee Rainwater & William Yancey's study refuting the Moynihan report published in 1968). Both of these works are crucial for their time as they lay out ideological structures which would affect Black families and, eventually, Hip Hoppers.

14   This is taken from an interview on case studies of African American churches in the Los Angeles area during the 1950–1968 era (c.f. Hodge 2010).

Black Christian churches created a social manifesto of living for Blacks: work hard, follow the rules, and love God. This type of dialogical hermeneutic was part of this hope and love mantra. Still, this is not discounting the fact that Blacks still felt isolated and sequestered in their spiritual journey here in America. Luke Powery in his book *Spirit Speech: Lament and Celebration in Preaching* notes that, "...African American people have not been at 'home' for centuries, ever since the Middle Passage. Within this exilic existence, blacks have been rejected by the landlords of the Americas, yearn for home, and seek to learn how to sing the Lord's song in a strange land" (2009, 6).[15] Therefore, we are reminded once again that simply because "jobs" were being created, there were still the very real issues of injustice, racism, and dehumanization of which many Blacks were reminded on a daily basis. This would create the foundation for the Civil Rights Movement of the 1960s, and especially the music, poetry, and spoken word which arose during that time. Even so, the social manifest for living was still a constant underlying theme which carried the philosophical spirit for the Civil Rights Movement (I will discuss this later).

Around the late 1950s and early 1960s, the beginnings of the first wave of what was to be called deindustrialization began to occur. Businesses began to find it more profitable to outsource their work, pay less in benefits, use cheaper labor, and ultimately generate larger profits for the shareholders. This adversely affected Black communities. What began to happen was a fragmentation of the middle class and a rise of people living in poverty. The American economy was beginning to change; it was shifting from an industrial to a post-industrial economy—one more focused on technology and highly skilled labor, which paid a lot more but required specialized training and education. Due to historic discrimination in colleges, many Blacks found it difficult to compete with peers with specialized degrees. The aerospace industry, for example, did not typically hire Blacks. Moreover, if the applicant did not have the necessary training, there was no point in applying. Todd Boyd notes, "We're not talking about people who had careers. We're talking about people who had jobs. If you have a job you are dependent on *that job*. So when that factory closes, you are in essence assed out."[16] By the late 1960s, most of those thriving factories had disappeared. In the wake of this loss, nothing was put into place for the thousands of workers now out of a job.

In 1968, there was full deindustrialization with many of these corporations leaving the U.S. to go to Mexico, India, and China (Sides 2003; Wiese 2004).

---

15   Also see Cheryl Sanders *Saints in Exile: The Holiness-Pentecostal Experience in African American Religion and Culture*. Oxford, 1996.
16   Interview taken from the DVD *Crips & Bloods: Made In America*.

The once hopeful and almost cheerful Black middle class was dismantled and was beginning to crumble. The Black generation born during the mid to late 1960s were in worse financial and social shape than the preceding generations. Moreover, these new generations were growing up without Black leaders and visionaries such as Martin Luther King, Bobby Seale, and Malcolm X. What was worse is that there were very few programs which could deal with the significant rise in Black families who were jobless. To add insult to injury, many Blacks—some of whom volunteered in search of work—were recruited into the army and fought and died in the Vietnam War which was raging during the late 1960s. During the height of the U.S. involvement in Vietnam (1965–69), Blacks, who formed only 11% of the population, made up 12.6% of the soldiers in Vietnam; the majority of these were in the infantry, and although some statistics differ on the figures, the percentage of Black combat fatalities was a staggering 14.9%.[17]

On Thursday March 10, 1975, eleven years after the end of the Civil Rights Movement, an entire section of the Los Angeles Times entitled "A Ghetto is Slow to Die" described this very real phenomena in the Black community. John Kendall researched families and the economic structures from 1963–1975 and stated that "The fearful live behind protective bars and double locks. High schools are graduating functional illiterates." He also asserted that "Little has changed in the basic conditions of the Black ghetto in 10 years since the Watts riots erupted..." The article was a sobering picture of reality which did not give a very promising future for anyone living in ghetto-like conditions, but principally for Blacks. Kendall continues to say that "Some black people have got businesses; some professionals have gotten into significant jobs. But if you talk about the masses or that guy who was in trouble in '65, it is more difficult now." The social manifesto that so many Black churches fought to create and instill was summarized in one word for life: survival.

In essence, once deindustrialization had begun and developed, large swathes of the Black community lay in financial ruin in its wake (Wiese, 2004). What little capital and access to education Blacks had, by the early 1960s, begun to wither away and create a distinct ghetto rife with anger and those searching for answers as to how and why this was becoming so depraved; it was a distinctive creation of societal separation and a disenfranchisement from the rest of American society. This societal separation and disenfranchisement was combined with factors such as police brutality—a fundamental element in the anger behind the Watts Riots in 1965 (Sides 2003), racism within almost every system in America, and social structures which pathologized Blacks as rebels,

---

17   Taken from *The Oxford Companion to American Military History* (1999).

communists, and those "outside" of American society. Additionally, the young people who were born during this time and who witnessed this societal shift would become the grandmothers and grandfathers of the Hip Hop culture that arose from these conditions.

Trust in politicans and government, nuclear heterogeneous families, White males as the symbol of the ideal "Christian," and "traditional family values" were all part of a thematic socio-theological meme for Americans during the late 1940s and 1950s. "Life" made "sense" to individuals and questions, doubts, mystery, and skepticism were frowned upon. Pathways to the numinous were "clear" and absolutized; morals were standardized and Christianity was the moral authority for deviant behaviors. There was a distinct shift in social, theological, philosophical, and even Christological ontology during the late '60s and early '70s. This shift was a direct result of the ensuing economic change for Blacks and also the reality that promises such as "work hard, and your dreams will come true" were shattered. For Blacks, a type of Great Depression set in, both financially and emotionally speaking. The new generation being raised in this ethos saw that the old way of life was not working and this new world in which they found themselves was one riddled with double standards, failed promises, destroyed social structures, and a government which seemed almost obtuse and belligerent towards them. An angry generation of Black and Brown youth were now culminating within the ghettos around the U.S. in the mid to late '70s. A new shift was taking place for Black and Brown youths' social and cultural expressions; in the womb of this shift, Hip Hop was taking form.

The Post-soul Emergence

Scholars such as Mark Anthony Neal (1997, 2002), Michael Eric Dyson (2001), Nelson George (1992, 1998, 2004) and Hodge (2010) use a more contextual term for what has come to be known as postmodernism: that term is post-soul. Post-soul is a rejection of soul era values, traditions, meta-narratives, theological accounts, and societal structures stemming from hierarchal systems attempting to control various societal areas (Alper 2000; Hebdige 1998; Kirk 2000; West 1993). Nelson George contends that, "Documenting the post-soul era is not about chronicling the straight line of a social movement, but collecting disparate fragments that form not a linear story, but a collage" (2004, ix). Further, the post-soul vernacular better suits the Black and Brown social structure (George 2004; Taylor 2007). Mark Anthony Neal tells us that, "...the political, social, and cultural expressions of the African-American community since the civil rights and Black Power movements" is essentially the point of birth for the post-soul era (2002, 3). Neal notes that these persons born and/or raised during this era came to age during the tumultuous 1980s, and had first hand witness to Reaganomics with its destructive forces in the 'hood. They experienced change from industrialism to deindustrialization, witnessed segregation to desegregation, went from strong clear notions of Blackness to nostalgic and metanarratives on Blackness, and even within these parameters of potential despair were still firmly in grasp of existential concerns within Black and Brown communities (Neal 2002, see Chapter 1).[18]

Therefore, the term post-soul and its era is one that encompasses the aforementioned, but also embraces the significance of race, class, and gender within its scope of ideology. Post-soul is the cradle in which Hip Hop is able to create its theological and spiritual sensibilities (Hodge 2010). Thus, for this book, we will contend that the post-soul era is the era in which Blacks and Hip Hoppers find themselves for the shaping of meaning, context, ontology, theology, philosophy, and spirituality. It is the era that best fits how Hip Hop began and formed its ideological positions.[19]

This period and shift from the soul era took full figuration during the mid to late 1960s[20] and it is there that we begin our discussion on the soul and post-soul development.

Soul & Post-soul Variations

The post-soul era is better understood by first understanding what the soul era was. The soul era arguably begins with the ending of World War II. It had several key elements to it that ring true and authentic to many who lived through some of the events that shaped it. Those key elements are:

---

18   Neal also contends that the post-soul era could be feasibly documented in its emergence with the rise of the 1980s "Reagan Right." It is because of this, Neal argues, that Reagan's policies further helped to instigate the advent of Hip Hop music and culture as Hip Hop became the most visible site of an already hostile and oppositional urban youth culture (Neal 2002, 102–103).

19   Admittedly, this is still a term under development and that, in the "postmodern" spirit, a singular term would not do justice to the current societal era in which we find ourselves living.

20   I argue that during this particular period, a shift and turn away from traditional modes of thought within Black traditions began to form. It began with Blacks standing up for their rights and refusing to conform to the social norms of White American society. Further, it was a time when some Blacks felt the power to speak up against Jim & Jane Crowism and the injustice which had befallen them for too long. It is also the era in which Hip Hop is, in essence, groomed and made ready for the coming storm of the 1980s.

- Connection to the faith community
- The soul culture which produced Marvin Gaye, Aretha Franklin, Jackie Wilson, Sam Cooke, and Donnie Hathaway
- It brought its religion's worldviews to the market place and public sphere
- It was nurtured in the womb of church, religious settings, and pastor-centered theologies
- They had optimism on their side and wanted to work with certain power structures to affect change

Faith and religious overtones mark the norms, values, and belief system of the soul era, especially in the Black Christian church. The soul era embraced an American Dream type of social element which many strived to achieve, and also produced a sense of morality rooted deeply in a King James Version of God.[21] It was a time in which the equation of life issues was A + B = C. Almost every time, in other words, life had answers and "clear paths" were evident eventually (e.g. Banks 1972; Battle 2006; Evans 1992).

Theologically, patriarchal respect and reverence characterized the soul era when it was uncommon for young people to question the authority of older men. Further, Black Christian churches were, in principle, a social structure for the creation of meaning, social representations of God, and spaces in which answers to life were eventually "found" (Hodge 2009; Pinn 2002).

The soul era took the values of post-World War II Black life and embraced it to its fullest. A "soulist" found themselves in a world which made sense, in one regard, and even though racism, segregation, and lynching were horrendous acts, life was still "black and white." The suburbanization and rise of American pop culture during the 1950s aided in creating a national social ethos in which life appeared to be "simpler" and "neater." *Father Knows Best, Leave It To Beaver,* and *Bewitched*, to name just a few of the growing television series of the time, made life seem compacted into a simple thirty minute fix. For the soulist, this made sense and helped to create a place for life, even if it was at the back of a bus.

In the soul era, the "enemy" was clear: White racism, segregation, and inequality. The Civil Rights generation (1945–1968) were united against these clear enemies who threatened to destroy the very fabric of Black and Brown life. The leaders of this time, Cesar Chavez, Martin Luther King Jr., Malcolm X, John Brown, Linda Brown, Ruby Bridges, and Medgar Evers were clear in their operative: destroy these enemies and create a "better tomorrow" (Jay and

---

21 To put this another way, a very rigid, fundamental, and binary view (sin vs. salvation) on theology and life.

Forman 1971). The soul era still had clear leadership, despite the declining financial status of many Black Americans, and this leadership had the ability to unify groups and masses.

The soul era inherited the struggles of previous generations of Blacks and urban poor who were united by several social and collective problems: struggle, pursuit of democracy, fighting the oppressive hegemony, justice movements, and a common working knowledge of God, typically rooted in Christianity (Hodge 2010; Jones 1973; Kirk 2000; Neal 2002). These social and collective adhesives were passed down, generationally speaking, and they galvanized young people around singularized leaders (e.g. King, Chavez) who "spoke for all" in the public sphere. This also created a sense of community among oppressed peoples, be they Latino, Black, or even women. The soul era had the public personalities to engage with, to learn from, and to embrace on many levels.[22] This will be examined further momentarily.

The post-soul era, by contrast, lost most of those leaders who were formidable and connected to the ghetto community. Further, within the post-soul era the "enemy" became muddled and unclear: was it the Vietnamese, classism, White people, or the FBI? To add an even stranger phenomenon, when segregation ended, what once was a thriving section of Black households and communities now became split. If a family had some aspect of economic refuge, they were more than likely to move out of the "ghetto" and into better neighborhoods, especially now that segregation had ended. While I do not contend that we need to return to a segregated world, one of the side effects of integration was the splintering of Black social classes and the separation of Black elites and lower class Blacks.[23] The post-soul era began in the late 1960s just as Black families were losing fathers and Black elites were moving out to the suburbs (Sides 2003, Wiese 2004).[24]

---

22   It can therefore be argued that, because of the loss of generational connectedness, social upheaval, and loss of historical connectivity during the late 60s and transition into the postmodern/post-soul era, the previous generation, which would become the first Hip Hop generation, was formed and created in a womb of dislocation, disenfranchisement, and a cultural anomie in which life was seen as misguided and with ambiguous direction. In this sense, the music and culture would in fact have much to say, both verbally and non-verbally, about these conditions.

23   A phenomenon Michael Eric Dyson describes as the Ghettoistocracy and the Afristocracy of Black classes (2005b).

24   Even social unrest was shifting during this time. Prior to the 1960s, rioting was typically Whites marauding through Black neighborhoods instilling on them violence in some shape or form, but the riots of the mid 1960s in Detroit, Oakland, and Los Angeles were Blacks revolting against the historical forms of injustice and racism in this country. From

Hence, one of the crucial differences between the soul and post-soul era was its connection to previous generations and historical narratives for life, community, and personal vision. This predominantly affected Black families (George 1998; Chang 2005). From 1965–1971, Black low-income communities were run by community groups such as the Student Non-Violent Coordinating Committee, the NAACP, and the Black Panther Party. There was a sense of social consciousness and awareness among the youth, and the old and young were still working side by side. The young were still attaining the knowledge from the preceding generations. These community organizations were committed to seeing change from within the Black community and from within the self—self-knowledge and self-awareness (Peralta 2008). Kumasi Brown, a South Los Angeles social activist and community historian tells us about this time that "all them youngsters were busy trying to rebuild their communities, trying to rebuild their futures, trying to figure out where the fuck do we go from here…together. And how do we create some sense of a future for our people?"[25] However, these community organizations, like the Black Panthers, quickly found themselves in the cross-hairs of government organizations like the FBI. According to recently declassified papers, the Black Panther Party was under constant observation and was deemed a "threat to national security," and was quickly labeled as both a "terrorist organization" and an "extremist group" which "advocated violence against American citizens."[26] These documents also reveal the fear and continual attempts, eventually ending in success, to destroy such community groups because of their "un-American" stance toward "Nationalism." To further this, almost anyone connected to such parties would be automatically followed, spied on, and deemed "hostile."[27] J. Edgar Hoover described organizations like the Panthers as "the greatest threat to the internal security of America."[28] Kumasi once again firmly asserts that "they [the U.S.

---

that point forward, "rioting" would not be the same, and most riots were in protest and rejection of "American" standards which many Black and Brown families living in the ghetto rejected and saw as a form of oppression (Sides 2003, Peralta 2008, Wiese 2004).

25   Taken from an interview with Mr. Brown on September 2010.
26   Taken from article 33 of 34 in the FBI vault files. http://vault.fbi.gov/Black%20Panther%20Party%20/Black%20Panther%20Party%20Part%2033%20of%2034/view (last accessed on 12/9/2011).
27   This was the case for two African American soldiers who showed interest in Black community development; they were followed and their activities were monitored. http://vault.fbi.gov/Black%20Panther%20Party%20/Black%20Panther%20Party%20Part%2033%20of%2034/view (last accessed on 12/9/2011).
28   Taken from an interview with Time magazine on Dec 14, 1970. *Nation: J. Edgar Hoover Speaks Out With Vigor.*

government] turned around and squashed those movements..." and some of the greatest and most energetic leaders of that time were either murdered, sent to prison, or fled the country in exile. Within a few years, between 1965–1970, many of the iconic leaders within the Black community were no longer there and a colossal void began settling in for Blacks. By 1971, there were very few remaining voices for Black youth to look towards, ghettos continued to swell, and Black Americans began a quick descent into extreme poverty, gang violence, and disenfranchisement.[29]

The youth born during this time were disconnected and disjointed from society. Moreover, with the rise in the absence of Black fathers during this time (Hattery & Smith 2007), Black youth found it difficult to adjust in a world which was not socially logical to them. Mr. Brown once again states, "...we passed by these children every day and paid no attention to them because we figured they'd be eventually taken care of. But, they watched us. We had the generations our parents came from and we had the personalities from that generation to connect with! To inspire us! We had something to attach ourselves to. They [the youth during this period] did not. They [the youth] were born in a state of suspended animation; they were totally disconnected and disenfranchised. They're like a planet out of orbit!"[30]

Therefore, it should stand to reason that the post-soul era was not formed in the womb of the church as the soul era was. The post-soulist did not have the connections to a "faith" community as did the soulists. Hip Hoppers, who are mainly the offspring of those from the post-soul era, had to develop their sense of being, their sense of life, their identity, and their values outside the church environment and, as Otis Moss states, "...it nursed from the breast of market forces and morally ambiguous political ideology" (2007, 11). Moreover, the post-soul offspring strongly critiques the status quo and institutions. Hip Hop is no different, which is one of the many reasons it has a difficult time finding solace in "church." The post-soul era was born during a time of deep urban difficulties and speaks for not just Hip Hoppers and Blacks, but also Latinos, poor ghettoized Whites, and disenfranchised Asians. Otis Moss once again states that:

> The truth is that many people of color, especially youth, are fighting for survival and attempting to gather meaning out of this strange land called

---

29 It is also interesting to note that at the same time these leaders were being extinguished in Black communities, the rise of the two infamous gangs, the Crips and the Bloods, grew exponentially (Peralta 2008; Sides 2003). We recommend reading Jeff Chang's chapter on the gangs of the Bronx (2005) as he also makes these connections.

30 Taken from an interview with Mr. Brown in September of 2010.

America. With the increase of police repression, demonization of people of color, introduction of crack cocaine, and the de-industrialization of urban centers, black people find themselves at a crossroads. Old tactics and strategies of change are now obsolete (2007, 113).

Paul Taylor, in his article titled "Post Black, Old Black" stresses that within the post-soul era, "new meanings have emerged: new forms of black identity that are multiple, fluid, and profoundly contingent, along with newly sophisticated understandings of race and identity..." (2007, 626), marking what Mark Anthony Neal contends as the "shift from essential notions of blackness to meta narratives on blackness..." (2002, 3) within the post-soul milieu. Additionally, post-soul Hip Hoppers largely find solace in an image which Todd Boyd describes as "The Nigga"—a rebellious, outspoken, system-rejecting, and irreverent yet proud and socially focused image of Black aesthetics, which revels in questioning, authoring and recovering some of those broken promises, often by any means necessary (1997, 13–37).[31] Thus, within the post-soul era, Hip Hop finds itself in a Marxist state of mind as it critiques the socioeconomics, social climate, and institutions of America.

Table 1 has a brief way of better understanding some significant components between the soul era and the post-soul era (Hodge 2010, 63–66).

These areas are by no means exhaustive. Yet they give us a place in which to begin and to better understand why Hip Hop helps to usher in post-soul tendencies. Moreover, Hip Hop begins new didactic conversations in regards to Christology, salvation, and Kingdom of God discourse.

Thus, for the post-soulist, life is unpredictable, mysterious, questionable. Systems will fail you and eventually, almost everyone will lie to you. When we contrast that with the soul era, we see a stark difference in attitudinal values toward life. Moreover, the two are almost at odds on issues of faith, God, and especially "church" (Hodge 2010).[32]

---

31   This image and characterization of Hip Hop only reinforces the notion that Hip Hop is hostile, secular, devoid of God, and immoral for those who reside in soul era worldviews.

32   While I will discuss this further in the coming chapters, it is important to note that Rap groups such as Public Enemy and NWA gave voice and breath to Hip Hop's post-soul aesthetic. These two groups were strongly criticized for their stance and critique on many social problems that existed and still exist today in the U.S. They also put a face on much of rap music that still exists today. The "ugly" side of post-soul is the commercialization and the pervasive and negative messages it sends to all people of color living in America. Public Enemy and NWA represented social critiques, yet, ironically enough, their critique was lost within the commercialization of the post-soul era while their "style" still remains. Many, who do not have a grasp on Hip Hop culture or who have never been to an inner

TABLE 1   *The differences between the soul era & the post-Soul era*

Soul era	Post-Soul era
Absolute	Non-absolute, majority thinking
Linear in reasoning & discourse	Non-linear; circular, triangular, & extremely visual
Hierarchal; top down power; order to power structures	Group centered & power is equally distributed and plural
Individualists; individualism is valued	Community based while still allowing for individual creativity & expression
Reasoning toward solutions and answers	Reasoning for relativistic approaches to answers
Solid conclusions	Ambiguity; life is a mystery
Answers that are solid and conclusive; everything can be explained	Uncertainty; everything does not have to have an answer
Racial & about categorizing ethnicity & class	Moving towards a Post-racial & post-classist society
Categorizing people, places, & things	Every person, place, & thing cannot be categorized and explained; there are people, places, and things that simply cannot be explained
God head is set	God is plural, existential, and mystical

Hip Hop & Postmodernism

It is necessary to have a brief discussion of Hip Hop and its relation to postmodernism. I realize that the term "postmodernism" has become quite stale in the academy and what was once a buzz word in the 1990s is now growing old. While I am not presenting an exhaustive study regarding this very important relationship, there are works such as Cornel West's *Prophetic Thought in*

---

city, see Hip Hop largely looking like these two groups: Black, exotic yet ominous, dark, and having an "in your face" attitude. This concept has brought billions of dollars to many corporations and has made large sections of the Black community a laughing stock and the butt of many jokes. The post-soul era's commercialization has made it "okay" to Niggarize the suburbs; films such as *Malibu's Most Wanted* (2003) are an example of this.

Postmodern Times and Lawrence Cahoone's *From Modernism to Postmodernism* which treat this extensively. It does however deserve some discussion at the very least in relation to Hip Hop.

Hip Hop, during the 1980s and 1990s, set the stage for public voices and a new form of music.[33] Russell Potter says that Hip Hop and Rap were one of the leading agents for postmodernism to develop; it was the music for the postmodern generation (1995). The music became the philosophical base for Hip Hop artists. In modernity, modern social theory sought a universal, historical, and rational foundation for its analysis and critique of society. For postmodernists, there is a rejection of that "universal" thought and message. Postmodern thinking rejects this "foundationalism" and tends to be relativistic, irrational, and nihilistic. Postmodernists have come to question foundations structured within systems and institutions, believing that they tend to favor some groups and downgrade the significance of others, give some groups power, and render other groups powerless.[34]

Cornel West also adds three significant changes in American culture that gave rise to postmodernism in the U.S.. West offers a genealogy of how this moment in time, postmodernity, came about.[35]

The first is the displacement of European models of high culture, of Europe as the universal subject of culture, and of culture itself in its old Arnoldian reading as the last "refuge." In this sense, the Eurocentric school of thought, in many ways made Blacks invisible and nameless. Within a Eurocentric hegemony there is a lack of Black power in the social sphere (West 1990). Yet, with the emergence of popular culture, forms of art such as rock and roll, jazz, and the blues, became vehicles in which Blacks gained voice and some power, relatively speaking, while shifting the Eurocentric authority and giving space for a new form of thought (West 1990, 32–33).

The second coordinate that West discusses is the emergence of the United States as a world power, through the means of slavery and the rise of capitalism during the nineteenth century. Consequently, the U.S. became the center of global and cultural production and circulation. This made it possible for America to grow economically and socioeconomically. John Hall says that "this

---

[33] Another reason Rap music is so appealing to contemporary generations is because, through postmodernism, one can express her or his self in a unique way and find a voice within that music. See Alper (2000), Anderson (2003), and Forman (1995).

[34] See (White 2002, 200), and also Stuart Hall discuss this cultural change in which Black popular culture developed in (1998, 21–25).

[35] These three points are adapted from West's essay, *The New Cultural Politics of Difference* (1990, 19–36).

emergence is both a displacement and a hegemonic shift in the definition of culture—a movement from high culture to American mainstream popular culture and its mass-cultural, image mediated, technological forms" (1992, 21–22).

The third area that West describes is the decolonization of the Third World, culturally marked by the emergence of the decolonized sensibilities (1993, 122–123). The world was becoming gradually autotomized. America was developing what we now refer to as popular culture and the rise of the inner city, of the ghetto, was developing as previously mentioned. The inner city was therefore set up to be a cultural hub, which I will reference later in this chapter. Nonetheless, the industrial revolution played a large role as urban areas grew, decolonization happened globally, and Black popular culture, which reflected the effects of the industrial revolution, grew in American popular culture.[36]

Consequently, the postmodern context has origins in pop culture and the media. The postmodern context has two very distinct characteristics. First, it is spiritual. This is an arguable point to make. Intellectuals such as Zygmunt Bauman (1998), Don Cupitt (1998), and Martin Heidegger (1996) would contend that postmodernism rejects modern spirituality and religion and begins on a quest toward some form of secularization. Charles Taylor would even assert that we do in fact live in a "secular age" with the advent of post modernity (2007). Yet, while these scholars have valid points, the postmodern (particularly the post-soul era) is still in search of a God, spirituality, and faith; it merely looks, acts, feels, and walks very differently to anything in modernity (Burnim 2006; Dark 2002; Detweiler and Taylor 2003; Drane 2000; Lynch 2005; Zanfagna 2006). Second, postmodernity presents a consciousness of pluralism on every level of social engagement. In other words, the postmodern age is a re-enchantment of the "forest" of life, society, the human experience, theology, spirituality, and faith. For the postmodernist, the "forest" is not managed, predicted, and produced away; the "forest" is a mystery. Moreover, for Hip Hoppers, the "forest" cannot be controlled by White managers who continue to dictate what is "right" and "wrong." Hip Hop, then, calls out that mismanagement, and proclaims the "forest" to be a fluid object that cannot be manufactured in cookie cutter ways.

The focus is on the spectacular,[37] on the edge, and on allowing the person to reach a higher level of knowledge (Cavazzini 2009; Cox 1984; Zizek 2008). Any

---

36 Also see James Cone (1997), on how the rise of the "suffering Jesus" came into play and how that played out in Black culture, and the urban gospel message (Chapter 6).

37 Graffiti art is one of the most powerful aesthetic expressions of postmodern Hip Hop discourse. This is very similar to what Emma Cavazzini argues in neo-avant-garde art in the postmodern global context (2009).

culture that focuses on the spectacular might be termed a transcendent culture. Life is over the top; the unreal is the real. Postmodernists are searching for the experiential and the transcendence in culture, which includes rap music.

4 Key Elements of Hip Hop & Postmodernism
Hip Hop has four key postmodern spiritual & liberating elements to it:

1. Restoration: Hip Hop is about restoring and recovering that true authentic self. This can come in many ways, but one aspect remains true, especially in many spoken word venues: the self needs to be restored and built up from its broken state.
2. Self-Awareness: Five Percenters will ask, if one does not have self-awareness, how can one know who one's true self really is? Therefore, much of the centrality of Hip Hop culture is about self-awareness and the development of the inner self.
3. Questioning Authority, Power, Control, & Institutions: this is probably the heart of Hip Hop culture. Countless rap songs do this in a manner which typically, once again, summons the *nigga* image that Boyd (1997) discusses. Hip Hop continues to ask the question "Whose authority, power, control, and institution should we follow, if any? And, what makes *them* right?" A powerful question that reaches into the core of postmodernism.
4. Recovering Empty Promises: Hip Hop is about making some "right" in a world that is not "right." Rap artists such as Tupac, Ice Cube, Chuck D, Eminem, and David Banner attempt not only to recover empty answers, but to also challenge the broken promises given by politicians, church officials, and people in control. Rap groups and artists such as Boogie Down Productions, A Tribe Called Quest, Brand Nubian, Public Enemy, NWA, Gang Starr, Tupac, Geto Boys, and Ice T were attempting a fundamental crusade to recover the empty promises made, in particular, from the American government, the social system, and churches. This crusade, of sorts, was fueled by the countless lies Hip Hoppers felt they had received in regards to not just the "American Dream," but also basic life existence (more on this in Chapter 3).

These four elements are very similar to what Dick Hebdige (1998, 374–381) describes as "The Three Negations" of postmodernism, which are also similar to Hip Hop and the post-soul era:

1. Against Totalization: Hip Hop culture is not in favor of one grand story, or in postmodern terms, "meta-narrative." Rap music calls out the faults

and errors of the previous and current generations' dogma on success, life, theology, love, hate, women, men, and sex. Hip Hop culture begins to dismantle this point of view by word and prose, and questions its substances. This is attractive to many urban youth, as they have been questioning this ideology since their emergence into this world. Paul Taylor once again suggests that there is a skeptical and suspicious orientation from "postmoderns" when narrating history (2007, 630). Moreover, Ihab Hassan tells us that, "chronicles of continuity...deny real change" by destroying creativity and diversity when they "fall into place on numbered pages" (1996, 383). Thus, Hip Hop looks upon dominant historical discourses with both suspicion and doubt.

2. Against Teleology: Hip Hop culture is against the "final word" from scholars and professionals that explain the origins and existence of the earth, God, religion, and humanity—especially if this comes from a Eurocentric perspective. Rap music calls out the monopoly of rich White males that have dominated most of Western Culture to this day.[38] Rap music and Hip Hop culture begins to deconstruct grand stories of beginnings and existence. Hip Hop culture increases the span of knowledge and brings back the mystery of faith.

3. Against Utopia: Hip Hop rejects almost any type of "happy ending" that does not ring true to the past forty years of ghetto life survival. For many urban youth, the reality of a suburban or "American Dream" utopia is not within reach. Still, Hip Hop creates space to, at the very least, engage in what life "might" be like (we will cover more of this in Chapter 4 in our discussion of the Hip Hop Jesuz).

Postmodernism is discussed here for several reasons. First, postmodernity gives Hip Hop a context, philosophically and pedagogically, in which to operate. Hip Hop artists' understanding of the 'hood, urban youth, and Hip Hop culture have postmodern qualities to them because they are elements of the post-industrial deconstruction in the U.S. and typically challenge the norms set forth by hegemonic dominant structures.

Second, Hip Hop is part of a postmodern shift in society. Hip Hop does not like the "norms" of the given societal structures, views them as oppressive and uses rap as a way to express those "beefs" with social authority. Hip Hop questions absolute truths, absolute authority, and believes deeply in community, which are all tenets of post modernity as argued by Lash (1990), Lyotard (1984), Kuçuradi (2004), and Kirk (2000).

---

38 See Neal (1997) & Gottdiener (1985).

And lastly, I desire to connect postmodernism and the post-soul era as I feel they are very analogous in nature and pedagogy. More importantly, postmodernism and the post-soul era fuel much of Hip Hop's growth and development over the last three decades. Therefore we feel it is important to engage in such discussions.

Chapter Summary

This chapter has been concerned with discussing and engaging with the social conditions in which Hip Hop's theological mantras were incubating for its creation as a global culture group. We explored and discussed Hip Hop's theological/spiritual tendencies and chronicled major events from post-World War II, the late 1960s, and the early 1970s which helped shape much of Hip Hop's Golden era. The soul and post-soul eras were also dealt with and we demonstrated the creation of both eras and their connections to postmodernism and Hip Hop.

Hip Hop was created in a space where dissention, questioning of authority, rebellious spirits, broken systems, and rejections of traditional modes of thought were all placed into one social stew and mixed together. The first generation of Hip Hoppers were from a generation that did not have the enlightening personalities of the '50s and '60s, nor did they have the connection to older compeers as previous Black and Brown generations had done. Further, Hip Hoppers embraced post-soul ideological structures as it provided the platform in which many felt they could express themselves and be heard in a way like never before.

The post-soul era brought with it a new manner of thought. American culture would never be the same once Hip Hop took hold of it. The post-soulist community is a group who does not see God in the same way as a soulist would, nor does that person trust that form of God. In contrast, the soulist views the post-soulist with suspicion, cynicism, and distrust. This will be a key part of our next chapter.

We now move to Chapter 2 which broadly looks at the theological messages within the Hip Hop cypher from a select group of key rap groups and artists. This chapter builds from Chapter 1 as there will now be an opportunity to sample the fruits from the post-soul era in the voices of Hip Hoppers. I will engage with artists during these societal shifts and demonstrate (1) their connections to our discussions in this Chapter and (2) their own post-soul worldviews on life, society, God, and the political structures in their context.

CHAPTER 2

God in the Cypher: Theological Narratives in Hip Hop

> I feel God smiling on me when I rap.
> "MIKE" (interviewee)

∴

> Shit, God is in the cypher. Ya feel me son? That's where God resides nigga!
> "JAMES" (interviewee)

∴

> The thing about Hip Hop today is it's smart, it's insightful. The way they can communicate a complex message in a very short space is remarkable.
> BARAK OBAMA

∴

At the heart of Hip Hop culture is a conglomeration of stories, allegories, life narratives, and messages constructed within these discourses. Hip Hop culture creates a canon that allows for those creating it to seek the spiritual and consciousness within their own context—a critical element to the DNA of Hip Hop culture. Conversely, language in Hip Hop contexts is powerful and creates space, significance, dialogue, awareness, and meaning. What stands out in the language of the rap music is the tension which exists between the current context and the desired 'life' one envisions. In the opening verse of Nas' song "Life's A Bitch" he describes part of this tension:

> Visualizin the realism of life and actuality
> Fuck who's the baddest, a person's status depends on salary
> And my mentality is, money orientated[1]

---

1 (Martin; Nas, and Premier 1994).

Here, Nas describes this tension within his current situation. He goes on to discuss these struggles in the chorus of the same song:

> Life's a bitch and then you die; that's why we get high
> Cause you never know when you're gonna go
> Life's a bitch and then you die; that's why we puff lye
> Cause you never know when you're gonna go
> Life's a bitch and then you die; that's why we get high
> Cause you never know when you're gonna go
> Life's a bitch and then you die; that's why we puff lye
> chorus #1 echoes at the end

Nas's chorus echoes the state of the mid 1990s when the Hip Hop classic album, *The Illmatic*,[2] was released. Only two years after the April 29, 1992 Los Angeles uprisings in response to the Rodney King verdict, there was a rise in gang violence, and a failure of the social system within urban enclaves. Nas's chorus echoes the sentiments, feelings, and state of mind for many Hip Hoppers living in these conditions. Still, within this discourse, Nas attempts to find peace and a space to process God. To this extent, Nas is wrestling with the ongoing narrative of the time: is there a God where I'm at?

A Hip Hop film[3] that emerges from this era and matches this sentiment—also one of the major films connected to the West Coast urban struggle and aptly dubbed as a 'hoodie film' (Boyd 1997)—is the Hughes brothers' debut *Menace II Society* (1993). In one scene where Old Dogg (played by a very young Larenz Tate), challenges the authority of his friends, Caine, a paternalistic grandfather who is proselytizing them concerning God and the need to follow "his commandments," poses the theo-ontological question: "Sir, I don't think God really cares too much about us. I mean, look where we stay at, it's all fucked up." Within this discourse, we find a deeper theological narrative of question, uncertainty, mystery, and doubt about a God "up there" who can reach "us" "down here" in the midst of chaos, violence, and a sense of being

---

2   This album is considered by many in the Hip Hop community as one of the best of the 90s. A classic album in its own right, Nas covers the socio-theological landscape of his time in this album and wrestles openly with being conscious and connected to God while still desiring fame, women, money, and power. It is a search for justice in the profane life (Spencer 1997, 107–110).

3   During the interviews, films/movies were discussed to connect with both the descriptive and normative approach to theomusicology to arrive at a clearer picture of what was happening in the setting and era.

forgotten. Old Dogg's question is re-told in the narrative form of rap music. Through the house parties, desire to have sex, and live large, the quest for understanding the why is grappled with in the stories rappers tell.

One of the descriptive factors in the context of the late '80s and early '90s was that of story. Yet, the question remains: whose story was being told? What group was being hailed as 'hero' and 'villain'? Moreover, who was the voice telling the story? For Hip Hoppers, it seems that a type of rhythmic code, of sorts, is being created—a code that allows for its member to distinguish what is being said and leaves outsiders baffled and wondering.

Hence, we have the signifier: the cypher.[4] For Hip Hoppers, the cypher *is* the story and narrative in rhythmic prose. The Hip Hop cypher is the message of its people. Scholars define the Hip Hop cypher as:

> The very term 'cipha,' signifies and exemplifies the international and global diffusion of Hip Hop Culture, as well as its social location as a universal, cultural free space to 'express yo' self.' 'Cipha,' in Hip Hop Culture derives from the language of the Five Percent Nation of Islam (Nation of Gods and Earths)—an indigenous form of Islam in the U.S.—where it is used, among other meanings, to refer to sites of learning and the construction and sharing of knowledge, with participants in the cipha 'building' truth and constructing a shared worldview, and themselves, in the process.
>
> The Hip Hop cipha, or some variation of it (sometimes referred to as 'spittin sessions' in areas of the South and elsewhere), is the foundation of Hip Hop rhyming, and remains central to Hip Hop. If Hip Hop were a material object, the cipha would represent Hip hop at its molecular level—it is the fundamental unit of analysis in the interpretation of Hip Hop Culture
>
> SPADY; ALIM, and MEGHELLI 2006, 10–11

One can note the power behind the significance of the cypher. Moreover, the socio-cultural molecular elements within the Hip Hop culture is all rooted in the cypher, according to Hip Hop scholars (One 2003; Watkins 2011; Zanfagna 2006). Spady, Alim, and Meghelli give depth to the art and cultural substance of the cypher.

Yet another definition of Hip Hop's cypher is:

---

4 Cypher is also spelled as cipher, cipha, and in some circles cypha. I will use Cypher as the preferred spelling.

> A cryptographic system in which units of plain text are arbitrarily transposed or substituted according to a predetermined code; or the key to such a system. In hip-hop, the cipher is a locale where artists of various backgrounds, commitments, and training come together in a linguistic battle of wit and passion, where 'aporetic flow' erupts into competing norms and continuous ad hominem assault. To 'cipher' is to decipher the motivations, positionalities, concerns, and roadblocks that make up the discursive power arrangements of a community. It is to 'play' a linguistic game of one-upmanship through deconstruction of your opponent and to embody and speak into existence the 'possibility of the impossible' task of what might be of critical, productive discourse—scholarship.
> MILLER and DRISCOLL 2013

This definition provides a more analytical approach to understanding the cypher. This definition gives insight regarding the themes with which this chapter will engage: deciphering the motivations, positionalities, concerns and roadblocks that make up the theological messages within Hip Hop.

These two definitions connect with the three analytical approaches to theomusicology: descriptive, normative, and predictive. To investigate the theological inferences, in this chapter I will begin by examining rap artists' cypher to determine the divine amidst the paradigms of pain, suffering, urban disenfranchisement, racism, hyper-sexuality, and the quest for hope.[5] Hip Hop provides a way to denote/suggest the feelings that one is experiencing within the current context in a symbolic and coded process. In rap music, it is a way of invoking the community and creating meaning. Ebony Utley (2012, 11) tells us that, "Rap music also contains traditional invocations in the form of public acknowledgements of God and prayers to God." Thus, part of the cypher is about acknowledging God within the code and rhythmic prose.[6]

But, is "God" really in the mix? How can a "God" allow such suffering if God is just, fair, and all loving? As one interviewee asserted to me, "Do we really want to follow a God that would allow such shit to happen to his people? I don't know man…[pauses] I don't know." We will keep this question in

---

5 I argue that Hip Hop has five central theological areas: (1) a theology of suffering (2) a theology of community (3) a theology of social justice (4) a theology of the Hip Hop Jesus, and (5) a theology of the profane. This chapter will assume these theological constructs given the data and theomusicological study of this book (Hodge 2010).

6 For a further study into the language of Hip Hop see Samy Alim's groundbreaking work investigating discourses and cypher codes within Hip Hop, *Roc the mic right: the language of hip hop culture* (Alim 2006).

tension—which seemingly follows the same line of thought that Old Dogg did in the film *Menace II Society* (1993)—and observe the context in which these theological inferences were created. Let us begin by examining rap artists' words, songs, and social context as they presumably journey to, for, and with God.

Theological Inferences

Let us consider the following artists as a sample for theological inferences within the cypher of Hip Hop: Ice Cube, Tribe Called Quest, Bone Thugs-N-Harmony. Digable Planets, Kanye West, Nas, Kendrick Lamar, and Remy Ma.[7] I specifically chose these artists because of their references in the interviews, their overall connections to a theological cypher, and their broader cultural popularity. Tupac Shakur was one of the top artists from the interviews, but Chapter 3 will cover Tupac more closely. I will also make reference to other rap groups who have significant theological references in their cypher such as Pete Rock & CL Smooth, DJ Premier, RZA, Brand Nubian, Gang Starr, X-Clan, Scarface, and Jay Z.

A Tribe Called Quest
Hyped as "the most intelligent, artistic rap group during the 1990s" by Hip Hoppers and music journalists alike, A Tribe Called Quest hit the Hip Hop scene at the height of the Golden Era in 1990 with the album "People's Instinctive Travels and the Paths of Rhythm." A Tribe Called Quest was made up of Q-Tip, Ali Shaheed Muhammad, and Phife and gave their audience an "alternative approach," as it was labeled by many Hip Hop pundits, to rap music. At a time when the genre of West Coast Gangsta Rap was growing and some were beginning to feel that Hip Hop was "losing its soul," A Tribe Called Quest was a group which added a different flavor to the rap rhythm and constructed heavy synthesized and drum machined songs. A Tribe Called Quest emphasized

---

7 I acknowledge that this list is male based and extremely lacking in female representation. This is not to suggest that the male dominance in Hip Hop is correct, nor condone it, but is merely following what the data in this research is telling us. Moreover, because male artists are often ones that get more radio play and publicity, they are typically the ones who get more of an audience and listeners. This is unfortunate and there are many female MCs who's message is strong and theologically based: Queen Latifah, MC Lyte, Eve, TLC, Missy Elliot, and at certain points Nicki Minaj. Further research and exploration is needed in this area. However, the scope of this research happened to fall upon a majority of male rappers.

lyrics and message over the actual song or 'beat'—a pattern which many East Coast rappers followed, and still do to some extent. The group desired to establish a sense of consciousness and Afrocentric self-awareness. They also questioned other rappers on their material regarding the edification of it and how it helped the community at large.[8]

Descriptively speaking, A Tribe Called Quest gave a space for this production of meaning at a time when popular culture was developing into the digital social context it has become now. Hip Hop scholars often note that Hip Hoppers create meaning in spaces of rap discourses (George 1998a; Hodge 2010; One 2003; Rose 1994; Utley 2012; Watkins 2011). Yet, much of this began with A Tribe Called Quest and their awareness and consciously themed messages.[9] A Tribe Called Quest is an infusion of Judeo Christian, Nation of Islam, and Zulu Nation theological constructs. Their music was reflective of that. Moreover, they called their listeners to not only a "higher calling," but also to fear respectfully that which is "higher than you" (meaning Supreme Being).

Three of their albums made it to *The Source*'s top 100 all-time rap albums: Low End Theory, People's Instinctive Travels and the Paths of Rhythm, and Midnight Marauders. When asked, "what theological inferences can you take from rap artists?" Hip Hoppers exclaimed regarding Tribe Called Quest:

- Q-Tip put it down for a nigga to realize that he needed to do better
- Tribe Called Quest? Whew [pauses] them cats was dangerous. Ya know? I mean, you couldn't have rap groups like that today. All niggas be like today is bitch this, I have money like them, but Tribe? Was like, fuck all that. God's got better plans for you...

---

8   Arguably, this was a time when "rap" was still young and "new" for record labels. Jeff Chang (2006) notes that the growth of rap also made for a growth in the desire to "make money" from it. Craig Watkins affirms this and asserts that when the record industry began publishing Sound Scan data and more money was offered to artists for talking about partying, drugs, and a "gangsta lifestyle," Hip Hop began to diminish in its overall character. Watkins (Watkins 2005, 33–41) calls this "Remixing American Pop" and points out that Hip Hop was on a fast course to record sales, money, and the loss of content. Therefore, to complement their "genius" status placed on A Tribe Called Quest, one might deduce that they were 'before their time' in discussing the problems associated with the record industry.

9   This is not to denote that N.W.A, Blacksheep, and the ensuing artists such as The Roots, Common, Mos Def, and Tupac did not have a social awareness or consciousness, but rather to suggest that A Tribe Called Quest was one of the first mainstream (meaning music is being played on power radio stations, MTV, and other popular outlets) rap groups to take their conscious-spiritual message to the public.

- Know thyself. Period. That's what Tribe Called Quest gave you. That's part of what God wants.
- I think they also inspired cats like Pac, Kanye, and Jay Z; A Tribe Called Quest was that deep.
- These bruthas [referring to A Tribe Called Quest] made you think about where you fit in the universe. They made you feel that God was still with you; even in the shit and mire of the 'hood.

In some regard we are reminded of Durkheim's' definition of religion:

> A religion is a unified system of beliefs and practices relative to sacred things, that is to say, things set apart and forbidden—beliefs and practices which unite into one single moral community...(1965, 47)

A Tribe Called Quest, in a manner, creates an ad-hoc system of beliefs and practices relative to sacred areas in Hip Hop such as respect for each other, consciousness, connection to the Earth, and an attempt to contextualize the deity for the practice of sacred things in uniting the Hip Hop community. In this sense, Hip Hoppers create sacred spaces within the music, on street corners, and attempt to make sense out of the disdain they feel coming their way from the rest of society. Yet, Charles Glock and Rodney Stark are correct to remind us, "What it means to be 'religious' is not the same to all men—either in modern complex societies or in even the most homogenous primitive groups" (1965, 18). Thus in this way, A Tribe Called Quest is, for their time and context, creating the sacred and profane for the Hip Hop community by manufacturing social consciousness and developing a native religious and spiritual awareness for urbanites living within reprehensible social conditions.[10]

In their album, People's Instinctive Travels and the Paths of Rhythm, the song "Youthful Expressions," offers insight to the cypher A Tribe Called Quest was

---

10   I find interesting what Hip Hop scholar Monica Miller notes as the social construct of "dirty" and "deviant" norms. In this sense, we can connect the construct of religion—on the one hand, often thought of as a 'moral' and 'righteous' aspect to society (following North American Evangelical norms). But Hip Hop constructs its own forms of sacred space. Are those truly that "dangerous" and "out of bounds?" Miller asserts that "...we are reminded that constructing Hip Hop as a 'danger' or 'risk' to the black community or society is less reflective of the actual dangers Hip Hop poses, and more representative of boundaries of properness, respectability, and morality. Socially constructed and fabricated social systems remain stable by (in) conspicuously including and excluding—reordering dirt that seemingly gets 'out of place'" (2013b, 26–27).

producing. Using a re-created sample[11] of Marvin Gaye's song "Make Me Wanna Holler"—a track critical in the youth revolt of the Black 1960s which contained critical discourse on conditions in the Black and urban communities—A Tribe Called Quest calls attention to the youthful voice needing to be heard. Here is a display of part of that cypher in the first verse of the song:

> The taste of nuthin, this does somethin
> Moms that knows that, says I'm frontin
> Call me Smiley, cuz I'm wiley
> Livin life like the life of Riley
> Smokin blunts with a boy named Bud
> We cough up your lungs, cough up your cud
> Put out fires, with a 40 ounce of water
> You know you oughta
> Dance to this, your girl you kiss[12]

Here, the cypher code is evident; done in a style which is both allegorical and metaphoric, the song uses poetic symbolism to get at the issues. What may appear as a call to smoke illicit drugs, marijuana in this case, is actually a play on discourse to challenge young people to think beyond just getting high. Moreover, when they exclaim that they "put out fires, with a 40 ounce of water," the play here is that they do not drink malt liquor, which is a stereotype of middle to low class Black males, but rather they drink water, which is refreshing. Near the end of the first verse, Q-Tip bellows his connection to the Zulu Nation[13]—an indigenous form of Afrocentric spirituality and theology rooted in Christianity and mysticism. This is a footnote of sorts, yet, it lets the listener know that there is spirituality at work.

The second verse continues the cypher toward identifying a youth voice:

> Jarobi:
> The economy...politics...police...everything
> Except for the youth
> But the youth about to come back

---

11 Music that is taken from another artist, but rather than sampling it, it is recreated by playing either the beat, notes, chorus, or combination of the latter.
12 (Quest 1990).
13 The references to the Zulu Nation are found throughout all three albums and are referenced at various times.

> Q-Tip (voice distorted):
> Alright, here they come
> Uh oh, uh oh, uh!
>
> Q-Tip:
> With expressions and I'm guessin
> 19 years is a youthful lesson
> Fallin skies babe, open eyes babe
> Can't you see what lays inside babe
> Makin mentions on this tension
> Rhythmic lovin, my profession
> Hips, they gyrate, scripts I narrate
> No banana, I ain't a primate
> Ain't no soul glo, just an afro

Here, again, symbolism is at work. Jarobi's opening line constructs the loss of thought and concern for the urban community. Rappers such as Tupac, Eve, Chuck D, MC Lyte, and Queen Latifa have all lamented the continued ignoring of urban issues by political officials. Yet, Jarobi offers a type of 'hope' for youth. They are coming back. Q-Tip follows. Note how he ends the last part of the verse: "Ain't no soul glo, just an afro." During this time of Afro consciousness of the 1990s—and for that matter ethnic minority self-consciousness—there was a push toward the natural and non-processed. For many Blacks, this was a shift from processed hairstyles such as perms and jerry-curls to a more natural look—in this sense, getting back in touch with their roots and African history. This particular reference is from the film starring Eddie Murphy and Arsenio Hall, *Coming To America* (1989). The character Darryl Jenks (played by Eriq La Salle), was a model for the shift against the processed hair look as he was the heir of the jerry curl and hair processing industry Soul Glo. Darryl represented the "American ideal" of Black success and his hair style therefore is one of the antagonists in the film towards the main character (Prince Akeem from Africa) who wears a natural look and is therefore, as the film portrays, closer to those African roots.[14]

The theological inferences for A Tribe Called Quest is trinary: personal awareness, social consciousness, and the challenge to seek a Supreme Being

---

14 Many rap groups such as X-Clan, Wu-Tang, Public Enemy, GZA, and BDP (Boogie Down Productions)—among many others—argued for a natural look between the years of 1988 and 1995. This push did not fade until the late 90s and is currently only found in small circles in the Hip Hop community. Yet, there is a continued push towards consciousness.

(preferably a contextual one in ethnicity). A Tribe Called Quest is attempting to awaken the "God" within the person and is relative to the time and context in which they are constructing their music. Their "genius" comes in both their grappling with all three domains in theomusicology (the sacred, the profane, and the secular), and their ability to, predicatively speaking, create a sense that the future of Hip Hop involved money, a loss of the artist's soul, and commercialization gone awry (Charnas 2010). Their message resounded: we need God in these "lost times" and a self-awareness is crucial.[15]

Yet, the tentacles of commercialism did not stop simply because A Tribe Called Quest was 'socially conscious.' In 1993, Q-Tip had a very small role in John Singleton's film *Poetic Justice* as Janet Jackson's slain boyfriend which led to other parts in Hollywood.[16] As several noted in my interviews, this was a shift toward 'Hollywood' and a push in the direction of 'success'—the very thing that A Tribe Called Quest argued and fought against. Q-Tip went on to have roles in several other films and television series. Meanwhile he continues to remain a part of the current and socially conscious part of Hip Hop. There are some who consider him a 'sell out' to Hollywood. This is an ongoing tension within the Hip Hop community, and hard core Hip Hoppers resist any forms of commercialization and becoming part of the mainstream. The group eventually broke up in the late 1990s.

Still, A Tribe Called Quest was a significant group who wrestled with the theological in their music. Their cypher was so coded in conscious imagery and God like symbolism and as a result, they remain a cornerstone in what James Spady, Samy Alim, and Samir Meghelli call The Gobal Cipha (2006).

We turn next to a group that many Hip Hoppers feel never got their true respect. Rooted in a heavily coded cypher and connection to a mystical, jazz/funk-infused, Black God, Digable Planets creates theological inferences in their push toward social consciousness and personal realization.

Digable Planets

As John Bush (2013), musician and writer at the music data base allmusic.com, notes, "Though they were not the first to synthesize jazz and hip-hop, Digable

---

15 In their song "8 Million Stories" on the album *Midnight Marauders*, the group wrestles and engages with the problems that youth face. In the end, while there is a clear connection with the pain, they call out to God, The Zulu Nation, and faith in God to help them and the last word spoken is "Mohammad" in reference to the Nation of Islam leader, Elijah Mohammad.

16 This was also a time when other rappers such as Ice Cube, Tupac, Ice T were making a shift into acting and starring in major roles in films.

Planets epitomized the laid-back charm of jazz hipsters better than any group before or since."[17] One of the most "unrecognized" "God centered" rap groups of the 1990s, as several interviewees told me, Digable Planets created a cypher that was complex, rich, theologically driven, and soaking with messages of self-awareness, realization, and a consciousness rooted in traces of Islam, Christianity, and Jewish theological constructs. As one of the "gems" of Hip Hop artists of the 1990s, Digable Planets was on a mission to create a space for youth, in particular, to realize their potential.[18] Further, Digable Planets represented a growing trend of rap groups using a blend of jazz, soul funk, and blues as their samples. Digable Planets were innovators in creating sounds that were simplistic in rhythm, yet had complex lyrics. Digable Planets were a group that held much "promise" for the culture of Hip Hop and gave credence to the Hip Hop cypher in every song.

Digable Planets formed in the early 1990s, when Butterfly (Ishmael Butler, from Brooklyn, New York) met Ladybug (Mary Ann Vieira, Silver Springs, Maryland) while attending college in Massachusetts. The two later connected with Doodlebug (Craig Irving, Philadelphia, Pennsylvania), in Washington, D.C., and began recording. Their mainstream hit, "The Rebirth of Slick (Cool Like Dat)," represented their cypher complexity:

[Butterfly]

We like the breeze flow straight out of our lids
Them they got moved by these hard-rock Brooklyn kids
Us flow a rush when the DJ's boomin classics
You dig the crew on the fattest hip hop records
He touch the kinks and sinks into the sounds
She frequents the fatter joints called undergrounds
Our funk zooms like you hit the Mary Jane
They flock to booms man boogie had to change
Who freaks the clips with mad amount percussion

---

17   Digable Planets was also a rap group which was frustrated with the political and economic state of the inner city. As children in the 1980s and twenty-somethings in the 1990s, the group pushed toward a stronger and more equitable government. The group was politically active during this time.

18   As is noted, much of the mainstream rap in the Golden Era was focused on youth and adolescents to become self-aware and be connected to a higher power (be it Allah, God, Jesus, or Buddha in some circles).

> Where kinky hair goes to unthought-of dimensions
> Why's it so fly cause hip hop kept some drama
> When Butterfly rocked his light blue-suede Pumas
> What by the cut we push it off the corner
> How was the buzz entire hip hop era?
> Was fresh and fat since they started sayin audi
> Cause funks made fat from right beneath my hoodie
> The puba of the styles like miles and shit
> Like sixties funky worms with waves and perms
> Just sendin chunky rhythms right down ya block
> We be to rap what key be to lock
>
> PLANETS 1993

Three points are worthy to note in this opening verse:

1. Space and place are located fairly early in the lyric. This connects to what Murray Forman discusses as the "symbolic meaning" within inner city localities. The importance of this is that it gives the listeners meaning and voice to their space—typically ignored in other media venues (Forman 2002, 42–46).
2. The push for natural and kinky hairstyles is once again mentioned and referenced. Digable Planets lobbied for a natural look and feel, a return to the roots of Pan African heritage which is also rooted in an awareness to God.[19]
3. The intersection of the sacred, profane, and secular is evident in the song's structure and by using strong language such as "shit" and "ass" to illustrate their points. Moreover, Digable Planets was a group who was able to interlace church like messages, rooted in real time life conditions on street corners and gated communities alike.

---

[19] The 1990s was also a stage where the "culture wars" gained momentum. Conservative Christian Evangelicals made a "stand" against rap music by issuing continued boycotts and pushing labels such as Warner, MCA, and Sony to drop rap artists who were speaking "foul messages" in their music. There was a cultural "push" that implemented those who were "Christian" in their theological belief systems to move away from more "secular" and "worldly" music. Hip Hop was at the top of these lists as conservatives felt it represented and advocated an immoral lifestyle (For a detailed account of this 'culture war,' see Craig and Taylor 2003; Heelas 1998; Lynch 2005). Rappers, while disagreeing with this type of message, did argue for a Third Eye Consciousness and some even felt that the influx of "gangsta rap" was a sign that Hip Hop was on a decline. Digable Planets, in a Yo MTV Raps interview, alluded to this.

Within this cypher, the real theological work is done in the construct of self-identity rooted in the Third Eye theological mantra of being aware. This cypher is strongly connected with Third Eye theology which searches for that 'Double Darkness' which surrounds the heart, according to Chon-Seng Song (1979, 18–21). There is a search which takes place for that higher Being—the creator—the Being which can open up that third eye which is connected to the heart and soul. Song, author of *Third-Eye Theology: Theology in Formation in Asian Settings*, tells us that "…in the process of the search for that Being, human beings become conscious of their spirituality, which relates them to that Being in a very special way" (1979, 17). This search for knowledge, consciousness, and a connection to a higher power, is precisely what Digable Planets and A Tribe Called Quest urge their audience to do even as they lose the urgency to keep up such a search.

In a song which seems torn out of current headlines, Digable Planets lay out their push for social action and what appears to be left-sided politics. The song "Femme Fatale" illustrates a strong affiliation with pro-choice worldviews, and a call for women to have more social capital and power. The song carries a preacher discourse and structure, and is laid out within the mixture of the sacred, the profane, and the secular. Here is part of that verse:

> lookin some kind of sad with tears fallin from her eyes
> she sat me down
> and dug my frown and began to run it down
> "you remember my boyfriend Sid that fly kid who I love
> well our love was often a verb and spontaneity has brought a third
> but do to our youth an economic state we wish to terminate
> about this we don't feel great, but baby that's how it is
> but the feds have dissed me
> they ignore and dismiss
> and the pro-lifers harrass me outside the clinic
> and call me a murderer, now that's hate
> so needless to say we're in a mental state of debate
> hey beautiful bird I said digging her somber mood
> the fascists are some heavy dudes
> they don't really give a damn about life
> they just don't want a woman to
> control her body or have the right to choose
> but baby that ain't nothin
> they just want a male finger on the button
> because if you say war they will send them to die by the score
> aborting mission should be your volition

> but if Souter and Thomas have their way
> you'll be standing in line unable to get welfare while they're out
> hunting and fishing
> it has always been around it will always have a niche
> but they'll make it a privilege not a right
> accessible only to the rich
> pro-lifers should dig themselves
> cause life doesn't stop after birth
>
> PLANETS 1993

Note the last few lines in this prose. These verses sear with a call to action for not only women, but for men in power. The song continues:

> to a child borne to the unprepared
> it might even just get worse
> supporters of the h-bomb and fire bombing clinic
> what type of shit is that? Orwellian in fact
> if Roe v Wade was overturned would not the desire remain intact
> leaving young girls to risk their health
> and doctors to botch and watch as they kill themselves
> I don't want to sound macabre
> but hey, isn't it my job
> to lay it on the masses and get them off their asses
> to fight against these fascists
> so whatever you decide make that move with pride
> Sid will be there (ladybug will be there, doodlebug will be there)

In the heat of the abortion debate, Digable Planets creates a space for Hip Hoppers (and others alike) to discover their significance in a media blitz geared toward making abortion an "immoral" decision and connected to religious and spiritual convictions. While that may be the case for some, Digable Planets are encouraging their audience to examine critically the issues surrounding abortion and to allow women to have the last word in that debate.[20]

The album ends with the song "Examination of What" where the group critically observes the current cultural context, and challenges their audience to contest the authority they hold true.

---

20   This is not to suggest that all in the Hip Hop community feel this way regarding abortion. There are those, as is the case with many issues, who feel strongly that it should not be allowed. Still, female Hip Hoppers such as Salt & Pepa, MC Lyte, Queen Latifa, TLC, and Eve have similar views to Digable Planets.

[butterfly]
one day...while I was sipping some groove juice I realised...that in the span of time we're just babies...it's all relative, time is unreal.

we're just babies, we're just babies, man (x 4)

Every man's a planet and the props are there to get it
insects roll together with the spirit in our orbit
life, it comes & goes and you do not punch a clock
I don't take shit for granted, I think of Scott la Rock
also of Tyrel and battles at the borders
my cousins in the joint and the homeless grippin quarters
the forests are all shrinking, this deepens to my thinkin
don't cover up the nappy, be happy witcha kinkin!
dwellin, yes, you're dwellin as the norm is itty-bitty
figure eighty-fitty for a smidgen of the city
in the serengetti, be ready for a box
but beware of the shanks and the pistols and the glocks
if your peoples don't getcha, you still ain't off clean
the politicians' mask is worse than Hallowe'en
I write the funky scripts so you know I got to kick 'em
now tell me who's the vics and tell me who's the victim

chorus [butterfly]

what is really what is really what is really what:
– if the funk don't move your butt
– and if the box don't make you hot
– and if the cats don't dig the raps
– if your life ain't got no spice
– or if the guns just wreck your fun
– or if some shouts ain't in the house
– or if your crew ain't down with you

The chorus reveals a cypher which essentially asks that "If your life isn't going well, look at the elements within it." This examination continues in the third eye stream and challenges those listeners to grow from their experiences. One must note that throughout the album (along with A Tribe Called Quest) the group does not condemn, cast judgment, or call out their audience for their lifestyle, but instead hopes to motivate them to "do better" or to "rise up" from the challenges surrounding them. They avoid the 'boot strap' narrative which so often falls upon Black and Brown communities to "do better" through a more committed work ethic and instead acknowledges the struggle, the fight, the social conditions, and need for a higher calling—even if that calling is merely to be a postal worker, a janitor, or a doctor.[21] This song is thematic for the time in which Hip Hoppers alike (Heavy D, Ice T, Blacksheep, Black Moon, Tupac) argued for in their messages and music: be yourself, seek a holistic life, seek God in the struggle, and be community minded.[22]

Digable Planets seeks to give the audience a pathway for consciousness, self-awareness, and voice in an oppressive world. Their music, message, and place on the Hip Hop cultural continuum are important because they give the Hip Hop culture a critical exposition of cultural events in a poetic manner while still creating room to think, act, and move forward with life—something that is critical in Hip Hop culture. Digable Planets broke up unexpectedly after 1994 and in ensuing interviews, members of the group pointed to issues within the music industry itself, which was reported by many other rappers. These involved tensions created when money is negotiated between managers, promoters, studio engineers, publicists, and within groups themselves. Even still, the group made an everlasting impression on the continuum of Hip Hop culture and are still peddled as a cornerstone.[23]

Nas

We turn next to an artist known as Nas—the Hip Hop "cypherologist"—as one interviewee told me. Nas was and still is a powerful force in the Hip Hop community. His debut album *The Illmatic*, is heralded as one of Hip Hop's finest and he carries on in the essence of Tribe Called Quest and Digable Planets,[24] but with a street edge and strong blend of the profane and secular. Nas calls on his community to not just think critically, but also to peer into the social double

---

21 In interviews, Digable Planets continued to focus on the true art of their music and what the deeper messages were. They stated that the music industry can corrupt and can take over your mind if you let it. Further, they were very critical of the "business" of the music industry and the cultural appropriation it could bring.

22 This was also thematic in other music genres such as Grunge and Alternative which Digable Planets, oddly enough, fit into those themes in many regards. They questioned authority, lifted up young people, called to a higher consciousness, and pushed their audience members to critically engage the times.

23 88% of my interviews still say that Digable Planets are legendary and pioneering in both their work and music.

24 Lady Bug noted in an interview that she had wanted to work with Nas because of this strong cypher and the social messages.

standards. Touted as a "legendary rapper" in the current era of Hip Hop,[25] and with album titles such as *God's Son*, *I am*, *Nastradamus*, and *Street Disciples*, Nas continues to construct both controversy and hope for many in the Hip Hop community while negotiating theological lines by blurring them in the profane and secular (as defined in the preface). Nas is a powerful force within Hip Hop culture and offers a myriad of messages which include theological implications, contradictions, love, sex, women, hope, social irony, and references to being the "best." Throughout the interviews, next to Kanye West and Tupac's name, Nas was mentioned and admired as if he was already canonized into the Hip Hop cultural continuum. Nas is a continuing force in Hip Hop culture.

What Nas brings is an unbridled intransigent East Coast confrontational approach to looking at the social, economic, spiritual, and political issues which affect most acutely the Black and Latino communities living in urban spaces. Nas' big hit was the song "The World is Yours" featured on this debut album *The Illmatic* (1994). With connections to the Tony Montana's mantra (in the film *Scarface*), "The World is Yours," Nas dances with what fame, money, and a life filled with success would be like. Theologically speaking, Hip Hoppers' concept of living a "good life" is not too far from a Western Christian view of heaven: gold streets, eternal life, mansions, success with "God," and a life without pain.[26]

In the second verse, Nas peers into the living conditions of those in urban areas:

Chorus: Nas, Pete Rock

[PR][27]   Whose world is this?
[Nas]   The world is yours, the world is yours
[PR]   It's mine, it's mine, it's mine
[PR]   Whose world is this?
[Nas]   The world is yours, the world is yours
[PR]   It's mine, it's mine, it's mine
   Whose world is this? "It's yours!"
   It's mine, it's mine, it's mine
   Whose world is this?

---

25   90% of my interviewees all saw Nas as both a legend, and in some regards, a true cypherologist given his current fame and continued success.
26   Pete Rock, also strongly connected to a theological philosophy in his music and life, was instrumental in the production of Nas' album and aided in the chorus of this song too.
27   PR: Pete Rock.

> [Nas] The world is yours, the world is yours
> [PR] It's mine, it's mine, it's mine
> Whose world is this?
>
> To my man Ill Will, God bless your life "It's yours!"
> To my peoples throughout Queens, God bless your life
> I trip we box up crazy bitches aimin guns in all my baby pictures
> Beef with housin police, release scriptures that's maybe Hitler's
> Yet I'm the mild, money gettin style, rollin foul
> The versatile, honey stickin wild, golden child
> Dwellin in the Rotten Apple, you get tackled
> Or caught by the devil's lasso, shit is a hassle
> There's no days, for broke days, we sell it, smoke pays
> While all the old folks pray, to Jesus soakin they sins in trays
> of holy water, odds against Nas are slaughter
> Thinkin a word best describin my life, to name my daughter
> My strength, my son, the star, will be my resurrection
> Born in correction all the wrong shit I did, he'll lead a right direction
> How ya livin large, a broker charge, cards are mediocre
> You flippin coke or playin spit spades in strip poker
> "It's yours!"
>
> NAS 1994

Note the chorus, which is a conversation that gives a sentiment of encouragement to the audience. Within the body of the verse, the God of Nas' cypher is revealed by looking at his daughter and the hope which lies within her. Conversely, Nas criticizes Christian theologies by stating that, "...all the old folks, pray to Jesus; soakin' they sins in trays of holy water..." For many in the urban areas, they felt abandoned by the "Church"[28] and Nas is one of the voices proclaiming that anger and sense of isolation.[29]

---

28   By "church" I am referring to the Christian church. The Black, Latino, and urban contexts are typically very connected to a Christian theological discourse. While Islam and the Nation of Islam are also strong and relevant, Christianity is still strong and prevalent. Ironically, because so much of dominant White Christian heritage and history is anti-Black and racist, containing a message that keeps ethnic minorities in a position of submission (Carter 2008; Rah 2009), so the Black equivalent contextualizes versions of Christianity which may, at times, contain some residue from The Nation of Islam. This could be one of the reasons rappers like Nas, RZA, and even Tupac are strong critics of main stream Christianity. We will look at Tupac's position on this in Chapter 3.

29   This is also what KRS-One told me in an interview, "Man, we was left by the Christians. It was our own people that didn't accept Hip Hop. That was the first place we went [talking

Nas claims that he is the "rebel of the street corner." Within that self-proclaimed mantra, Nas offers strong critiques. Yet, similar to A Tribe Called Quest and Digable Planets, Nas does not advocate violence and derides Black on Black crime. In the song "Represent" his cypher argues for the alternative:

> I drink a little vodka, spark a L and hold a Glock for
> the fronters, wannabe ill niggaz and spot runners
> Thinkin it can't happen til I, trap em and clap em
> and leave em done, won't even run about Gods
> I don't believe in none of that shit, your facts are backwards
> Nas is a rebel of the street corner
> Pullin a Tec out the dresser, police got me under pressure
>
> Represent, represent!! (repeat 4X)
>
> Yo, they call me Nas, I'm not your legal type of fella
> Moet drinkin, marijuana smokin street dweller
> Who's always on the corner, rollin up blessed
> When I dress, it's never nuttin less than Guess
> Cold be walkin with a bop and my hat turned back
> Love committin sins and my friends sell crack
> This nigga raps with a razor, keep it under my tongue
> The school drop-out, never liked the shit from day one
> cause life ain't shit but stress fake niggaz and crab stunts
> So I guzzle my Hennesey while pullin on mad blunts
> The brutalizer, crew de-sizer, accelerator
> The type of nigga who be pissin in your elevator
> Somehow the rap game reminds me of the crack game
> Used to sport Bally's and Gazelle's with black frames
> Now I'm into fat chains, sex and Tecs
> Fly new chicks and new kicks, Heine's and Beck's

Here, in this cypher, Nas is calling his audience—particularly the young ones—to look beyond the violence and guns to a life of money, women, weed, and success. Embedded in this song is a message for those who want to live in

---

about the Black Church]...but they closed their doors; wouldn't even allow us to have events in their spaces. That's the politics that needs to be discussed which have not. The only ones that were open to us [speaking of the Hip Hop community] were the Hare Krishnas. They the ones who opened the doors and offered us space. So, for Christians that want to criticize Hip Hop [pauses], they need to look back at their own damn history."

a state of disarray; jail time and unconsciousness will follow. In a metaphoric stance, Nas uses the very thing he is challenging the listener to think twice on, by lyrically nuancing with them. On the surface, it appears like a "party" song, but, as one moves beyond that, there is much more to it. Yet, Nas is holding in tension items that society calls "bad" such as weed, illicit sex, and their connection back to God (3rd verse).

Nas is currently making albums, his theological overtones are influential and his albums such as *I Am* and *God's Son* offer insight to his own self-canonization in Hip Hop.[30] Nas continues to call his audience to a higher form of thinking, but doing that from a local perspective—the street corner and 'hoodie spaces. Nas' 1999 song and ensuing video for "Hate Me Now" on the album *I Am*, featured Nas on a crucifix and exclaiming tones of martyrdom within the rap industry. The song stirred much controversy and some YouTube versions even had disclaimers. Nas' use of the Jesus image is part of the Hip Hop appropriation of Christ (more on this in Chapter 5). In the video, Nas carries a cross, has lacerations across his face, and wears a crown of thorns. Crowds of people throw stones at him and yell. Nas creates a space in which he connects with the suffering of Jesus by comparing it to his life in the music industry and media world. The video cuts back from Nas entering a club and performing as a lavish individual to the martyrdom of the cross. Nas uses messianic imagery and symbolism in which he positions himself as a messenger and prophetic voice for the Hip Hop community.

This demonstrates the power within Nas' music, message, and transmediated ideology.[31] Moreover, he has continued to criticize dominant forms of religion who, as he has stated in numerous interviews, are tyrannical and oppressive. Nas does not shy away from any of this and keeps it "100" as an interviewee told me.[32]

---

30   It is an interesting note that Tupac, whom we will discuss further in Chapter 3, did not always have a positive outlook on Nas. Tupac felt Nas was "fake" and "two faced." In several interviews, Tupac strongly criticized Nas and called him a "sell-out." Tupac, known as the 'Ghetto Saint,' often said that Nas was only in the "rap game" to save his own "ass" and that he was out for money. An interesting note to make as he is one of the few rappers from the Golden Era who is still making albums and profiting from Hip Hop. He also did not succumb to the pressures of the music industry so duly noted by rap artists Digable Planets, Tribe Called Quest, Blacksheep, DJ Premier, and Onyx. This is not to suggest that Nas is indeed a 'sell-out.' But it is something to consider.

31   The use of digital & social media to create story and message.

32   Hip Hop vernacular for being real, authentic, and transparent with your persona and message.

Next, we will look at a rap group which openly beheld and pirouetted with Satanism, death, the afterlife and Christianity: Bone Thugs-N-Harmony. We enter a West Coast sound and theological treatise that considers what the afterlife may be, especially in an environment where death is so prevalent: the urban context.

Bone Thugs-N-Harmony

West Coast sounds—strong baseline, melodic rhythms, and an emphasis on a 'hard-core' sound—took the public stage when N.W.A. released their now infamous song "Fuck The Police." Followed by Dr. Dre's 1992 album *The Chronic*, West Coast rappers became widely known and artists such as Snoop Dogg (Now Snoop Lion), Tupac, and Bone Thugs-N-Harmony took the stage in a rap game that up until that point, was dominated by East Coast rappers. Bone Thugs-N-Harmony entered an area with which few dared to engage during the mid-1990s and became one of the few mainstream rap groups of the time who dealt directly with death, the Devil, evil, and God in the context of the afterlife.[33]

The years between 1994 and 1997 saw rappers such as Bone Thugs-N-Harmony dealing with issues like death and loss. Iconic rapper Eazy E died of AIDS on March 26, 1995, Tupac on September 13, 1996, and Biggie Smalls was murdered on March 9, 1997. All had the Hip Hop community searching for answers and asking the questions: where are they now, and why? Bone Thugs-N-Harmony confronted questions about death, violence, and the ensuing afterlife head on. Anthony Pinn describes their perspective as a 'Nitty-Gritty-Hermeneutic' (1995, 114–117) in regards to suffering and the problem of evil.

Further, they were arguing, in essence, what Terrence Tilley suggested— that 'theodicy' creates hardships (1984, 304), and theologian attempts to respond to the question "why does evil exist in God's good world?" damage the very faith they hope to secure (Pinn 1995, 113). Moreover, Bone Thugs-N-Harmony seeks to argue that theodicy fails to explain evil because of the tension of having a 'Good God' in a world (and context) that is clearly evil. Tilley further asserts:

---

[33] Between 1994 and 1997, a time many Hip Hoppers do not care to remember, artists such Red Man and Onyx openly commercialized death within the context of vampires, zombies, and Satanic imagery. It was a short lived era, but nonetheless, an era which saw some rappers push back from Abrahamic faiths and look into a darker realm of understanding supernatural power.

...to write a theodicy is not merely to express a wish. Such writing is an illocutionary act which is not merely an expressive act, but a declarative act which makes 'true' what is only a wish. One of the evils of theodicy is that it effaces the differences between the world that theodicists wish to be (a world wherein God reigns) and the world that is (1991, 249)

Therefore, Bone Thugs-N-Harmony, in a Hip Hop manner, challenges the notion that says "God is in control of all." They are constructing alternative theories by looking into Ouija Boards and mysticism. They are able to confront the trivialization of death, pain, struggles, and life problems (Song 1979, 32–33) by mainstream theologies of the afterlife while providing a contextual approach to this problem.[34]

Take, for example, Bong Thugs-N-Harmony's song "Crossroads" in their 1995 album *E 1999 Eternal*.[35] In it, they ponder the questions of life and death. The song begins with a call to consciousness and awareness that a life on the streets will only lead to bad consequences. Moreover, the group asks the all-important question "What-cha' gon do when you can't run no more?" The first lyric states:

> Let's all bring it in for Wally, Eazy sees uncle Charlie
> Little Boo, God's got him and I'm gonna miss everybody
> I only roll with Bone my gang look to where they lay
> When playing with destiny, plays too deep for me to say
> Lil' Layzie came to me, told me if he should decease well then please
> Bury me by my grand-grand and when you can, come follow me
> THUGS-N-HARMONY 1995

---

[34] In the same regard, many urban dwellers, especially younger ones, see death as an almost welcome event and space. In other words, "something has to be better than this hell we live in." It was common during this era to entertain death as a welcomed event—as a resting place and space to find loved ones. This may, in fact, connect with that 'bad' theodicy in which Tilley argues against. Yet, I would argue that it offers some a sign of hope that this life is not the end and that there is a 'better tomorrow' waiting for you on the other side. Christina Zanfagna records that "to claim your suffering in the moment, to truly feel it and accept it, is a powerful act of self-attestation" (2006, 8).

[35] As a co-producer on this album, I can attest to the fact that Bone Thugs-N-Harmony was in fact attempting to wrestle with death and the theodicy within it. They had issues with the failed answers their Black parents—who were rooted in charismatic Pentecostal Christianity—had for them in regards to death and God. They struggled with the recent deaths of Eazy A and Tupac and wanted a stronger answer than "It was God's will." Thus, in this album they wrestled with death, evil, and the presence of 'God' within those areas.

In this lyric we see the rapper Bizzy begin to deal with the death of his grandfather. He is speaking to his listeners, stating that "God has got him" as if to say that somehow his granddad is in heaven now.[36] Moreover, Bizzy wishes to be buried next to him so that they can spend the physical death—that is being buried in the ground—together.

The rapper Layzie follows with:

> God bless you working on a plan to Heaven
> Follow the Lord all 24/7 days, GOD is who we praise
> even though the devil's all up in my face
> But he keeping me safe and in my place, say grace
> For the case to race with a chance to face the judge
> And I'm guessing my soul won't budge
> Grudge because there's no mercy for thugs
> Oh what can I do it's all about our family and how we roll
> Can I get a witness let it unfold
> We living our lives to eternal our soul aye-oh-aye-oh

Here Layzie encourages his listeners to have a relationship with God, work on their "plan" for entry into heaven, and to see death as only a gate into another dimension. The video makes the lyrics alive and allows the viewer to see that even with a life that is less than perfect, one can still become an angel and go to heaven.

The video begins with a Black funeral in a church. The grieved parents are sitting in front of the church grieving the loss of their loved ones, when all of a sudden a man wearing black leather comes down the front of the aisle, but is only seen by the mother of the lost one. The man dressed in black—presumed initially to be death itself—then lifts the spirit of the young man out of the casket and carries him out. The mom is beside herself. However, with one glance from death, she stops yelling and crying. All of this is taking place while the song "Mary Don't You Weep" plays—an old Negro Spiritual sung during death ceremonies.

The video continues showing death taking lives, one by one, while the artists also continue asking the question of all Hip Hoppers, what are we going to do with our life? The "Crossroads" then becomes more apparent near the

---

36   This is no revelation either; most people believe they are going to heaven when they die in an ABC poll done on the subject "heaven" in 2007. Most see their loved ones in heaven as opposed to hell.

end of the video. Initially, we are not sure of the intentions of this ominous figure. He continues to take lives. He even takes a baby, much to the protest of its parents.

By the end of the video, we see death going up a long mountain and following him are the souls of the people he has touched—all silhouetted in white. In this group is the fallen rapper Eazy-E. At the top, Bone Thugs-N-Harmony are singing and bearing witness to death bringing up all of these souls. The video then shows that death is not all that "scary." He drops his black jacket, while still carrying the baby he took, and his wings are then revealed and people are led to heaven. Bone Thugs-N-Harmony then contend that we will meet our loved ones at the crossroads. Moreover, they are in a better place.

Bone Thugs-N-Harmony are pertinent and important to the Hip Hop Community because, simply put, they bring a highly divergent perspective to Hip Hop that explores dimensions of death and violence in ways that other rap artists are not able to do. There is an admiration in Hip Hop with regards to death. It is valued, feared at times, and also glamorized in the ghetto. Dyson writes:

> The sheer repetition of death has caused black youth to execute funeral plans. In its response to death, black youth have reversed perhaps the emblematic expression of self-aware black morality. Martin Luther King Jr.'s cry that "every now and then I think about my own death." They think about it constantly and creatively. With astonishing clinical detachment, black youth enliven King's claim that he didn't contemplate his death "in a morbid sense." They accept the bleak inevitability of death's imminent swoop—which, in truth, is a rejection of the arbitrariness we all face, since death to these youth is viewed as the condition, not the culmination, of their existence. Black youth tell funeral directors to portray their dead bodies with a style that may defeat their being forgotten and that distinguish them from the next corpse (2001, 227).

Bone Thugs-N-Harmony represent a crucial engagement with death, suffering, and the relationship of Satan to life, death, and the divine. In this engagement, Bone Thugs-N-Harmony allows a broader path to be followed in which one realizes that death is not constrained inside the theological mantras found within Abrahamic faiths.[37] In fact, what this group does is modify that and

---

37 This engagement is not without its criticisms. Three of the interviewees stated that Bone Thugs-N-Harmony were "devil worshippers" and that their own personal faith prevented them from listening to much of their material. When probed further as to what was holding them back from listening to more of the music, the interviewees all stated their fear

grapples with the real idea that a devil and/or evil presence might actually be at work side by side with good forces in the death process. Bone Thugs-N-Harmony represent a group of Hip Hoppers willing to move beyond the norms and previously established beliefs concerning death and ask what the devil's role is in all of this.

Kanye West

Kanye West has risen to a socio-theological status within Hip Hop that few other rappers have attained. "John," in my interviews, stated that Kanye was indeed the "new Tupac." Another interviewee, "Lady J," told me that Kanye represented a newer, more practical approach to the Christian God. In Ebony Utley's (2012) work, Kanye's name was the highest on the list of "spiritual rappers" beating out Tupac.[38] Kanye, who worked as a producer and musical arranger for artists such as Jay Z and John Legend, was raised in a Christian home. His music is a reflection of the influence of artists from the Funk era, such as The Commodores, Kool And The Gang, Marvin Gaye, and myriad of '80s popular culture artists such as Tears For Fears, Cyndi Lauper, Pet Shop Boys, and Peter Cetera. He is a musician at heart and combines samples, live drums, electronic rhythms, and musicianship to all of his music. His first mainstream album, *The College Dropout* (2004),[39] made headlines as he addressed the issues of salvation, Jesus, Jesus' love, sin, and the profane with his song "Jesus Walks." Here, Kanye continued the conversation which Tupac had started in regards to heaven, final destinations, and Christological manifestations in indigenous settings.

"Jesus Walks" is a song about contextualizing a "good news" message that for too long had been a White, Western, perfected image of deity to which many from urban centers could not aspire nor connect (I will discuss this further in Chapter 5). Rappers have had a keen feeling toward the historical Jesus because of the persecution he endured and the narrative of suffering of his story. Kanye's song acknowledges the secular and the profane within the

---

of evil and what they defined as "demonic forces" within the music. This adds to the argument that extreme Christian evangelists such as G. Craig Lewis claim that "all Hip Hop is of the Devil." Bone Thugs-N-Harmony is, of course, at the top of those lists.

38 This could signify a shift in the way newer generations espouse and respect deity within Hip Hop moguls. For the last two decades Tupac has been the primary rapper who represents a "God Connection" but as of recent times, Kanye, Kendrick Lamar, and in some circles even Jay Z, are beginning to represent the broadening of this title. Time will tell how newer generations will view Tupac and endear him to theological and spiritual pursuits.

39 Kanye did release a less known album called *I'm Good* in 2003, but this was a "mix-tape" and did not receive much radio air time.

sacred.[40] The song begins with an opening designed to seek a higher personal consciousness:

> Yo, We at war
> We at war with terrorism, racism but most of all we at war with ourselves
> (Jesus Walks)
> God show me the way because the Devil trying to break me down
> (Jesus Walks with me) with me, with me, with me (fades)
>   WEST 2004

The beginning of the song sets the tone and demarcates a search for a Jesus who can "walk with him" and help in the war.

In the second verse, Kanye begins to uncover that contextualized "good news" and offers up an image of Jesus that detours from the standard Evangelical one. It is the Jesus that Hip Hoppers appear to identify with.

> (Jesus Walks)
> God show me the way because the Devil trying to break me down
> (Jesus Walks with me)
> The only thing that I pray is that me feet don't fail me now
> (Jesus Walks)
> And I don't think there is nothing I can do now to right my wrongs
> (Jesus Walks with me)
> I want to talk to God but I'm afraid because we ain't spoke in so long
>
> To the hustlas, killers, murderers, drug dealers even the strippers
> To the victims of Welfare for we living in hell here hell yeah
> Now hear ye hear ye want to see Thee more clearly
> I know he hear me when my feet get weary
> Cuz we're the almost nearly extinct
> We rappers are role models; we rap we don't think
> I ain't here to argue about his facial features
> Or here to convert atheists into believers
> I'm just trying to say the way school need teachers
> The way Kathie Lee needed Regis that's the way y'all need Jesus
> So here go my single dog radio needs this

---

40   It is not just this particular song with which Hip Hoppers are able to relate. Kanye's constant comparisons to Jesus, suffering, martyrdom, and being crucified is yet another pathway through which Hip Hoppers connect with his "Christ like" image.

> They say you can rap about anything except for Jesus
> That means guns, sex, lies, video tapes
> But if I talk about God my record won't get played Huh?
> Well let this take away from my spins
> Which will probably take away from my ends
> Then I hope this take away from my sins
> And bring the day that I'm dreaming about
> Next time I'm in the club everybody screaming out
> WEST 2004

Note the implications that Kanye makes in this verse: a call to secularized individuals (hustlers, drug dealers, strippers), a space for those who are labeled as profane (killers, murders), and the beginnings of journey toward a Jesus that can relate to them. Kanye also skirts the issue of race and reminds us that "skin color" does not matter to him; he is in pursuit of the actual relationship and the "need" for a higher power—a God, a deity that is relatable and reachable (Hodge 2009; Utley 2012; Zanfagna 2006).

Still, even within this veneer of perceived genuine spiritual pursuits, Kanye struggles with some of the same issues other rappers have regarding misogyny, nihilism, and a hyper braggadocio. In a 2013 interview with Hip Hop DX, Kanye stated that, "I ain't your fucking role model. Don't label me that. I'm an artist. Period. That's what I do. Don't expect anything else from me." Hip Hop DX columnist Omar Burgess describes Kanye as a "walking contradiction" yet also asserts, "I think the fact that he generally embraces the inconsistencies in his ideology makes for some interesting tension within his music" (Burgess 2013). That "tension" is precisely what makes Kanye a strong secular and profane articulation of theological matters.[41]

In his 2013 New York Times interview with journalist Jon Caramanica, Kanye deals with this tension himself:

---

41 This also connects with Kanye's 2005 statement during a Hurricane Katrina live telethon regarding George Bush's response to the victims of the hurricane. It was a sign that Kanye was not going to "play nice" in regards to social issues. Moreover, there was his live interruption of Taylor Swift during the MTV 2009 Music Awards. Kanye, a Black man, "rudely" interrupted a "White woman" at her moment of glory. This controversy has also created a Christological brand for Kanye as many in the Black and Latino community felt that this "interruption" was exactly what Whites have done for decades to Blacks and the fact that he had the nerve to do this and speak up for another Black woman who did not win (Beyoncé). It gave him not only social credit, but also a messianic one—a "voice" of the voiceless.

> I don't have some type of romantic relationship with the public. I'm like, the anti-celebrity, and my music comes from a place of being anti. That was the album where I gave people what they wanted. I don't think that at that point, with my relationship with the public and with skeptical buyers, that I could've done "Black Skinhead" [from "Yeezus"]
>
> Cited in Caramanica 2013 interview with KANYE WEST

Kanye sees himself as this model for this tension and, conversely, also views himself as a sort of Hip Hop hero. He continues:

> I am so credible and so influential and so relevant that I will change things. So when the next little girl that wants to be, you know, a musician and give up her anonymity and her voice to express her talent and bring something special to the world, and it's time for us to roll out and say, "Did this person have the biggest thing of the year?"—that thing is more fair because I was there.

Some bloggers and scholars view Kanye's confidence as arrogance and pride, while almost all of the interviewees saw him as a visionary and modern day prophet.[42] Kanye does, however, present a contradictory stance on some issues—especially regarding gender.

In his 2013 album *Yeezus*, Kanye drew critics when he called himself "God." While a lot of the album deals with a strong involvement with indigenous forms of theological inquiry, much of the hyper male posturing is done on the backs of women. Kanye describes oral sex and ejaculation on women as normative for sexual exploration and dances in the controversial space of religion and sexuality as if it were a good space. But women are not in power within this space. Does that still make him a Jesus figure? In an online article Ebony Utley tells us that:

> Throughout the album, West asks audiences to embrace a similar "and without contradiction" acceptance especially of his social commentary about race and his social disdain for women.
>
> West's album is filled with typical rap posturing. No successful rapper has ever spent an entire album rapping about how he can't read, can't get a job, and can't keep a girl. Rap is a fantasy world, where men's success is premised on making their wildest dreams seem true. The catch comes

---

42 A term typically reserved for artists such as Tupac who were able to future cast events.

> if you're a black man without any real power. How do you convince an audience that you do have power when the fashion world won't take you seriously, detractors upbraid you for having a baby with Kim Kardashian, and people publicly make you apologize for words and deeds you're not sorry for. Well, apparently, West came up with an answer in the 48 hours he spent finishing lyrics for the album. You accrue power by taking it from someone else. Thus, women take the brunt of West's anger usually via some (oral) sex exchange.
> UTLEY 2013

These present some contradicting posits for Kanye. Still, the Christian Jesus was not without controversy either. The relationship to Martha, the adulterous woman at the well, the strong words toward the Syrophoenician woman, and the absent teen years of Jesus all leave an open gap for ideas surrounding the historical Jesus.

Still, Kanye continues to push forward and his 2013 album makes numerous references to God and the connections that he has to God. This, once again, is in continual tension with the sacred, profane, and secular (Spencer 1990, 1991a) and allows a more comprehensive view of the complexity surrounding religion in Hip Hop contexts. Utley again, reminds us:

> Does this type of misogyny, which, let us be fair, is common in rap, undermine West's religious allusions? No. Both religion and rap are notorious for perpetuating patriarchy and heterosexism. Any system designed to empower must do so at the expense of someone else. Whether it's a believer over a nonbeliever, whites over blacks, men over women. How does a new slave get his power back? He becomes "a dick instead of a swallower" and "fucks a Hampton spouse." Does that excuse West from his cavalierly sexist commentary? No. But a man obsessed with Jesus does so because he wants to imitate the power of Jesus. When rap and religion turn to power, there will be hierarchy, and the person controlling the story will always come out on top (2013).

Thus, Kanye's religious dance continues and in that dance the search for power is critical—albeit at the expense of misogyny. Yet, what makes Kanye West such an appealing figure, not just for Hip Hoppers but for American popular culture in general, is that he is, in his public persona, transparent and hostile towards dominant forms of norms—especially as it relates to religion and spirituality. At the same time, Kanye represents the human experience and is contrary, proud, hypocritical, and arrogant. This is true though of many well-known pastors, priests, rabbis, and religious leaders; no one gets a pass and is "all perfect."

Ice Cube

This brings us to our next artist, Ice Cube. Michael Eric Dyson calls him "Gangsta rap's visionary" (1996, 172–175). Ice Cube, former member of the group N.W.A., is indeed a visionary. One of the few who was able to parlay his fame and wealth from the Golden Era of Hip Hop into contemporary notoriety, Ice Cube's theological discourse is complex, controversial, Afrocentric, and a strong part of Hip Hop's hostile Gospel.

Ice Cube, born O'Shea Jackson, began his career in Los Angeles, California during the mid-1980s at a time when Hip Hop and rap music were in their teen years. Ice Cube was a member of the group N.W.A.[43] and wrote, aided in the production, and played a lead role in the group. Ice Cube, so called to assert his cool "like ice" modus, was raised in a well-educated two parent family. During the time of N.W.A.'s rise, the crack epidemic ravaged many urban enclaves and South Central Los Angeles was at the center. Police brutality, police scandals, and political corruption were all matters that N.W.A. were dealing with. Moreover, they were one of the first West Coast rap groups to put the West Coast sound—strong baselines, melodic keyboards, and little use of samples—into the public sphere to give the Hip Hop world a taste of sound which had never been heard before. Ice Cube was also one of the select few to come out of the Hip Hop Golden Era and still be a marketable force today.[44] Ice Cube is Hip Hop's "visionary" simply because he was able to work the music industry and create a business that few rappers have been able to do. In other words, he became independent and a respected name in both film and music—something that he was advocating from the beginning of his rap career.[45]

---

43   N.W.A. stand for Niggas With Attitude. A term which continues to be a part of the overall essence of Hip Hop including other ethnic groups such as Latinos, Asians, Middle Easterners, and even poor disenfranchised Euro Americans such as Eminem Macklemore (Kelley 1994).

44   Arguably, some critics of Ice Cube have encouraged him to stay in the background and that his style of music no longer "fits" the current state of Hip Hop. Still, Ice Cube continues to press forward and is one of the few ethnic minority owners of a film and media production unit: Cube Vision.

45   Underground artists (who preferred to remain unnamed for this book), revealed to me that Ice Cube stole much of his rapping style from other local artists in the Los Angeles underground rap scene. In Los Angeles, he was booed him off stage at The Good Life Café when he was rapping like the other rappers. They claimed that the broader Hip Hop

GOD IN THE CYPHER: THEOLOGICAL NARRATIVES IN HIP HOP

Theologically speaking, Ice Cube had strong criticisms of dominant forms of religion. While his debut solo album, *AmeriKKKa's Most Wanted* (1990), concentrated on social, political, educational, and cultural issues facing mainly Black youth, his sophomoric album[46] *Death Certificate* (1991) more openly connected with the Zulu Nation and Nation of Islam faith while openly challenging Christian faiths. Most of Cube's criticism was that of involvement and engagement of Christian churches in urban spaces—especially ones where drugs, nihilism, and loss of hope were prevalent. In other words, Cube asked the following questions which attempted to solve the theological and ecclesiological conundrum: if there are churches on every corner in the 'hood, if there are truly "God fearing people" in the community, and if prayer really "works," why do the current conditions continue to exist and where is the redemption from Jesus?[47]

Songs such as "A Bird In The Hand," "When I Get to Heaven," "Go To Church," and "Enemy" strongly and openly critique a Christian form of deity, salvation, and forms of redemption. Although Cube never proselytized the beliefs of the Nation of Islam; the messages were present in his music. As someone who has stayed with his first wife, maintained a stable home for his children, avoided being killed, and kept a steady fan base for over twenty years, Ice Cube is a powerful figure and representation of a "moral" life which those religions tend to promote.

In his album *Death Certificate*, Cube embodies Nation of Islam and Zulu Afrocentric morality in response to pain and suffering. The album is divided into two parts: death and life. The first part deals with social issues plaguing urban males. This section ends with death and gives way to life (birth) by opening up and condemning Uncle Sam and the nationalism which exists within that mantra.[48] The second part, life, is much more aggressive in its racialization of God and the use of the signifier "devil" in reference to White people. These are strong theological connotations, which come from the Nation of Islam, and

---

       community did not know this and that Ice Cube had created his image on "false pretenses" especially in light of his upbringing in a stable, middle class, two-parent home.

46   Ice Cube released an EP album in 1990 titled *Kill At Will*.

47   Albeit most of the time Ice Cube referred to the Western White image of Jesus and focused on a more Islamic version of God.

48   Typically this is an ideology that asserts a "God and Country" stance and is often associated with White America, White versions of Christianity, and a pro-America values based system which tends to overlook the accomplishments of ethnic minorities in its history (Heyward 1999).

which refer to White Americans as devils.[49] The life side of this album has a strong position of social consciousness, awareness, and activism, but does so in a manner in which those who live in extreme urban oppression, social deprivation, and social isolation can relate. This album is a blue print for the belief systems of the Nation of Islam,[50] done in rap prose.

For example, in his song "My Skin is My Sin," Cube clearly articulates a posture against White national Christian religion:

> I Get Around like Tupac, just bought a new Glock
> And I want what you got
> So please give it up so I can live it up
> Just like the rich but I still eat grits
> I don't know karate
> But I can still beat the dog shit out of Nazis
> You claim you want to put in work
> Plotting to blow up a church
> See you devils are all the same
> You'll gun down a congregation in Jesus' name
> Using me as a scapegoat, well cracker don't sleep
> Far from a goat, more like a black sheep
> Lamb of God, and it's odd
> That Allah is a man that don't need a tan
> And you can't stand when I talk like that
> And why do black men have to walk like that?
> Cause we swing low like a chariot
> And now I got Harriet all on my dick
> Cause my shoe size is much bigger than a motherfucking 10
> My skin is my sin
> My S-K-I-N is my S-I-N ["Burning our black skin"] [Repeat 2x]
>   CUBE 1994

---

49 The rationale behind this is the result of four hundred years of slavery, violence towards Blacks, creation of laws benefiting Whites, Jim & Jane Crow laws, and the ensuing racism which, as some in the Nation of Islam would argue, they created. Thus, the resulting ideology behind this is that a group who could produce this kind of hate, violence, and oppression, must be in cahoots with the devil, thus the reference and label.

50 Throughout many of his early albums, Ice Cube interjected extended interviews with Malcolm X and other Nation of Islam leaders; he would juxtapose these with the message in his music and was a strong critic of White Jesus.

Notice the lines Cube draws between a Nation of Islam God and the Christian God regarding racial representations. Cube invokes sexual imagery as a form of power over White women. This "taking back" of power is consistent in rap artists who rap about Afrocentric forms of self-awareness and self-consciousness. It is not clear, currently, if Cube still feels the same regarding race, gender, and religion.

That said, Cube is not without his own misogynistic, homophobic, and gender biases that are in need of discussion and examination. Statements like "real black men are not gay," constant references to women as "bitches" and "hoes," and the association of being a "man" solely by engaging in heteronormative practices are issues that Ice Cube listeners, and the Hip Hop community as an entirety, must face. His constant connection of a "real man" as that of a provider, leader, heterosexual, and ruler over women does not chime well with post-soul worldviews. Moreover, Hip Hop feminists tend to view Ice Cube as a sort of male relic who, while having powerful and motivating ideas to move out of oppression, racism, and social isolation, tends to focus on males who are heterosexual and dating within their own race.[51]

However, these values are not very different from those of the Black community in general. Still, Cube, even though more strongly associated with The Nation of Islam and Zulu, tends to have a more rigid mindset on relationships, family, and intimate relationships (most Abrahamic based faiths have tendencies toward this worldview too). Ice Cube is an external expression of that worldview, and while his views on social change are progressive, his views—along with other male rappers—on women, LGBTQ peoples, and non-traditional methods of family life are typically frowned upon and seen as both "out there" and, at times, non-spiritual.

Still, the significance of Ice Cube in Hip Hop culture is important as he continues to be a strong voice for the 'hood and urban communities in general. While his method of approach may be skewed, theologically, in some areas, his commitment to social change is strong. Cube's cypher is that of progress and

---

51 Cube would make references throughout his albums in the 1990s of not marrying outside the Black race and that money, fame, and fortune could turn Blacks to marry White women because Black women were not as attractive. As the interviews continued, I was able to find strong belief systems which argued for heterosexual, same race, traditional gender role relationships which were typically associated with the Black and Latino community. In other words, while Blacks tend to vote democratic and more liberally, familial and religious ties continue to be focused on more conservative, traditional, and rigid belief systems—which include a disdain toward homosexuality and the LGBTQ community.

a life rooted in spiritual convictions.[52] Cube has remained a voice in certain areas against the privatization of prisons and was a strong critic of the former governor of California, Arnold Schwarzenegger.

Kendrick Lamar

Cube helped in opening up the door for our next cypherologist, Kendrick Lamar. Lamar is a recent addition to the Hip Hop cypher and is still very young in his craft. Yet, he has invoked many to view him as a sort of secular, profane, and sacred Hip Hop icon who is taking up the mantle that Tupac left. Let us turn now to Lamar's theological cypher.

Still young and in need of more examination and research of his life, lyrics, and overall theological cypher, Kendrick Lamar has risen to the top of Hip Hop in a relatively short amount of time. At the age of twenty six (in 2013), Lamar has, as many of the interviewees exclaimed, "picked up the Tupac mantle" and carried it on. His songs "Tammy's Song" and "Keisha's Song" are continued conversations of Tupac's "Brenda Has a Baby" and give greater and more graphic details in regards to the struggles of many abandoned and disenfranchised Black women living in urban regions. Lamar, as "Kelly" stated in an interview late summer of 2012, is "the future of Hip Hop. He is a breath of fresh air, ya know? I mean, he's still got some songs in there that dog women out, but, for the most part he could be someone who could really be a voice for women in this male run game called Hip Hop." Kelly's thoughts have been shared by other interviewees as well. What Lamar brings is youthfulness, energy, and a message which deviates from the normal one in contemporary commercialized rap (money, hoes, and sex). Lamar also combines the sacred, profane, and secular in a tightly woven social knot which creates a type of nitty-gritty hermeneutic in which his audience members are able to relate to and engage.

Lamar is a post-soul rapper and came of age during the late 1990s when rap music and Hip Hop was at its end in the Golden Era. More importantly, Lamar was raised in a post 9/11 America and has benefited from the use of technology

---

52 Some have made the suggestion that the Ice Cube of 1990 would be an enemy of the Ice Cube of today. Cube does not live in South Central anymore and has created a big name for himself within both the film and music industry. One might argue that he has "sold out" by moving out the 'hood and remaining silent publically on many of the social problems facing Black Americans such as the Trayvon Martin issue, gentrification, Obama and race, and issues facing the LGBTQ community.'

and the Internet.[53] Lamar is also a rapper whose legacy was assured with pioneers such as Dr. Dre, Snoop Lion, Ice Cube, and MC Eiht among some of the noted names. They symbolically "passed the mantle" onto Lamar in a closed meeting and ushered him in as the new Hip Hop Don—a title typically reserved for veteran rappers and Hip Hoppers.[54] Lamar gives a taste of reality to his music and adds new dimensions to the West Coast musical genre.

Lamar is a product of the post-Golden Era shift when Hip Hop became more commercial and in pursuit of economic prosperity (Watkins 2005). Moreover, in this era, much of the elements of Hip Hop have been eroded, according to some scholars (Neal 1997; Nelson 2007; Rose 2008). Yet, Lamar brings in a new wave of engagement with family, racial issues, God, and a new reality of what a theological purist might look like within the post 9/11 landscape. Lamar begins to deconstruct and challenge what Monica Miller refers to as the Black Church and the "spirit of market maintenance" (2013b, 77–81) in his body of work. Lamar does not "otherize" those who do not fit and look like the expected norm of a spiritual and theological persona.[55] In fact, like Kanye and Tupac, Lamar welcomes them in and asks them to partake in the liturgy he offers in his music.

Songs such as "Heaven & Hell," "Ronald Reagan Era [His evils]," "Overly Dedicated," "The Heart Pt.2," and "Growing Apart [From Everything]" all wade into the issues of sex, religion, and human life. Let us examine the opening verse in "The Heart Pt.2:"

> Sitting in the studio thinking about which mood would go
> right now, freestyle or write down, whatever
> And still I come up clever, I just need to free my thoughts
> and Lord knows that I know better, but I ain't perfect
> I ain't seen too many churches or know them Testament verses
> You should either hear me now or go deaf
> or end up dead, die trying and know death
> Might end up dead, swallow blood, swallow my breath

---

53 This is not to suggest that Lamar is the only rapper who came of age during this period; nor is it to suggest that Lamar is a "lone rapper" who is not without the community of the underground in Hip Hop. However, Lamar is one of the few commercialized rappers (having been on MTV, BET, and consistently selling albums in the top ten) who is able to connect theological queries with real life and still maintain an audience and sell albums.

54 Sources stated that the gathering was small and that Lamar was at the center as if the group was laying hands on him and "commissioning" him to "go forth."

55 I will expand on the concept of 'other' in Chapter 5.

> Fuck a funeral, just make sure you pay my music respect nigga
> I mean that from the bottom of my heart
> You see my art is all I have, and victory tastes sweet
> even when an enemy can throw salt
> Still knock 'em out the park like a fucking tow car
> Let bygones be bygones, but where I'm from
> we buy guns and more guns to give to the young
> LAMAR 2010

Lamar is allowing himself a level of transparency in this song while acknowledging the social issues plaguing the community. Coming from South Central Los Angeles, Lamar is accustomed to the violence in urban centers. However, this song in particular acknowledges the "humanity" within the religious experience and gives space for non-perfected personalities to create congruence.

Lamar, having been raised in a Black Christian home, is accustomed with many of the Black Christian traditions, but is also aware of the realities of the human condition which he labels as "sin." Thus, in several regards, he is following Miller's critique of the Black church and "market maintenance," and asking why Black churches do what they do in the manner that they do. Lamar also, like Tupac, criticizes the Black church for the money it takes from its people, especially in low-income communities.[56]

Take for instance, the cover art on Lamar's 2011 album, *Section. 80*. The album's title is in focus, but just to the right of it is a Bible that has a blunt and cigarette lighter on top of it, with more books underneath. To the left of that is a loaded gun clip, condoms, lipstick, a stack of money and a faded out lamp. To the front of that is a pipe and a medicinal marijuana container next to the paper which states the album's title. Lamar's use and imagery of the sacred, profane, and secular is well balanced. Sex, drugs, religion, violence, and pleasure all in one album cover reveals that Lamar is dealing and contemplating with serious issues. The album itself is no less an engagement with those issues and Lamar's cypher is weaving the sacred, profane, and secular as the album cover suggests.

Lamar's 2015 album, *To Pimp A Butterfly*, is a mixture of soul, funk, jazz, the spoken word, and rap connected to the Golden Era of Hip Hop. This album

---

56 Two informants close to Lamar have said that Lamar is "pissed off" at the Black church for what he calls a "misfortune of events" in regards to what Black pastors have created in the 'hood comparing the lavish cars some drive to the economic bondage in which they keep some of their parishioners. This information was only made available for this research and I have kept the names hidden.

holds in tension good, evil, sin, and the sacred; it is a well-balanced album for the theomusicologist. The ending has a poignant and moving interview with Tupac. The editing is done in a manner that allows you to believe that Tupac and Lamar are in the same room[57] discussing social issues which are still relevant in 2015: the injustice toward young Blacks, racism, and the tension as to what defines a Black male. *To Pimp A Butterfly* is a masterful album which dances on the platform of evil, and names it "Lucy." Lamar creates a post-soul conversation and allows the listener to wrestle with that as well. Lamar was noted as saying that this album was created in the wake of Ferguson, Missouri and Trayvon Martin (Singleton 2015).

While Lamar is up and coming, we are challenged with references to women solely as sexual objects—even as a devil named Lucy in *To Pimp A Butterfly*. Hip Hoppers, men in general, have a difficult time straying away from generalized objectifications of women. Part of it has to do with many of them being raised in urban, working class, blue collar communities which tend to be fairly conventional and inelastic when it comes to gender roles, gender behaviors, sexual orientation, and overall perceived "moral values." These cultural codes, if you will, are embedded in religious customs (which are typically Christian although Islamic religions tend to prescribe strict "moral codes" for women and men). They are often negotiated through behaviors which must fall within the cited norms of the given context—which are often stacked against women (Althaus-Reid 2000, 2004). Lamar, among other male Hip Hoppers, are simply following the customs of his upbringing and many like him are socially, politically, educationally, and economically "progressive." The "progressive" typically ends with gender and sexual orientation, making for a contradicting message regarding equality and justice.[58]

Women in a male dominated genre and culture such as rap music have a difficult time establishing even pro-women agendas—let alone a feminist one— and are often both overlooked and labeled as a "dyke" or "lesbian" for confronting misogynistic behaviors and lyrics (Hurt 2006; Neal 2005). As the research in this book has shown, while female contributions are plentiful in Hip Hop, by sheer dominance, males draw the most attention and the female voice in the

---

57 That particular interview from Tupac is believed to have been done in late 1995 by an unknown interviewer from *Vibe* magazine.

58 An underground rapper who is beginning to engage the gender and sexual orientation issue is Jasiri x from Pittsburg. While the scope of this book does not allow me to expand on many underground rappers like him, it is imperative to mention such Hip Hop male rappers who are taking up such an undertaking, often with very little to no commercial radio airplay.

Hip Hop cypher is not as prevalent as it is on the underground scene. In other words, women in Hip Hop, while strong in the underground scene, do not get the credit they deserve within the global Hip Hop cypher. Therefore, we turn next to one of the few women of Hip Hop that gets recognition as a mogul, artist, and spiritual advisor, Lauryn Hill.

Lauryn Hill

We end with the lone female voice in this line up of Hip Hop cypher, Lauryn Hill. Hill, who began her career with the group The Fugees, went solo and in one album, created a powerful name for herself in the Hip Hop cypher. Regaled as the female prophet of rap, the mere mention of her album *The Miseducation of Lauryn Hill* made Hip Hop mogul Quest Love cry in a B.E.T (Black Entertainment Network) documentary on Women in Rap. Her album made history and became an instant Hip Hop classic. Each interviewee saw her as a type of Hip Hop "campus pastor"[59] who was able to challenge the soul beyond anything any ordained minister could do. Hill never did create an album that complemented her first solo album. However, with one album, she created something that reached out to the Hip Hop community which has lasted for almost two decades. As Dave, an interviewee, stated:

> Lauryn was like…man…she was like a damn pastor who preached faith in a time of doubt. That album [*The Miseducation of Lauryn Hill*] was that for me. I use to listen to that when I was going through my divorce. She was my counselor and therapeutic space. Whew. God used her for sure.

Hill created a space for those who were hurt, disenfranchised and disinherited to find meaning and, essentially, God. She brawled with God and the pain she had—and still has—in her life of broken promises, failed relationships, questions regarding faith, and the reality of being a Black woman in the U.S..

In her song, "Ex-Factor," she dances with issues surrounding love within a committed relationship:

> It could all be so simple
> But you'd rather make it hard
> Loving you is like a battle
> And we both end up with scars
> Tell me, who I have to be

---

59 In relation to Hip Hop being a community similar to a college campus.

> To get some reciprocity
> No one loves you more than me
> And no one ever will
>
> Is this just a silly game
> That forces you to act this way?
> Forces you to scream my name
> Then pretend that you can't stay
> Tell me, who I have to be
> To get some reciprocity
> No one loves you more than me
> And no one ever will[60]

The song goes on to discuss the failures of relationships and the pain associated with those "loves lost."[61] Hill dances with the premises of pain, love, and faith. Where is God during these times? This is powerful to the Hip Hop community because it does not attempt to answer fundamental existential questions decisively, and allows those who listen to grapple with ambiguity.[62] This is an essential mantra for the post-soulist: to grapple with the ambiguity of who God is and move beyond linear step-by-step processes (e.g. do "this" X amount of times, and then "that" will happen) to resolution and into an enlightenment of who God is (with ambiguity and doubt). Hill capitalized on this.

Still, Hill did not simply "leave it there." She would take part of that ambiguity and mix it with divinity:

> Father you saved me and showed me that life
> Was much more than being some foolish man's wife
> Showed me that love was respect and devotion
> Greater than planets deeper than oceans
> My soul was weary but now it's replenished
> Content because that part of my life is finished

---

60 Lauryn Hill, "Ex-Factor," *The Mis-Education of Lauryn Hill* (1998).
61 Throughout the entire album, Hill has interludes where ethnic minority teens are being interviewed and asked about what they think and believe love is. The answers are both amazing and rich and also continue to give voice to a marginalized group. Hill knew this and wanted to have this on her album to have that "youthful voice."
62 This is an ongoing theological discussion in regards to doubt, faith, and the search for God. For a real time look into the power of music within this discussion, see Tom Beaudoin. 2013. *Secular Music and Sacred Theology*. Collegeville, Minnesota: Liturgical Press.

> I see him sometimes and the look in his eye
> Is one of a man who's lost treasures untold
> But my heart is gold I took back my soul
> And totally let my creator control
> The life which was his to begin with[63]

Hill is able to fade into that gray theology in which many—especially those within urban enclaves—live and reside spiritually. "I Used To Love Him" is a song that interweaves with these issues.

In the song "Doo Wop (That Thing)" Hill, conversely, challenges "backsliders" and "lukewarm" believers alike:

> Talking out your neck, saying you're a Christian
> A Muslim, sleeping with the Gin
> Now that was the sin that did Jezebel in
> Who're you going to tell when the repercussions spin?
> Showing off your ass because your thinking it's a trend
> Girlfriend, let me break it down for you again![64]

Here, Hill takes a stance to call out the doubletalk within religious people and the call to live a better life—if that is in fact what one is saying they want to do. Hill hermeneutically calls out the negativity and double life[65] in a manner to which people will listen. T.J., an interviewee notes:

> When I heard that song, I was convicted...cause that was me! I was living that lifestyle. I was saying I was Christian and living a life of sin...ya know what I mean? Shit, Lauryn called me out through that album and helped me to live a better life for God...shoot, better than any preacher could ever do.

TJ went on to exclaim that Hill was instrumental in his faith formation and development. Six others also referred to Hill as being their "pastoral guidance" in a theological journey with God.

---

63   Lauryn Hill, "I Used To Love Him," *The Mis-Education of Lauryn Hill* (1998).
64   Lauryn Hill, "Doo Wop (That Thing)," *The Mis-Education of Lauryn Hill* (1998).
65   Very similar to Wilbert Shenk's account of Visser 't Hooft with his his five-fold response to neo-paganism in the West (2001, 78–80); an interesting connection.

Within Lauryn Hill's discourse, appeal, and connection with God, her theological pursuits, once again, end when it comes to LGBTQ issues and gender constructs. While Hill was facing charges of tax evasion and dealing with her own psychological matters, Hill released a single titled "Neurotic Society" and, what is troubling is that it makes comparisons to society's ills by connecting them to being "girl men" and "drag queens."

> We're living in a joke time
> Annotate, metaphorical coke time
> Commerce and girl men
> Run the whole world men
> Bold, drunken debauchery
> Old world brutality
> Cold world killed softly
> Whole world run savagely
> Greedy men and pride fiends
> Program TV screens
> Quick scam and drag queens
> Real life's been blasphemed

Monica Miller wrote an Op Ed piece in response and asserts:

> "Neurotic Society" proclaims again that Babylon is falling—thanks in part to tricksters like "girl men," "drag queens," and the lies of "social transvestism." Whether or not Hill is merely using these comments as examples of the smokescreens and sleight-of-hands that pervade this "Neurotic Society" is unclear. Beyond intention, these sorts of statements suggest that society is in a shambles because it's been taking too many cues from the LGBTQ community, acting like "girl men," "drag queens" and "transvestites." Is her beef with oppressive society or is her issue with people who don't abide by a traditional family structure? For those who don't feel me, would it be okay if her song criticized "neurotic society" for acting like "N-----s," "mammies" and "jezebels?" No! Then why does she think it's cool to critique society by using stereotypes about a community that suggest the community isn't as valuable as another.
> MILLER 2013a

Hill follows a pattern that many rappers, as we have discussed preciously, follow: LGBTQ's non-traditional male norms, and heteronormative values are cherished. When connected to faith, spirituality, and religion they become moral, ethical, and spiritual values which tend to send vexing messages comparatively to the social conscious content that many rappers have. This is a pattern in much of the music Hip Hop has, and while this is not the overall worldview within Hip Hop culture, it is a prevalent one and one that is typically connected within the Abrahamic faiths which are predominant throughout Hip Hop culture.

Does this take away from the messages that Hill sings about and lives for? No. On the other hand, it does present a perplexing case of juxtapositions that rappers who espouse a theological motif seem to not be able to move beyond in regards to heteronormative and hypermasculine traits.

Chapter Summary

The ongoing theodicy debate of a good God that allows "bad things" to happen to "God's people" is one that will continue for decades to come. Old Dogg presents a valid theological query in a contextual manner which cannot be overlooked by simply saying it is "God's will." He questions God's will. Rappers, as it has been demonstrated in this chapter, also struggle with that—living life in the secular and profane, yet attempting to produce some semblance toward and with the sacred. All this, as we have seen, is done in context. The God in the cypher is a journey down that theological path toward a life that is better than the current one that is had—one that helps in opening up a deeper knowledge of the self. That in and of itself is a spiritual journey for most Hip Hoppers and the Hip Hop community.

This chapter examined these eight rappers for their theological cyphers within the Hip Hop cultural continuum. While each one is neither a "God" or a perfected model of the ideal Hip Hop messianic, they do present themes which not only the Hip Hop community, but also society in general needs to contend with.

In Chapter 3, we will look specifically at one Hip Hopper: Tupac Amaru Shakur. While Chapter 1 was a broad look at the social conditions, Chapter 2 gave examples from within those conditions and geographical locations. Chapter 3 will explore the life, music, and theological messages within one of Hip Hop's most known and respected artists to this day and allow his theomusicological message to speak within the sacred, profane, and secular.

CHAPTER 3

Hip Hop's Totemic Prophet: Tupac Amaru Shakur

God has cursed me to see what is real. He has cursed me to see life as how it should be.

TUPAC, interview with Ed GORDON

• • •

Here on Earth, tell me what's a black life worth. A bottle of juice is no excuse, the truth hurts. And even when you take the shit, move counties, get a lawyer, you can't shake the shit. Ask Rodney, LaTasha, and many more. It's been goin' on for years, there's plenty more. When they ask me, when will the violence cease? When your troops stop shootin niggaz down in the street Niggaz had enough time to make a difference Bear witness, own our own business Word to God cause it's hard tryin to make ends meet.

TUPAC, in "I Wonder If Heaven got A Ghetto"

• • •

I think that if you take the 'O's out of 'Good,' it's 'God,' if you add a 'D' to 'Evil,' it's the 'Devil.' I think some cool motherfuckers sat down a long time ago and said let's figure out a way to control motherfuckers.

TUPAC SHAKUR

• •

Tupac Amaru Shakur.[1] Even the name causes many Hip Hoppers to stand still and pause for a moment. When asked what he did on hearing the news of Tupac's death, Marlon Wayans stated that he cried like his momma cried when

---

1 I must note that fifteen of the interviewees noted that Biggie Smalls was also considered to be a prophet and Hip Hop spiritualist. Only releasing a total of four albums (which pales in comparison to Tupac's arsenal of albums), Biggie is still noted as one of Hip Hop's moguls attempting to work out the profane and secular in sacred spaces. More research is needed on the spiritual significance of Biggie.

Marvin Gaye was murdered. Young girls and boys who were not even alive during Tupac's life remember and adore him as if they had grown up in his era. Further, even mildly liberal parents today (who were teens in the 1990s) pause and think about the effect Tupac had on their own lives.[2] Tupac was iconic. Recalling Tupac's accomplishments at such a young age, Quincy Jones recalls his death by stating that if Martin Luther King Jr. had died when he was twenty-five, he would have been a struggling Black Baptist minister. Malcolm X would have been a street hustler, and he himself would have been a struggling trumpet player. When Tupac died at twenty-five, he left a legacy of life, love, rage, pain—and theology. "Tupac was touched by God, not very many people are touched by the hand of God."[3]

What makes for such an iconic figure? What makes him what some scholars call an urban theologian (Dyson 1996; Hodge 2010; Watkins 2011)? What makes Tupac's music, life, and poetry continue to ring true eighteen years after his death? Is there something deeper and more meaningful in Tupac's lyrics which are infused with a type of ghetto spiritual essence and urban contextualized spiritual authority entrenched in the murky waters of the profane and the sacred?[4] This chapter will argue that there is.

Tupac was more than just a fad or an "estranged artist." He had a mission and message that few are able to embrace. The cost is high: life. Tupac saw life and culture beyond the routine and ordinary; he approached life full of passion, rage, anger, love, thoughtfulness, and even carelessness. He was the product of a post-soul society which had been groomed on the ambiguous consumer culture of the 1980s (Covert 2003). In this consumer culture, Tupac became a type of popular critical pundit for the Hip Hop community—which was established early on in Hip Hop culture in its critique of U.S. social structures—particularly religion and economics. He was a by-product of the post-revolutionary Black spirit alive in the early 1970s.[5] He was the voice of the ghetto/'hood, marginalized, oppressed, and downtrodden,[6] connecting

---

2 As seen in my 2004–2008 interviews on Tupac's theological mystique in (Hodge 2009).
3 Interview taken from the DVD documentary *Thug Angel: The Life of An Outlaw* (2002).
4 I argue that for too long religious discourse and rhetoric has placed a polarized stance on "good" and "evil," the sacred and the profane. However, what emerges in the Post Soul context is a type of third area: the area in between the good and the evil, the sacred and the profane, hence making this ground quite murky and diluted—this is the world in which Tupac found God. (For further review see :Iverem 1997; Miles 2001; Pinn 2002; Reed 2003).
5 See also Anthony (Pinn 2002) in which he discusses the effects of the civil rights movement, post soul creations, and post-revolutionary elements for the Black church and Black theology.
6 While this was Tupac's main audience, there have been numerous suburban, wealthy, White people who connected with Tupac's message simply because they themselves were

God to a people who would never imagine gracing the pristine hallways of a church. He related God, culture, Hip Hop, life, pain, and even "sin" to Jesus, and forced the listener to deal with those issues while providing an accessible pathway and access to a God that was not marred with a blonde-haired, blue-eyed embodiment of perfection. Tupac's God was the God of the 'hood. As Cheryl Kirk-Duggan so eloquently states of Tupac, "...amid his deep hurt and alienation, he often expressed profound religious sensibilities—a kind of street spirituality that invokes traditional faith categories [and] ranging from irony and sarcasm to humility and sincerity, aware of the life and death issues that people face daily on the street" (Kirk-Duggan 2009, 214).

This chapter is concerned with demonstrating the post-soul theology of Tupac Amaru Shakur,[7] while providing an alternative space for those who do not fit the White evangelical model of "finding God" to *seek* God. This chapter will utilize the elements of a method called ethnolifehistory[8] in conjunction with

---

marginalized, oppressed, and or downtrodden by parents and or other structural forces similar to those of the urban poor.

7 Tupac did have his issues. He was aware of these personal failures as it related to his own anger, hurts, and pain. Moreover, Tupac struggled with both sides of the coin: the positive and the negative. On one side, there is the hopefulness of the African American community in one person, while on the flip side there are elements of his life that grind that hopefulness to a saddening halt. That said, this chapter illuminates the gospel message of Tupac. There is more than enough negative press on Tupac on the Internet and from his critics who saw him as a negative "Black male." What I argue here is that Tupac creates an actual theological space for those who have been overlooked so that they can connect with God. I am not asserting that we accept Tupac as a perfected person; he was human and had his errors. However, within those errors, we find God and Christ at a deeper level, a level many of us are not willing to go to because it involves elements of the blasphemous.

8 Ethnolifehistory is a method which charts and considers the varying peaks within a person's life which can then be translated into potential periods, eras, and stages by focusing in on: (1) the creation of life eras and their development and transition from one major event to the next, (2) key moments which help to shift one era to the next (i.e., what regression may occur and are there identifiable overlapping eras which may also affect the person or culture being studied?), (3) transitional effects on the subject from one era to the next (i.e., are there eras or moments which create stress, joy, or mourning for the person? If so, how might such instances be interpreted over and against what is happening in the larger society and culture?) And lastly, (4) how these eras, the shifts, and the effects of such changes impact the cultural products under study. I am persuaded that the multi-method of ethnolifehistory, that is, its utilization of interviews (active, structured, semi-structured), case studies, ethnographic processes, and discourse analysis, make it a promising methodology for religion and Hip Hop studies. Ethnolifehistory not only methodologically pushes religion and Hip Hop studies beyond lyrical and aesthetic analysis but also includes close ethnographic attention to underutilized sources in the current terrain of religion and Hip Hop studies such as interviews, for

theomusicology to examine Tupac. From this data, there are five major eras which shaped Tupac's life music, poetry, and theological themes. Those five eras are:[9]

1. Military Mind (1971–1980)
2. Criminal Grind (1981–1988)
3. The Ghetto is Destiny (1989–1992)
4. Outlaw (1992–1995)
5. Ghetto Saint (1996-Present)

Moreover, this chapter looks at the intersection between the sacred and the profane theomusicologically, a place where Tupac resided daily and where he found a lot of meaning from pursuing the numinous. It was a space outside the traditional environment of "church" and a space for the "thugs," the "niggas," and the "'hood rats." This chapter will illuminate the neo-sacred theology[10] of Tupac which he, in turn, was asserting as a contextualized theology of and for the 'hood. It will demonstrate that there is much to engage with and learn from, theologically speaking, in the "dark matter" (that which is labeled

---

example. Attention beyond a sole focus on the lyrical and aesthetic dimensions to consider the lived realities and geography of an artist's life seldom considered might offer a more expansive window into how and why meaning or religion is constructed and plays particular roles, taking on different shapes at certain moments in an artist's life. For example, might religious references and uses proliferate in an artist's cultural output at particular "highs" and "lows" of their life or craft? What might be of value in considering and focusing on events of significance within an artist's life for such queries in particular, and the study of religion and Hip Hop more generally? Might this method help to adjudicate material previously deemed "theological," "spiritual," or "religious" by other studies in religion in Hip Hop? Might the method of ethnolifehistory categorize such prior classifications as merely coincidental or as a product of the religious marketplace? In light of such possibilities, ethnolifehistory takes into account and concerns itself with questions such as: How might particular events in an artists' life develop and change over time? How might such occurrences affect and influence religion in/and Hip Hop culture as a whole? How long do certain periods in an artists' life last? How and why did it come about? How does the larger cultural context affect significant periods? (Hodge 2015).

9   For a detailed and comprehensive review of each life era and how I arrived at these eras see (Hodge 2010) on Tupac's missiological gospel, in which he discusses the major changes from era to era and how Tupac emerged and defined himself through each one.

10 This term is used to define the intersection of the profane and the sacred, a space which has elements of both deity and sin while yet pointing to divine edification in the midst of chaos, pain, blasphemy, and irreverence.

as evil, debaucherous and/or sinful of life), within what seems apparently blasphemous.[11]

Tupac & the Post-soul Context

To begin, we must define four terms. First, post-soul in the macro sense of an entire culture differs somewhat from micro post-soul as applied to Tupac as a singular individual. Tupac, as this chapter will argue, is a post-soul personification of the rejection of norms, hegemonic authority, and dominant religious structures that inhibit community building (Alper 2000; Bauman 1998; Cox 1984; Cupitt 1998). Henceforth, the post-soul is the era which began in the late 1960s and early 1970s that rejected dominant structures, systems, and meta-narratives which tended to exclude ethnic minorities and particularly the 'hood. The post-soul era rejects linear functional mantras[12] and embraces communal approaches to life, love, and God. The post-soul context was formed in the cocoon of a social shift which broke open the dam to the questioning of authority, challenging the status quo, asserting one's self-identity in the public sphere, and questioning group leaders.[13] The post-soul embodies a more urban, ethnic minority, Hip Hop worldview. Therefore, while still recognizing the societal shift that occurred during those years, the post-soul is a more multicultural/ethnic approach to post modernity and the issues it raises.[14]

---

11   This chapter takes up the argument begun by Benjamín Valentín in regards to sketching cultural theology and the importance of relevant cultural figures within a theological space. While Valentín argues for a Latino cultural theology, I would argue that Tupac is part of that process even though he was African American, and that many young Latinos in particular saw Tupac as part of their own cultural geography. For instance, Valentín asserts that Latino youth realize that culture matters. There are more ways in which they are being oppressed and which affect Latino lives than simply economic factors: cultural imperialism, racism, sexism. Tupac covered these in his music and felt connected to this type of critical cultural discourse from him (Valentín 2009, 39–40).

12   Sequential based reasoning, linear worldviews (first this, then that, lastly this, etc.), and simplistic answers.

13   (As discussed in:George 1998b; Hodge 2010; Neal 1997, 1999, 2002; Pinn 2002, 2010).

14   For example, books such as (Best Steven 1991) fall short of mentioning the social, religious, and cultural shift that the Civil Rights Movement brought to the American public sphere. Moreover, (Betts 2004a,) does not mention—even briefly—the contributions of Hip Hop and Rap moguls. In the work of Lash (1990a); (Lash 1990b), Gil Scott Heron, Ray Charles, and even the television show *Fresh Prince of Bel Air* were never mentioned in the literature. While each of these represent major changes and social shifts, they were not engaged. The Post Soul, as argued in Chapter 1, is therefore a parallel conceptual framework

Second, post-soul theology is the theology of the post-soul context. Its vernacular prioritizes a connection with a God of the oppressed and disenfranchised. Post-soul theology seeks to better understand God in the profane, the blasphemous, and the irreverent. Moreover, it makes God accessible to humans in a multi-ethnic and inclusive way while still recognizing the atrocities committed in the name of religion (Hodge 2013b).

Third, many renowned evangelical theologians have argued that we live in a "secular" culture. However, within the post-soul context, spirituality makes its reemergence and seeks to discover God in the ordinary. This pathway is foreign to traditional methodologies of salvation. The neo-secular is a mixture of sacred and profane spiritual journeys pursuing God in a space outside traditional forms of worship.

Fourth, the neo-sacred is rooted in the post-soul theological context. This sacred space embodies city corners, alleyways, club rooms, cocktail lounges, and spaces/places which are extraneous to many who call themselves "Christian." The neo-sacred is Tupac's message to the pimps, the hookers, the thugs, the niggas—those overlooked by society, missionaries, and many church-goers. The neo-sacred is concerned with finding God in the post-soul socio-ecological landscape and making God accessible for all.

For Tupac, a new type of theological discourse was needed in the face of severe economic, social, and political disparities. For example, in one of his first songs, *Panther Power*, Tupac bellows:

> As real as it seems the American Dream
> Ain't nothing but another calculated scheme
> To get us locked up shot up back in chains
> To deny us of the future rob our names
> Kept my history of mystery but now I see
> The American Dream wasn't meant for me
> Cause lady liberty is a hypocrite she lied to me[15]

Tupac calls out the very fabric of the "American Dream" (home ownership, being educated, affordable health care, and day care)[16] and challenges its

---

    including those excluded voices and creating space for artists like Tupac. Tupac asserted time after time that race played a role in the historical discourse of people, and the post soul aids in filling that void.

15 "Panther Power" The Lost Tapes. (1989/2000).
16 These four "American Dream" taxonomies are what (Block et al. 2006,) describe as the four main constructs of the "American Dream," and how the exponential increase in

apparent mythology for the ghetto poor. Where is God in all of this? Where is justice for those who do not live the commercialized embodiment of "the good life"? Tupac asserts the neo-sacred within this pain and disillusionment in a song titled "Lord Knows":

> I smoke a blunt to take the pain out
> And if I wasn't high, I'd probably try to blow my brains out
> I'm hopeless, they shoulda killed me as a baby
> And now they got me trapped in the storm, I'm goin' crazy
> Forgive me; they wanna see me in my casket
> and if I don't blast I'll be the victim of them bastards
> I'm losin' hope, they got me stressin,' can the Lord forgive me
> Got the spirit of a thug in me[17]

At the same time, Tupac realizes that this is not the way life was supposed to be. He is fully aware that God has not intended people to behave in an inhumane fashion. He calls out to God in a post-soul style, decrying his lifestyle:

> Fuck the friendships, I ride alone
> Destination Death Row, finally found a home
> Plus all my homies wanna die, call it euthanasia
> Dear Lord, look how sick this ghetto made us, sincerely
> yours I'm a thug, the product of a broken home[18]

In these lyrics, Tupac "does what he has to" in order to survive within these types of injustices, while still asking the poignant theological questions of God in the face of suffering. Tupac presents a voice to engage culture, deal with conflict, create cohesive narrative, generate community, dispel the traditional powers, and call people to a different level of engagement with God. Cheryl Kirk-Duggan would say that "like James Baldwin, Shakur confronted black suffering with a moral ire" (Kirk-Duggan 2009, 219). For those who would argue that this type of approach to life is vile, immoral, and "sinful," Tupac would reply that only God can judge him:

---

all four of those areas between 1973–2003 have almost eliminated the middle class. For Tupac, and many other Black scholars, the poor, the ghetto, and African Americans are at the bottom of this avalanche of misery.

17   "Lord Knows" Me Against The World (1995).
18   "Letter To The President" Still I Rise (1999).

> Oh my Lord, tell me what I'm livin' for
> Everybody's droppin' got me knockin' on heaven's door
> And all my memories, of seein' brothers bleed
> And everybody grieves, but still nobody sees
> Recollect your thoughts don't get caught up in the mix
> Cause the media is full of dirty tricks
> Only God can judge me[19]

Blues music had a similar sense. Contextual, relevant, gritty, and with reflections of Black lives in the White supremacist South, many White conservatives and religious Blacks dismissed the blues as evil, sinful, and altogether vile. Teresa Reed reminds us that "…blues singing was associated with the brothel, the juke joint, and the dregs of black-American society…" (Reed 2003, 39). Still, despite the stench of "sin," Reed (Reed 2003, 39–40) argues that the "…religious commentary is salient in the blues text…these lyrics treat religion in a way that yields two important kinds of information: integration of secular thought with sacred and…the postbellum shift in black-American religious consciousness." Tupac's music is merely a continuation of this postbellum shift, now with rap music (Hodge 2010).

A great example of part of this shift came in the late 1960s and early 1970s, when a heated debate was brewing that Black theology had no relevance and merely reflected an "angry" and "hateful" message from Blacks (e.g. Cone 1997a). Black theologian Herbert Edwards, in response to claims from some White theologians that Black theology was not a valid theological approach, argued that Black theology provided contextualization, a voice, and offered a way for those who had previously been either dismissed by White evangelicals or forcibly assimilated to their tradition. Tupac begins to create such a Black theological space.[20]

Tupac argues the inadequacy of the previous and existing theologies for the present crisis: poverty, recidivism rates for young urban males, racism, and classism. Tupac never once questioned, blasphemed, or cursed the name of God or Jesus. What Tupac did do was to call out religious officials, traditionalized churches (churches practicing hyper-traditionalism and adherence to the

---

19 "Only God Can Judge Me" All Eyez On Me Disc 1 (1996).
20 Edwards, while discussing Black Theology, argues that in order for theologies to have a concrete basis they must prove the inadequacy of the preceding theologies, establish and prove their own adequacy for the present, and must establish continuity with the primordial, normative expressions of the faith (Edwards 1975, 46–47).

"letter of the law"), conventional forms of religion, irrelevant theologies, and current methods of evangelism.

Tupac was not a trained theologian, pastor, or evangelist[21] in a way one would recognize with the formal rigor of the seminary. Tupac did not have the eloquence of a T.D. Jakes or the patois of a Baptist preacher. Still, Tupac was able to connect God to the streets and give those who had never heard of God a vision for what their life could be like. For Tupac, and others like him, lacking formal seminary training never disqualified him, or others, from doing "God's work." Still, Tupac never really came to any solid conclusions about a theology of the 'hood. He began the discussion, but because of his early death, never finished the mantra of a ghetto Gospel.

> We probably in Hell already, our dumb asses not knowin'
> Everybody kissin' ass to go to heaven ain't goin'
> Put my soul on it, I'm fightin' devil niggaz daily
> Plus the media be crucifying brothers severely...[22]

This aptly-titled song "Blasphemy" was a rejection of a form of Black theology that places the pastor at the center of the church, creates a pious stature for him (and it typically is a him), and discourages honest questions and doubts from emerging within the congregation (Pinn 2010). Tupac not only challenges but shatters the status quo by placing context and reality into his message within this song. He further states:

> The preacher want me buried why? Cause I know he a liar
> Have you ever seen a crackhead, that's eternal fire
> Why you got these kid's minds, thinkin' that they evil
> while the preacher bein' richer you say honor God's people
> Should we cry, when the Pope die, my request
> We should cry if they cried when we buried Malcolm X
> Mama tell me am I wrong, is God just another cop
> Waitin' to beat my ass if I don't go pop?[23]

---

21   In my 2008 research, 19 of the 20 of the interviews stated that Tupac was their "pastor" and had a connection to theology. They told me that Tupac was a prophet because of the way he could interpret theological matters and make it "clear" for them (See Hodge 2010).
22   Tupac, "Blasphemy," The Don Killuminati: The 7 Day Theory (1996).
23   In this verse we can also see Tupac connecting with mainstream theological thought by asking the serious questions of God. In other words, is God just another White,

Tupac continues shattering the status quo of "nice" theological answers by offering up metaphorical comparisons:

> They ask us why we mutilate each other like we do
> They wonder why we hold such little worth for human life
> Facing all this drama
> To ask us why we turn from bad to worse is to ignore from which we came
> You see, you wouldn't ask why the rose that grew from the concrete had damaged petals
> On the contrary, we would all celebrate its tenacity
> We would all love its will to reach the sun
> Well, we are the roses
> This is the concrete
> And these are my damaged petals
> Don't ask me why
> Thank God, nigga
> Ask me how[24]

In one of his greatest theological songs, "So Many Tears," Tupac pushes past the "milk" theology, described by Paul in 1 Corinthians 3:2, and enters into a mature theological stance on life:

> Now that I'm strugglin' in this business, by any means
> Label me greedy gettin' green, but seldom seen
> And fuck the world cause I'm cursed, I'm havin' visions
> of leavin' here in a hearse, God can you feel me?
> Take me away from all the pressure, and all the pain
> Show me some happiness again, I'm goin' blind
> I spend my time in this cell, ain't livin' well
> I know my destiny is Hell, where did I fail?
> My life is in denial, and when I die,
> baptized in eternal fire I'll shed so many tears
> Lord, I suffered through the years, and shed so many tears.[25]

The post-soul context requires one to disembody and deconstruct current theological mantras which continually hold up tradition. Pain, injustice, and

---

conservative Republican, wanting me to fit in and wear suits and ties like I've been told and have seen? Is there a place for the real nigga and thug in heaven?

24 "Mama Just A Little Girl" Better Dayz disc one (2002).
25 "So Many Tears" Me Against The World (1995).

racism force the post-soulist to look beyond the "standard" and ask God for more. Simplistic answers are rejected and despised. It gets God off the hook too easily to say "just pray about it,"[26] and in times of pain and injustice, everything needs to be on the hook, including God. The procedure is quite simple: have a conversation with God, be real, and do not be afraid to use strong language to describe your pain:

> Was it my fault papa didn't plan it out
> Broke out left me to be the man of the house
> I couldn't take it, had to make a profit
> Down the block, got a glock, and I clock grip
> Makin G's was my mission
> Movin' enough of this shit to get my mama out the kitchen and
> why must I sock a fella, just to live large like Rockefeller
> First you didn't give a fuck, but you're learnin' now
> If you don't respect the town then we'll burn you down
> God damn it's a motherfuckin' riot
>
> I see no changes, all I see is racist faces
> Misplaced hate makes disgrace to races
> We under I wonder what it take to make this
> one better place, let's erase the wait state
> Take the evil out the people they'll be acting right
> Cause both black and white are smokin' crack tonight
> And only time we deal is when we kill each other
> It takes skill to be real, time to heal each other
>
> Pull a trigger kill a nigger he's a hero
> Mo' nigga mo' nigga mo' niggaz
> I'd rather be dead than a po' nigga
> Let the Lord judge the criminals
> If I die, I wonder if heaven got a ghetto[27]

---

26   Pinn (1995) describes this type of theological process as nitty gritty hermeneutics, pushing past the basics of theology and into the depths of life to ask God "tougher questions." Acceptance of pain is put into context and the hermeneutic moves into the "nitty gritty" of life.

27   Lyrics taken from the song "I Wonder if Heaven Got A Ghetto" (Original Hip Hop version) R U Still Down disc one (1997).

For Tupac, the goal was to create a manner in which a portion of society who had been forgotten, those living in urban enclaves, could still be human and have meaning. In his song "Searching for Black Jesuz," Tupac and the Outlawz search for a deity that can relate to them, one who "smokes like we smoke, drink like we drink."[28] In the song "Picture Me Rolling," Tupac questions whether or not God can forgive him. He asks, "Will God forgive me for all the dirt a nigga did to feed his kids?"[29] In this neo-sacred element, Tupac begins to ask the longstanding theological question: what does forgiveness really look like for sinners?

For the post-soulist, this process of searching for God in the mystery, the hurt, the pain, and then finding God in that heinous mixture is a welcome breath of fresh air compared to the avoidance and three-point sermons that so much of evangelical theology has become. It is the heart of dialogue and the very place God is experienced. In fact, almost anyone who has experienced deep loss and pain, in which God's hand felt distant, can relate to this. For example, "White Man's World" combines Tupac's request for heavenly favor and reprisal in a process similar to the Psalms: "God bless me please...Making my enemies bleed."[30] Within those statements much more is at work—a fundamental attempt to make God accessible in a social structure which has been forgotten and left for dead.

More of the neo-sacred and post-soul theology arises in songs such as "Hail Mary." The song suggests a liturgical prayer, beseeching listeners to follow God and to "follow me; eat my flesh."[31] While it might appear that Tupac is asking his listeners to see him as "God," in fact Tupac was acting as a type of pastoral go-between. In several interviews from the early 1990s, he made reference to people in the 'hood not always having a clear path to God, and that in that absence of such a path, if he was the only pathway, then so be it.[32] Tupac made it clear he was not God or Jesus, but merely a conduit and a beacon to a contextualized Jesuz.[33]

---

28   2Pac & The Outlawz, "Black Jesus," *Still I Rise*, 1999, Interscope Records.
29   Tupac interview with Vibe Magazine, approximately 1995.
30   Tupac Shakur, "White Man's World," *Makaveli-Don Killuminati: The 7-Day Theory*, 1996, Deathrow Records.
31   Tupac Shakur, "Hail Mary," *Makaveli-Don Killuminati: The 7-Day Theory*, 1996, Deathrow Records.
32   Tupac interview with Vibe Magazine, approximately 1995.
33   Note the letter "S" has been dropped to demonstrate the contextualization of the Christ figure for the 'hood. And the letter Z at the end of Jesus' name was added to give a portrait of a Jesus that could sympathize and connect with a people that were downtrodden and broken. The letter Z is consistent with Hip Hop's vernacular to change words and phrases

Tupac fills part of the vacancy for those who doubt. In the song "Po Nigga Blues," Tupac poses a question to God which oozes with spiritual doubt: "...I wonder if the Lord ever heard of me, huh, I need loot, so I'm doin' what I do."[34] In other words, will God really forgive me when I am practicing socially unapproved standards of living? Dyson reminds us that "...Tupac's religious ideas were complex and unorthodox, perhaps even contradictory, though that would not make him unique among his believers" (Dyson 2001, 204). Part of that vacancy felt in the 'hood also comes with images of heaven: streets of gold, mansions, pearly gates, and a God who is "perfect"—these may be too much for the person living on streets riddled with potholes, in project housing, around broken gates, and with White racist images of God. Paulo Freire boldly states that within situations of oppression, the main goal of the oppressed should be to "...liberate themselves from their oppressor" (2000, 28). Tupac was helping to create that pathway for liberation.[35]

Tupac had a post-soul theological Gospel message for his fans, community, and society, embodying both the sacred and the profane. Tupac owned a lot of his own "sins" and shortcomings which, in post-soul contexts, creates a kind of transparency and authenticity. His listeners could identify with a marred, scarred, profanity-ridden, and broken ghetto "preacher." Within that profanity, an attempt to create honest communication between God and humankind is at work. Tupac and E.D.I. contend, in the song "The Uppercut," that "I'm a product of the pimp, the pusher, and the reverend...we all lost souls trying to find our way to heaven."[36]

Dyson asserts that "Tupac aimed to enhance awareness of the divine, of spiritual reality, by means of challenging orthodox beliefs and traditional religious

---

to fit the context and enunciate words for a Hip Hop community. The Z also represented a Jesus which was not only "above" in theological discussions, but also "below" in reachable form. The Z gives new dimensions to the portrait of Christ and validates the struggles, life, narrative, and spirituality for many Hip Hoppers. (Hodge 2010, Chapter 6)

34 Tupac, "Po Nigga Blues," *Loyal To The Game*, 2004, Amaru Interscope Records.
35 It is interesting to note that within my interviews, a theme of liberation from traditional church arose from the interviewees. "To move away from," "get out from under," "and "move out" were all phrases from respondents, when asked "How has Tupac's music, poetry, and spirituality affected you theologically?" These phrases were part of a larger discussion on how contemporary religion had become corrupted and lost its "edge" in life. Whether or not race was a factor in this response was not analyzed. This would be something for further study, but there is a clear implication here that the interviewees felt they needed to move out from their current theological situation, and that Tupac helped them to do just that.
36 Tupac, "The Uppercut," *Loyal To The Game*, 2004, Amaru Interscope Records.

practices." (Dyson 2001, 204). Tupac's "gospel," in essence, was a mature one that sought to better apprehend God in the core of a world gone askew.

Locating Tupac's Gospel

Tupac's "good news" about life in the 'hood is a type of "indecent theology" that Marcella Althaus-Reid discusses in *Indecent Theology: Theological Perversions in Sex, Gender, and Politics*,[37] as grand narratives of God have collapsed in the 'hood, creating parallel narratives that are contextual and relatable are crucial. Tupac's gospel, at its core, seeks to give marginalized urban dwellers (and poor Whites as well) a voice to God and a place for meaning in unbearable conditions. Tupac is an indirect "theologian," bringing a neo-secular message of God's love to the 'hood and contextualizing epistemological processes—in other words, constructing a new knowledge set of life in the 'hood for a generation raised in the Crack Cocaine milieu. Jamal Joseph notes that Tupac had a huge heart for people to understand a better way of living, to know positive role models, and to be critical thinkers (Jospeh 2006, 16–23). There are three gospel messages within his music: the gospel of hold on, the gospel of keeping your head up, and the gospel of heaven having a ghetto.

First, the gospel of hold on encouraged those who have given up or are about to give up on life or other people (e.g. Iverem 1997). Tupac encourages his listener to see that there is hope for a brighter tomorrow:

> God
> When I was alone, and had nothing
> I asked for a friend to help me bear the pain
> No one came, except God
> When I needed a breath to rise, from my sleep
> No one could help me... except God
> When all I saw was sadness, and I needed answers
> No one heard me, except God
> So when I'm asked...who I give my unconditional love to?
> I look for no other name, except God[38]

---

37 See (Althaus-Reid 2000) as she discusses an "indecent" approach to theology by questioning the authority figures within that religious structure and allowing new voices to emerge (in her case, a feminist perspective on religion).

38 2-Pac read by Rev. Run, "God," *The Rose That Grew From Concrete Vol.1*, 2000, Interscope Records.

In this poem, entitled "God," Tupac calls out to God and asks for a conduit. He finds it in the midst of hurt. James Cone calls this type of process "revelation" and argues, "For black theology, revelation is not just a past event or a contemporary event in which it is difficult to recognize the activity of God. Revelation is a black event..." (Cone 1990, 30). In this poem, Tupac takes on the revelation and looks for no one else but God.

In the song "So Many Tears,"[39] Tupac begs God not to forget a nigga, "...Lord I suffered through the years and shed so many tears...dear God please let me in."[40] There is a paradoxical optimism in the midst of extreme pain, hurt, despair, and violence.[41] Tupac calls the person to seek a better way and higher level of understanding.

The gospel of keeping your head up was a frequent theme in Tupac's discourse. Howard Thurman stated that one of the ingenuities of Balack slave culture was the ability to not diminish hopes, dreams, or visions to immediate experience. The immediate experience may by hurtful, problematic, nefarious, and even abusive but one must foster, encourage, manifest, and manage the future vision that allows one to escape the immediate consequences of despair. Hopelessness occurs when one has the inability to imagine a different future (Thurman 1976). In this gospel Tupac is essentially making sense of immediate pain and suffering. He would say, "Yes, I'm holding on, but where do I look?"

Tupac wanted his fans to know that the ideology of "keeping ya head up" was not done in vain. In the face of extreme opposition and hurt, there was still a way to move forward. Even when things seemed as though they could not get any better, Tupac would tell his fans that there was a better way. Life did not end on the experience of the immediate event; one's errors and successes were not necessarily their defining moments (Cone 1997a, b; Kain & Abel 1996).

> If I upset you don't stress, never forget
> That God isn't finished with me yet

---

39 Tupac Shakur, "So Many Tears," *Me Against The World*, 1995, Amaru/ Interscope/ Jive Records.

40 This mindset is no different than what slaves had to deal with and their vision that God would eventually help them. Luke Powery (Powery 2009) asserts that the spirit of lament is combined with celebration and that they go hand in hand.

41 This ideology connects with a concept that Rudolf Otto calls "The Mysterium Tremendum" (Otto 1950, 12–24), the mysteriousness of what God did in spite of an appalling situation. For Otto, this meant that "A God comprehended is no God." (Otto 1950, 25). In other words, holding on does not always mean that it will make sense or will even "feel right." This was an area for Tupac that helped him deal with the bigger picture of sin and the brokenness of humankind.

> I feel his hand on my brain
> When I write rhymes I go blind and let the Lord do his thang
> But am I less holy?
> Cause I chose to puff a blunt, and drink a beer with my homies
> Before we find world peace
> We gotta find peace and end the war in the streets, my ghetto gospel[42]

Tupac attempted to bring a pragmatic type of hope for the 'hood through his music instead of traditional hymns. Tupac replaced them with the Thug Life mantra and his message of encouragement in hard times (Hodge 2009, 278–284).[43]

Regarding the authority of what is from God and what is not, Dyson writes:

> …countless sacred narratives are hardly distinguishable from contemporary rap… The prophet Jeremiah belched despair from the belly of his relentless pessimism. And the Psalms are full of midnight and bad cheer. This is not to argue that the contrasting moral frameworks of rap and religion do not color our interpretation of their often-opposing creeds. But we must not forget that unpopular and unacceptable views are sometimes later regarded as prophetic. It is a central moral contention of Christianity that God may be disguised in the clothing—and maybe even the rap—of society's most despised members.
>
> DYSON 2001, 208–209

Tupac was part of this long tradition of lament, praise, and life in the secular, or what James Cone calls the "secular spiritual" (Cone 1992, 68–97).

In the song "Hold Ya Head," Tupac encourages those who are in prison, in pain, and lost to hold on and keep that head up in times of trouble. Through weed, alcohol, and even illicit sex, a post-soul theology arises:[44]

> The weed got me tweakin' in my mind, I'm thinkin.'
> God bless the child that can hold his own

---

42   "Ghetto Gospel" Loyal To The Game (2004).

43   This was one of the reasons why Tupac was so calm, almost at peace, with the knowledge of his imminent death (Jospeh 2006). Tupac was fully aware that life did not end here. Even though he did not have it easy and his situation was nefarious, there was a better place in heaven set for him.

44   For those who practice moralism, they begin to look outside its confined view of what a Christian looks like. Jesus Himself was considered a heretic, a blasphemer, and a profane individual for his views on spiritual matters (c.f.Miles 2001).

> Indeed, enemies bleed when I hold my chrome
> Let these words be the last to my unborn seeds
> Hope to raise my young nation in this world of greed
> Currency means nothin' if you still ain't free
> Money breeds jealousy, take the game from me
> I hope for better days, trouble comes naturally
> Running from authorities 'til they capture me
> And my aim is to spread mo' smiles than tears
> Utilize lessons learned from my childhood years
> Maybe Mama had it all right, rest yo' head
> Tradin' conversation all night, bless the dead
> To the homies that I used to have that no longer roll
> Catch a brother at the crossroads…
> Plus nobody knows my soul, watchin' time pass
> Through the glass of my drop-top Rolls, hold ya head![45]

In the song "Still I Rise," Tupac laments to the Lord that the struggle is almost too much to bear; pain and misery parade his life and the journey seems like it will never end. Yet, in the end, still I rise. "Tupac sounds out that in times of trouble; God is with you, so keep your head up. Even the words in that phrase, 'head up' is meant to persuade one to look unto the Heavens from which our help comes" (Hodge 2009, 264).

Lastly, the gospel of heaven having a ghetto was a prolific thought in Tupac's worldview, contextualizing heaven and making it accessible for people who do not subscribe to Euro-Western theology. Tupac even calls himself the "ghetto missionary." In an interview on B.E.T. Tupac states:

> If I can't be free, if I can't live with the same respect as the next man, then I don't wanna be here. Because God has cursed me to see what life should be like. If God had wanted me to be this person, to be happy here, he wouldn't let me feel so oppressed. He wouldn't let me feel so trampled on; you know what I'm saying? He wouldn't let me think the things I think. So, I feel like I'm doing God's work, you know what I'm saying? Just because I don't have nothing to pass around for people to put in the bucket don't mean I'm not doing God's work; I feel like I'm doing God's work. Because, these ghetto kids ain't God's children? And I don't see no missionaries coming through there. So I'm doing God's work. While Reverend Jackson do his shit up in the middle class and he go to the White

---

45   "Hold Ya Head" The Don Killuminati: The 7 Day Theory (1996).

House and have dinner and pray over the president, I'm up in the 'hood doing my work with my folks.[46]

Here Tupac expresses not only the divisions of class within Black society, but also within its theological walls.[47] Tupac knows it is his mission to bring a Gospel to those who have been left out and have not been invited to the anticipated heavenly party with its unspoiled clean streets. The thought then is this: if life continues according to plan, heaven will have cops waiting to "beat our ass" the minute we walk through the gates. Therefore, Tupac decided to ask the question, Does heaven have a ghetto? In other words, can I be accepted in this realm that has continually told me I am neither worthy nor acceptable? Can I be taken for my own worth as I am, or do I have to enter through the back so as not to disturb the residents nor mar the fine linen?

The great writer, mystic, and theologian Howard Thurman asks the relevant and almost irreligious question regarding religion and its message to the poor and disheveled: "What does our religion say to them?" (Thurman 1976, 13). Thurman's challenge says:

> I can count on the fingers of one hand the number of times that I have heard a sermon on the meaning of religion, on Christianity, to the man who stands with his back against the wall. It is urgent that my meaning be crystal clear. The masses of men live with their backs constantly against the wall. They are the poor, the disinherited, the dispossessed. What does our religion say to them?
> THURMAN 1976, 13

Tupac took the challenge and attempted to create a Gospel message for those poor, disinherited, and dispossessed peoples living in the urban enclaves called the ghetto. Tupac created a transcendental space for the thug, the nigga, and the pimp to find God.[48]

---

46   Taken from an interview on BET by Ed Gordon in 1994.
47   This is an ongoing debate and issue within Black culture and the Black church. For a further discussion see (Dyson 2005a; Lincoln and Mamiya 1990; Pinn 2002).
48   These types of questions create theological conundrums in contemporary evangelical theology, which echo vagueness and ambiguity regarding God's love to marginalized peoples. Therefore, the Hip Hopper, the ghetto person, and Tupac himself pose a new question: if social structures and systems have failed us, wouldn't the church and religion follow suit? Tupac could no longer sit by and accept a traditional view of Jesus or Christianity. Tupac needed a stronger theology than that, a Christ who could accept the thug and the marginalized person. This was the outcry in songs like "I Wonder if Heaven

Tupac's answer to his own question, "Does heaven got a ghetto?" is yes! However, not in the literal sense. Tupac never said that there is poverty, crime, gentrification, and homelessness in God's Kingdom. The term is used figuratively, symbolically, as if to ask, "Is the Gospel big enough to fit everyone who wants to fit in, and can God handle me if He really created me?" Tupac resoundingly said yes. He encouraged his audience, as a pastor would their flock, to see that there was a different image of heaven and that there was room for those that did not fit in a traditional evangelical (and at times White) theology.[49]

> Who's got the heart to stand beside me?
> I feel my enemies creepin' up in silence
> Dark prayer, scream violence—demons all around me
> Can't even bend my knees just a lost cloud; Black Jesus
> give me a reason to survive, in this earthly hell
> Cause I swear, they tryin' to break my well
> I'm on the edge lookin' down at this volatile pit
> Will it matter if I cease to exist? Black Jesus[50]

Toward a Theology of Tupac the Post-soul Prophet

Tupac was not perfect. He was baptized in the dirty waters of marketing, social representations of blackness, stereotypes of the gangsta, the tattooed thug, and the poor Black child. He was not Jesus incarnate, nor was he the "perfect" role model for everyone. Before he left for prison, he told Jada Pinkett Smith that he wanted to quit thuggin' and give up on rap and solely do acting (Dyson 2001, 215–216). However, Tupac ended up embodying the same Black male image he had fought so hard against for so long: the cyclical prison inmate, the nihilistic Black male, the paranoid pessimistic urbanite.

It is within these conflicts that this paradox between the sacred and the profane arises—a post-soul theology with Tupac in the middle. Tupac embodied both sin and deity. Within this contradiction, there is both good and evil, sin and salvation, dirt and cleanliness all at work and having the ability to create a

---

Got A Ghetto?" and "Black Jesuz." These were expressions of a deeper search for God and spirituality. These were also fundamental questions of who God really is—questions that many of us ask ourselves such as are we really "saved?" (Hodge 2009, 264–265).

49   This is also something I discuss at length in my chapter on engaging the theology of the profane in *The Soul Of Hip Hop* (Hodge 2010, 159–164).

50   2Pac & The Outlawz, "Black Jesus," *Still I Rise*, 1999, Interscope Records.

fuller religious person, one who is honest about both the "good" and the "bad." This is the human struggle. Tupac, in this sense, was no different to Paul. While Tupac knew what was right and how to do the right thing, he did not do it because his flesh was weak (Romans 7:7–24). Still, within that weakness, he sought to find space to find God and Jesuz. This is a large part of post-soul theology. Tupac gave us this gospel and let people know that he was not the way; he was only pointing the way to Jesuz.[51]

Chapter Summary

This chapter has been concerned with Tupac Amaru Shakur and establishing his hermeneutical, ecclesiological, and numinous pursuits throughout his music, poetry, and life cycle. In this chapter, I have argued that Tupac was one of the only rappers within the Hip Hop community and continuum who has earned, at least at the time of this research and publication, the title of 'ghetto saint' and 'urban prophet.' His music searched through sexuality, manhood, pain, violence, revenge, hate, anger, love, hope, nihilism, and a pursuit of God in a contextualized manner. Tupac was the externalized secular discussion of transmediated discourses of religious pursuits within the Hip Hop community. Tupac was and still is a prophetic and totemic symbol within Hip Hop and urban communities.

Yet, Tupac was still human, and contradictory to his own belief system at times. He wanted "peace," yet was in a passionate feud with Biggie Smalls, Sean Puffy Combs, and Nas—claiming on several occasions that he had 'fucked Biggie's wife.' Moreover, there was the issue of his own personal demons of insecurity, self-worth, and lack of stability which gave Tupac an unsteady persona at times and an image in the public sphere which said he was just a 'thug'—the literal definition and not the one Tupac had imagined with T.H.U.G.L.I.F.E..[52]

Yet, even within this contradiction and seemingly hypocritical ethos, Tupac remains "prophetic" to many. Possibly, it is because he was so transparent with his faults and shortcomings that he became one of Hip Hop's most respected artists and voices. Perhaps it was because he intertwined God (the sacred), and his own life (the secular), with a realist form of 'life' in urban context (the profane) that made him into the ghetto theologian he was. Tupac's painful past

---

51   This connects to John the Baptist in John 1:19–32 in the Christian Bible, where John denies that he is the One and that the one who comes after him is Jesus, who gives life eternally.
52   The Hate U Give Little Infants Fucks Everyone.

might have given him the artistic insights to create music, poetry, and messages that could relate to his audience and within the Hip Hop continuum.

We will now explore that pain, violence, and suffering which helped create an artist like Tupac. Chapter 4 will explore the contexts in which this violence exists and the socio-religious rhetoric associated with it. Chapter 4 is crucial in that it will establish that violence is relative, that the meta-narrative of retribution for that violence and suffering is associated with the dominant culture, and that those within urban communities who engage in violent retribution are typically shunned.

CHAPTER 4

Violence, Death, & Suffering in Hip Hop Context

> I shouldn't have to live in two Americas. I should be living in the same America as everybody else!
> — MOS DEF

⁂

> What he [the police] doesn't realize is that every day he's feeding me a spoonful of hate. That's my diet. A spoonful of hate. Every day. It's only a matter of time before I will erupt; or upon whom I will erupt on. Will I attack myself, will I attack my brother, or will I attack the source of what is causing my hate?
> — KUMASI BROWN

⁂

> The whites have always been an unjust, jealous, unmerciful, avaricious and blood-thirsty set of beings, always seeking after power and authority. To my no ordinary astonishment, [a] Reverend gentleman got up and told us (coloured people) that slaves must be obedient to their masters—must do their duty to their masters or be whipped—the whip was made for the backs of fools, &c. Here I pause for a moment, to give the world time to consider what was my surprise, to hear such preaching from a minister of my Master, whose very gospel is that of peace and not of blood and whips, as this pretended preacher tried to make us believe. What the American preachers can think of us, I aver this day before my God, I have never been able to define.
> — DAVID WALKER, in DAVID WALKER'S *Appeal*

⁂

The Hip Hop community regularly experiences violence, death, nihilism, and war-like conditions. One might argue that this is at the center for most of the social critique Hip Hop has towards dominant societal structures and systems. Equality, justice, fairness, impartiality in the law, and a social voice is where many Hip Hoppers—especially the underground community—push towards and give a lot of their energy. Sally, one of the interviewees, recounted to me stories of the economic injustice she faced which then led to her having to prostitute to make ends meet. From there, she detailed a world that seemed to end for her. It was one 'John' after the next to get just enough money to buy herself some 'ramen noodles' to eat. Tim voiced to me that as a child he assumed life was murder and death until his guardians moved him to another part of the city. Tim learned early on in life that it was about survival and that 'death was around every corner.' Both Tim and Sally affirmed that Hip Hop was their voice, their solace, and their community to which they could relate and in times of deep depression, it was also their "spiritual outlet."[1]

Hip Hoppers typically come from communities filled with stories such as these.[2] Also, since the Hip Hop community comes from largely urban ghettos, the music is a reflection of that lifestyle and social conditions so it tends to be just as 'gritty' and raw. This "rawness" in approach and prose leans towards conflict and tension, and pushes back from dominant figures in society such as politicians, religious celebrities, and hegemonic pundits who view this "rawness" as a threat to society, moral living conditions, and ultimately the safekeeping of the "nation state" (Rose 1994; Quinn 2005). Critics of Hip Hop have argued that rap lyrics are often:[3]

- Too violent
- Misogynistic[4]
- Promote racism, hate, and violence
- Against law enforcement
- Promote anarchy
- Teach 'Black Power'
- Teach youth to hate White people
- Destroy 'moral values' with youth
- Corrupt the minds of the youth
- Not fit for consumption.

---

1 A theme that is also echoed in my earlier research as well (Hodge 2009, 2010).
2 This is not to overlook the suburban, White phenomena in Hip Hop in which artists come from "well-to-do" backgrounds and are not familiar with the more harsh conditions of urban living.
3 A sample taken from headlines from MSNBC, Fox News, CNN, and Time Magazine between 1998 and 2011.
4 This is also a criticism of many feminists, womanists, and social activists of mainstream Hip Hop too. This critique is not limited to conservative voices. As noted throughout this book, misogynist lyrics are a concern and an issue within Hip Hop culture as a whole.

These criticisms come when rap lyrics condemn the conditions in which many of them find themselves living, and are frequently in reaction to the injustice which caused those conditions to begin with (e.g. economic inequality, political corruption, police brutality). Hip Hop Blacks, Latinos, disenfranchised Whites, and Asians are inclined to have critical responses to the President of the U.S., law enforcement, politicians, and U.S. history which they feel is not reflective of their narrative and experience. The videos and lyrics, in turn, are a reflection of that felt injustice, which then incur the social criticisms listed above. It is a cycle indeed. Still, the critique is one that rappers feel is unwarranted since the very accusers of their music are some of the same perpetuators of the injustice, oppression, disenfranchisement they are experiencing.

Further, within this nebula of injustice, oppression, and disenfranchisement, what are the ontological, hermeneutical, and numinous meanings which occur? Does God exist within evil and violence? How is God invoked for violence in micro-settings such as Hip Hop culture? Abrahamic faiths typically view suffering and violence in redemptive ways if, (1) the individual or group is morally upright and 'right with God,' (2) suffering for 'God' and/or 'Christ' is warranted under martyrdom conditions, and (3) the call from God causes that individual/group to suffer in relation to that 'call.' Yet, what does it mean when injustice causes the violence as seen on April 29, 1992 when South Central residents in Los Angeles received the "not guilty" verdict from the high profile case of the Rodney King beatings? Or when Troy Davis, a Black man, was found guilty of killing a police officer and sentenced to death in 2011, when no physical evidence was ever recovered and the eyewitness who allegedly saw Davis shoot the officer was known for taking deals with the police to lessen his jail time and later recanted his testimony? More recently, what does it mean when a transit officer shoots and kills Oscar Grant while he is handcuffed, only to receive nine months jail time? An even more recent racially contested event: the acquittal of George Zimmerman who brutally murdered Trayvon Martin, a young Black male who Zimmerman pursued and then shot and killed after an alleged 'scuffle' between the two, in which Zimmerman claimed self-defense. How does 'God' fit into these injustices?

One response to this is that pain and suffering produces a stronger person. Emilie Townes suggests a perspective on pain, in Wells-Barnett's work, which argues that pain and suffering are both revitalizing and fruitful.[5] Townes finds Audre Lordes' distinction between the pain (a "process of pointing toward

---

[5] According to Townes, redemptive suffering is theoretically rejected. "Wells-Barnett joins those who reject suffering as God's will and believe that it is an outrage that suffering exists as all" (Townes 1993, 171).

transformation") and suffering (a continuous "cycle" of reliving pain) both insightful and helpful (In Pinn 1995, 68–70). Lordes challenges the labeling of pain and suffering. Anthony Pinn argues that, "Pain, like suffering referred to as redemptive, fuels efforts to break the cycle of oppression using past experience and lessons. That is to say, pain denotes the consequence of socially transformative activity" (Pinn 1995, 71). For Lordes, in this context, "Pain promotes self-knowledge which is a tool for liberation and wholeness...Pain names suffering as sin and plots a strategy to defeat sin" (Townes 1993, 197). So, in this view, pain might provide the insight and pedagogy, as Pinn would suggest, necessary to achieve the liberation from that pain and call out the systemic "sin" within. Social activism, advocated by Wells-Barnett, is an attempt to bring a type of justice to the situation and to seek liberation actively by ending the cycle of oppression and pain, according to Lordes.

This is what some rappers are after: calling the "sin" out within the systems or people that produced it. The linguistic shift may have occurred in how we label and define pain and suffering, but the conditions and systems which produced it for Hip Hoppers and the urban community remain the same.[6] It is a type of distributive justice in which some rappers such as M-1 from Dead Prez assert as necessary in order for pain and suffering to be alleviated while still calling into question the "sin" within the systems. For example, in reaction to the dilapidated education systems, Dead Prez tell us:

> They aint teachin our families how to interact
> Better with each other, knowhatimsayin? They just teachin us
> How to build they shit up, knowhatimsayin? That's why my niggas
> Got a problem with this shit, that's why niggas be droppin out that
> Shit cuz it don't relate, you go to school the fuckin police
> Searchin you you walkin in your shit like this a military compound
> Knowhatimsayin? So school don't even relate to us
> Until we have some shit where we control the fuckin school system
> Where we reflect how we gon solve our own problems
> Them niggas ain't gon relate to school, shit that just how it is
> Knowhatimsayin? And I love education, knowhatimsayin?
> But if education ain't elevatin me, then you knowhatimsayin it ain't

---

6 The ideology and worldviews behind suffering are vast. Ida Wells-Barnett, for example, does not make a clean break from the notion that suffering can be redemptive and continues to advocate for the idea that there is redemptive suffering (Wells-Barnett 1970; Wells-Barnett 1995; Wells-Barnett 1969), along with other scholars as well (Spencer 1990; Reed 2003; Paris 1985; Odum 1968).

> Takin me where I need to go on some bullshit, then fuck education
> Knowhatimsayin? At least they shit, matter of fact my nigga
> this whole school system can suck my dick (2000).

Notice the "raw" critical hermeneutic that the group uses towards education. In essence, Dead Prez both advocates for actual education and critiques the social injustice (which causes variable amounts of pain and suffering) within the educational system and lets the system know that this cannot be tolerated any more. At the end is a vehement line that calls the educational system out if it cannot do what it was intended to do, and that is actually to educate.

In situations in which the suffering produces death, Hip Hoppers, much like Old Testament stories, call for an eye-for-an-eye to avenge that death. Rappers such as Ice-Cube and Geto Boys will exclaim that Hip Hoppers (Blacks in particular) should take up arms in certain regards in response to violence against them. N.W.A.'s now thematic song 'Fuck The Police' was in reference to police brutality yet, at certain points, it also advocates for retaliation against those same officers.

Still, there are others in the Hip Hop community, such as Lauryn Hill, Will Smith, Mace, Rev. Run, and at times MC Lyte, who argue for Martin Luther King Jr.'s position of agape love to affect the oppressors' moral conscience. In this view, uprisings, retaliations against police officers, aggression and violence towards the oppressor are not methods which should be encouraged and/or utilized. King himself was convinced that hope, love, and redemption were the essential values that Black Americans (and in turn those who are being oppressed), should take in order to gain support and realize justice. One of King's seminary papers demonstrates this ideology:

> Who can deny that many apparent evils turn out in the end to be goods in disguise? Character often develops out of hardship. Unfortunate [sic] heredity and environment conditions often make for great and noble souls. Suffering teaches empathy.
>   Jr April 15, 1960, 419

The "love your enemy" approach has been popular for many and is widely accepted within mainstream society as being "moral" and "just." In other words, this position, one of loving your enemy and showing the "oppressor" love, is valued and promoted as "good" and "just" which often times fits well into conservative Western Christianity. Malcolm X, among others, did not always share this position and often advocated for armed resistance—one that is regarded as both controversial and "unacceptable" for those who are oppressed. Still

King's ideology of agape love is popularized often by even right-winged conservatives such as Glenn Beck who in 2011, staged a "march" on King's birthday for "America's safety" (safety against what he labeled as 'terrorism,' 'liberal laws,' and the 'eroding of American values').

The critique of this view is that the oppressor (be it the dominant White or White Supremacist systems) can deem violence as both legal and necessary against those oppressed, any time it desires. The oppressor can even make it 'theologically sound' if they so choose. However, when the oppressed 'fight back' and respond, they are seen as immoral, unjust, and not following the 'teachings of Jesus.' This critique is a consistent one within Hip Hop culture of those arguing for violent reactions to violent actions. King has, over the last two decades, received criticism from Hip Hoppers such as Ice T, Ice Cube, Black Moon, Mos Def, X-Clan, RZA, and even Tupac at certain points for this 'love' of your enemy. Billy, an interviewee states, "Why the fuck should I love the person who fucking hates me? Huh? You tell me that? Shit don't make no sense kid. No fucking sense!"[7] In response, rappers have evoked the vision and writings of David Walker, a free Black who argued for Black slaves to rise up against their masters and revolt, claiming that he himself had visions from God who urged him to do this (Pinkney 2000).[8] Further, King's view on suffering, that it is in fact redemptive, raises the concern of a God who would allow such suffering while allowing such "justice" for those who are doing the persecution. The Hip Hop community, along with scholars through the ages alike, wrestle with this notion of a "just God." How can God be all-loving and all-knowing yet allow such injustice to the very people that follow him (Pinn 1995; Pineda-Madrid 2001)?

This chapter seeks to inspect the context, lyrics, and overall messages within the Hip Hop community and individuals and rappers who criticize their living and social conditions which produce violence, pain, and suffering. In other words, why rap/sing about violence? Are the lyrics violence or merely on par with, for example, artists such as Bono who openly criticize politics and social living conditions? Are rappers' response to their social world merely

---

7   This type of mantra also imagines the race of Jesus Christ, who history withstanding, is popularized to have 'loved' everyone. Black Hip Hoppers often feel as though a White image of Christ is just another White Supremacist waiting to oppress them in the same manner as those here on Earth. Moreover, White Jesus is often seen as a "punk" or "pussy" because of his perceived stance on non-violence. In Chapter 5 we will examine this further, but it bears noting at this juncture.

8   Some also argue that it is only a matter of time before those who are experiencing pain, suffering, disenfranchisement and oppression will revolt and use armed means for that revolt. Just how long does one take being slapped in the face before slapping back (Fanon 1968)?

a reflection of the context in which they are living? Is violence relative, therefore, when violence is in response to something that the dominant group deems as "just" as, for example, our response to the attacks on 9/11? What is life like in the midst of war-like conditions that are invisible to the public eye? Is retribution (an eye-for-an-eye) a possibility? Does God stand by the oppressed? Let us begin this chapter by examining violence and the context in which it is produced. How does U.S. nationalism, combined with a discourse of religion, create "justifiable" violence domestically, and towards other nations and cultures? How do discourses of national violence become "acceptable" when it affects the majority? These will be questions we begin to observe in this chapter within the Hip Hop context and continuum.

Violence in Context

It is important to discuss the discourses and pathological mantras which shape how and when violence is used and when that violence is justified, especially when religion is invoked. Violence and responses to violence are relative and are labeled "just" and "unjust" by the groups within any societal structure. Violence, when done in response to what a state or government defines as a "just cause," can not only be accepted but may be deemed "holy" and "moral." More importantly, once the public and/or society has deemed war and violence acceptable in the name of "justice," the line connected to God becomes easily visible (Tuman 2010, 67–72). For example, following the attacks after 9/11, the war was deemed a "holy war" from certain media outlets. To compound that, President Bush repeatedly stated that he had "prayed" and "asked God" regarding his decision to invade Iraq. This type of socio-religious discourse aids in creating acceptance for the murder of children and innocent by-standers as a result of this "holy war." The acceptance of "God's will" is further used to ignore violence against non-dominant religious groups such as Muslims. Violence, in this sense, is then seen as a form of "justice" against "those people." Further, Wade Clark Roof in his article "American Presidential Rhetoric from Ronald Reagan to George W. Bush: Another Look at Civil Religion" reminds us that civil religious rhetoric can be just as dangerous as the violence itself because it involves both nationalism and constructs of identity (Roof 2009).[9] This union of religious-political rhetoric tends to create myths and fantasy

---

9   We look at presidents here because, arguably, they have some of the biggest influence over political, religious, and economic rhetoric. As noted in Coe and Domke (2006) and Tuman's (Coe and Domke 2006; Tuman 2010, 122–126) works, presidents greatly influence how a nation

within the public arena in which God is "on our side" and "with us" while being completely "against them," almost increasing the need for more violence against "those people." These myths are powerful ideological vehicles for any people group and society, particularly in the issuing of violence through military force (Tuman 2010; Roof 2009).

A type of social mythology is created in the 'nation-state' which creates a 'just' action when it is harmed or threatened. This, when combined with God and religion, offers a troubling mixture of ideology, identity, and theodicy which would suggest that "God's nation" is in fact "set apart" and given the "right" to invoke "war" on those that "persecute it." In the eyes of God, this would be considered just. Roof once again tells us,

> The myth of a Chosen Nation arises out of the Hebrew Bible and suggests that Americans are exceptional in having a covenant with God: they are the New Israel in the language of the early Puritans. A second myth of origin—Nature's Nation, emerging out of the Enlightenment and Deism—gave rise to the notion that the United States arose out of the natural order, and that the country reflects the way God had intended things to be from the beginning of time. Building upon both of these foundational myths, the Millennial Nation myth implies that God chose America to bless the nations of the world with the unfolding of a golden age. The last two are obviously complementary: one looking to the beginning of time, the other looking to the end of time (2009, 288).

Roof gives a troubling view of how this type of mantra can create a dangerous mix of violence in the "name of God." If one believes they are in fact "God's nation," actions from that "Godly nation" will in fact be sanctioned by God. Further, any suffering and pain resulting on the "other side" from these said actions, is overlooked and considered just. What would you expect from attacking or harming "God's chosen people?"

Myth, in this sense, becomes very dangerous as it tends to lead to more violence all in the "name of...." However, it touches close to one's identity and if we have learned anything from the American Religious Identification Survey, it is that religion and personal identity are closely tied together. Couple that with a nation's leader who is "God's servant" evoking socio-religious rhetoric at a time of fear, panic, and social threats, and you have a powerful discourse which can

---

state recognizes not just "terrorism" and its "evils," but also to the extent the people within that system will agree to violence, war, and death to those who "oppose" "God's nation."

be positioned to end in accepted levels of violence and suffering. Roof places it like this:

> Myths are the means by which a nation affirms its deepest identities and frames its rationale for political action; they are the elementary, yet profound, stories giving meaning and purpose to the collective life of a people; they evoke the imagination, so crucial to national self-understanding. Functioning largely at the unconscious level in the minds of citizens, they are activated though ritual, and particularly during times of national threat…(2009, 287)

In this quote, Roof articulates the strength of myths as a public looks upon national threats as a threat to God "himself." Moreover, when leaders fall in love with the idea of "how it should be" and the idealization of "what God wants," the instinct to kill, murder, and destroy is powerful and contentious. Roof says, "in such moments myths are easily absolutized, or turned into hardened, reified realities taken to be literally true…." As historian Richard T. Hughes (Hughes 2003) points out, in such moments of fear and panic the myth can be a comfort for them.

Religious rhetoric,[10] in turn, is socially constructed and maintained by establishing religious roots (Tuman 2010, xv). For example, Roger Smith noted that George W. Bush Jr. used more religious rhetoric after the 9/11 attacks than any other president to date. "George W. Bush has used more religious rhetoric than his predecessors and has used it in distinct ways" (Smith 2008, 279). More specifically:[11]

> Ronald Reagan initiated a new era in which "God" references per presidential address more than doubled compared to presidents from FDR through Jimmy Carter. George W. Bush ranks highest in references per address and references per 1,000 words, exceeding even Reagan. In contrast, though Bill Clinton and George H.W. Bush invoked God more often

---

10 This religious rhetoric and religious-political discourse is also associated with the construct of terrorism, especially when it gives reason to topple a government as a result of being labeled a "terrorist" and "harboring terrorist." These discourses affect the way a nation views killings and murder; it is almost as if a pass has been given once the stigma of terrorist has been issued (Matusitz 2013, 53–69; Tuman 2010, 122–126).

11 Also see Kevin Coe and David Domke's (Coe and Domke 2006) work on presidential discourse and the ascendancy of religious conservatives for an even broader examination of socio-religious rhetoric in the context of justified violence.

per address than pre-Reagan presidents, their rate per 1,000 words was roughly that of those predecessors. The second Bush and Reagan also adopted the prophetic posture in 47% of their addresses, compared to 0% for pre-Reagan Democrats, 5% for pre-Reagan Republicans, and 15% for the first Bush and Clinton, all statistically significant differences. Both presidents, but especially Bush, made prophetic statements most often in relation to the role of the United States in promoting freedom in the world (2008, 280).

This type of rhetoric and public discourse flirts dangerously with what Coe and Domke (2006) note as "Divine vision for U.S. foreign policy." As the president is the "head of the nation," so too often follows the public opinion. Politics and religion, however, is nothing new in the public sphere of the U.S. Billy Graham is noted as one of the first Western Christian Evangelicals to begin urging presidents to "convert" and "choose a religion" for the "moral state of the nation."[12] This picked up speed during the 1960s when President Kennedy claimed Catholicism as his religion (a controversy at the time). It continued throughout various presidents, bringing this rhetoric into the present where we see little to no line between church and state. The socio-religious rhetoric runs dangerously close to that of countries such as Iran and Afghanistan where religion, state, country, and Allah are one and the same. Thus, it has become simpler for presiding presidents to invoke "prayer," "war," and "God" while still having most of the nation support them in that decision.

On a macro level, people want "pay-back" and retribution when they feel wronged or attacked. This sense of payback often takes the form of maximum revenge, particularly after national events such as 9/11, ISIS attacks on U.S. citizens, and events that get labeled as "terrorism." In other words, the public wants vengeance and they want it immediately. This vengeance is justified when "innocent lives" are taken and, especially, when the dominant society is struck at the very center of what they believe to be sacred (e.g. economic and religious symbolism). Therefore, the notion of an "eye for an eye" is warranted and desired against anyone who would come against "us" and attempt to destroy "us." Rhetoric such as freedom, taking back, never forget, one nation, proud, American, God's country, and our nation are ones that strike at the public's religious formation and identity. These, in turn, create a contagion effect of 'mob-rule' which after the events of 9/11 have created a "new world" where

---

12 As noted in the documentary *God In America* which documents the rise of Billy Graham by noted scholars, and examines the connections between church and state (Belton 2010).

violence against those "bad guys" is accepted and at times required.[13] More importantly, the Brown skin of those accused of "terrorism" and their "foreign ways" and "savage lifestyle" give the public even more of a license to kill, murder, and seek the level of retribution "God" has required them to seek (Hughes 2003; Coe and Domke 2006; Tuman 2010).

In this creed of an "eye for an eye," violence is almost expected and even desired in response to violent acts against "us." While there was public outrage for the war in Iraq, the main reaction from the public was support for the war because it was "just" in the sense that it was in retaliation—being that the U.S. is thought by many as "God's Country." The ensuing logic was that this was, in fact, an attack against "God." This type of violence is accepted and even required by the public.

These worldviews and ideologies are troubling, vexing, and problematic, to say the least. It benefits those in dominant structures and gives way to those in positions of racial dominance to perform violence in the "name of God." They ignore truth and give precedent to myths as absolute certainty, and do so under a religious guise.

Yet, when those in urban communities suffer similar violence, suffering as a result of hegemonic systems of oppression, or incur a death that does not affect the larger society (e.g. gang related shootings or the death of Black males), it is not seen nor valued as important by the public at large. The concept of non-violence has typically been used toward Blacks and urban ethnic minorities in the face of violence against them. Still, the broader U.S. uses violence as a means of "peace" and legitimizes that violence as normative. In extreme cases such as 9/11, it is part of "God's retribution" toward those defined as enemies. As is the case in the Baltimore uprisings, discourses such as "stop the violence" and "we need peace in our city" were heard, yet rarely is that same treatise used toward the police and systems which produce death and pain like the deaths of Freddie Gray, Tamir Rice, Trayvon Martin, or Laquan McDonald.

Whose pain, suffering, and story is the one that gets valued, told, supported, and avenged? Is it wrong that gang members engage in some of the same retaliatory methods that the U.S. military uses when one of "their own" is killed? Is it morally wrong to say that one death is valued over the other? How does one contend with a God which appears to be on "one side?" In this state of a double standard ethos, voices have emerged to call out this injustice within Hip Hop

---

13 For example, bumper stickers and t-shirts that display "Terrorist Hunting License" or "The Marines: We arrange a meeting between Terrorists and God" are typical discourses which skirt the lines of socio-religious rhetoric and, tinged with humor, give an opportunity to "kill" those who are "bad" and make it socially "ok" to do so.

culture and rap music. Tricia Rose (1994, 78–85) tells us that "rap arose in a postindustrial city context in which artists and listeners are able to shape their own social community through the music." Moreover, Rose (1994, 34) also says that Hip Hop is a source for youth for alternative identity formation and social status in a community with "war like conditions." Michael Eric Dyson has argued that Hip Hoppers were able to conjure up a certain type of capital from the misery and pain of inner city living. Dyson contends that "Hip-hoppers joined pleasure and rage while turning the details of their difficult lives into craft and capital" (1996, 177). Hip Hoppers have called attention to the ghetto and argued that it too, is valid, real, and worthy of the same retribution and vindication of which the broader U.S. is worthy, even if it means acquiring that vengeance by violent means.

Once again, Ice Cube narrates that "…it's time to take a trip to the suburbs, let em see a nigga invasion, point blank on a Caucasian. Cock the hammer then crack a smile, take me to your house pal" (AmriKKKa's Most Wanted 1991). In this song, Cube describes what might happen if ignoring such issues continues. As noted in Chapter 2, in Cube's third album, he converts to Nation Of Islam and acts as God's agent within his songs to bring "death to all White Devils" who are non-believers of Allah. To the naked eye and ear, one might consider this to be "obscene" and "too violent." Yet, these are very similar discourses to those of Ronald Reagan, George Bush Senior, and George Bush Jr. in describing the "insurgents" who invaded "our country" (Coe and Domke 2006; Smith 2008). One must ask, what is truly the difference?

Such narratives closely resemble the violence in patriotic speech in which attacking and killing is celebrated and venerated through other religious discourse. In other words, hegemonic violence is celebrated and glorified, but insurgent and urban violence is not. The uprisings that took place in Baltimore after the death of Freddie Gray at the hands of yet another police unit is a precise example. Pastors, celebrities, and pundits on both sides of the aisle had prescribed memes for the protesters in Baltimore. "Why are you doing this," "Stop the violence," and "You don't get nothing out of violence" were all memes sent to the protestors. Former NFL player Ray Lewis even recorded a video pleading with "his people" to "stop the violence" and that "this is not the way." Yet, did these same voices have the same message to the Baltimore police department? Was there national outcry and prescribed memes for the armed security units attacking peaceful protestors? Yet airstrikes and drone attacks are celebrated when a nationally defined "enemy" is attacked.

The U.S. military has killed thousands of Iraqi civilians and that will be defined and branded as heroic, but when American civilians die it is an atrocity. Moreover, if the police gun down unarmed black youth, that's "Okay"; if rappers talk about anger and revenge in a manner not approved, they are "animals" and "predators"—a threat to public safety. What's the difference? None. And the Hip Hop community, along with many others in socially conscious communities, sees and knows this well: that we live in a racist, hierarchical society.

Processing Pain & Violence

Rappers and Hip Hop culture approach pain and violence in different ways. Rappers such as DMX talk about the struggles of forgiveness in his song "Look Thru My Eyes." He states:

> Lost all control, my shoulders hold a lot of weight
> Just like first I'm sold an eight, then told it's not an eight
> But then it's out of state, and it's too late for changes to be made
> That's what I get for fucking with strangers in the shade
> This is it, that nigga's got to give me a place
> For the same reason that fate, chose to give me away
> Take away hate, now I'm supposed to love the one that cursed me?[14]

In this part of the track we see DMX dealing with having to forgive a person who has been adversarial towards him. Now he has to enact some type of forgiveness. He ends the verse and song by letting the listener know that his life is a conflicted one—one that has a good side, but also a side that struggles with the "ugly." This type of suffering and pain is a mixture of suffering because of the individual personhood and suffering for something you as a person have done in life. This is complex, yet DMX continues to challenge his listeners to see life is not only hard, but also full of paradoxes.

DMX continues with suffering because of social, political, and spiritual oppression. In the song, done in spoken words, in Prayer III, he states:

> Let us pray
> Lord Jesus it is you, who wakes me up every day
> And I am forever grateful for your love...
> ... this is why I pray
> You let me touch so many people, and it's all for the good
> I influenced so many children, I never thought that I would
> And I couldn't take credit for the love they get

---

14   From the album *It's Dark And Hell is Hot* (1998).

> because it all comes from you Lord;
> I'm just the one that's givin' it
> And when it seems like the pressure gets to be too much
> I take time out and pray, and ask that you be my crutch
> Lord I am not perfect by a longshot—I confess to you daily
> But I work harder everyday, and I hope that you hear me
> In my heart I mean well, but if you'll help me to grow
> then what I have in my heart, will begin to show
> And when I get goin,' I'm not lookin' back for NOTHIN'
> Cause I will know where I'm headed, cause I'm so tired of the Sufferin'
> I stand before you, a weakened version of, your reflection
> Beggin' for direction, for my soul needs resurrection
> I don't deserve what you've given me, but you never took it from me
> because I am grateful, and I use it, and I do not, worship money
> If what you want from me is to bring your children to you
> my regret is only having one life to do it, instead of two
> Amen[15]

Here, we see DMX confessing to God the pain of living a life that is difficult to live. DMX creates a sense of suffering that listeners who have gone through similar events can connect with and relate to. He begs God for direction, even more in times of trouble.

In the same fashion, the rap group The Outlawz paints a picture of suffering because of something the person has done in life. Napoleon in the first verse states:

> I know this young nigga who love to keep his gun in his pants
> 14, little Ant will snatch your shit to enhance
> He lost his moms at a early age, pops was cracked out
> His brother ran a drug house where they slept with they Mac's out
> And where we from, fuck them basketball teams
> And your neighborhood PAL cause it's all about makin' cream
> He stayed dirty, copped a clip for thirty
> He'd rather be sellin' drugs early instead of young, black and nerdy
> He had his hard hat, born ready for war
> This young nigga heart's gone and I saw this before

---

15 From the album *...And Then There Was X* (1999).

> He lived day by day, prey by prey, stray by stray
> Blunted on Chancellor Ave. 380 hallway
> He bought a AK and I know he gon' sway, it ain't no damn way
> That this young nigga can turn his life around, mang
> Now where is God when you need him, he's internally bleedin'
> Little Ant's barely breathin' but he gotta stay eatin'
> So he robs again but this time he all smoked out
> He put his finger on the trigger and let the death fly out
> Some man got hit, he's layin' on the pavement stiff
> Blood drippin' from his face and he drownin' in it
> Now what a surprise that little Ant can't come around
> That it's his own man dead on the ground
> Dead on the ground[16]

Here, Napoleon creates a story for the listeners to see the reality of the streets on individuals. Here, pain and suffering is a result of someone making poor choices and decisions—or so it would seem. The song echoes with a call to "turn from your ways" because if you do not, then the resulting consequences could be unfavorable for you. This verse could also connect with suffering as a result of forces and problems you cannot control, and suffering from social, political, and religious oppression. These last two could be subsets of the first area of suffering which, when all combined, form a complex and multifaceted dimension to suffering in the Hip Hop context.

Thus, the Hip Hop community engages with suffering and pain; it understands it and relates to it. Its art is a reflection of that suffering and pain. Its artists have backgrounds in it and the Hip Hop continuum was, as has been argued, established to create an alternate mode of engagement with that pain in spiritual means (Alim 2006; George and National Urban League. 1990; Hodge 2009; One 2003).[17] Accordingly, Hip Hop, in a theological sense, finds

---

16 "Lost And Turned Out" from the album *Neva Surrenda—The Rap-A-Lot Sessions* (2002).
17 I also argue in my previous work (Hodge 2010), that Hip Hop creates a theology of suffering in context. Hip Hop defines suffering in one of five ways. (1) Suffering because of circumstances that you cannot control (e.g. financial hardships, family drama, physical ailments, mental disabilities); (2) suffering for a cause in which you believe deeply (e.g. socio-political issues, social justice concerns, racial matters); (3) suffering because of the individual personhood (e.g. people hate you because you have money, fame, prestige, or are simply doing well in life); (4) suffering as a result of something you as a person have done in life and/or something someone has done to you (e.g. past mistakes, current mistakes, life errors or for something good that you did but are now being persecuted for it,

deep meaning in spaces that help process that pain in bits. Christina Zanfagna (2006, 2–3) notes in her research that Hip Hoppers undergo "ecstatic experiences" in spaces such as concerts, spoken word venues, and battle raps. Pain is processed and dealt with in community too; one cannot suffer alone and in the pain of it.

While these artists mentioned above deal with pain in personal and small group settings, what about criticism of the hegemonic systems? The president? The systems that cause the pain? Finally, how does one contend with a Hip Hop God who gives a call to "action?" Let us turn now to explore Hip Hoppers The Geto Boys, Pastor Troy, and Ice T to peer further into pain and suffering from the Hip Hop context. It will then be demonstrated that these artists construct meaning within the violence and war-like conditions in which they have both grown up, and have seen throughout their lives. In the music they justify the retaliatory violence, connect with a God who can relate to their experience, and provide context and reasoning behind the violence and ghetto wars.

Contemplating Violence in Context

The tension between a "just God" and "no God" is palpable from those within the Hip Hop community who struggle in seeing a God who would allow such misery and pain upon a group of people.[18] So, a rapper like Pastor Troy is one who merges these ideological structures of God into one. Pastor Troy, an Atlanta based rapper who went underground after an open feud with rapper Master P, holds the tension of the problem of good and evil and does so in

---

and/or the good and bad within intimate relationships); and (5) suffering as a result of social, political, and/or spiritual oppression (e.g. beginning a new mantra of belief or creating new paradigms for people to see the world differently and society not dealing well with that).

18 This is also related to the suffering and pain that groups such as Blacks have endured in the U.S. The struggle between a "righteous God" an "angry God" or an "absent God" and an "apathetic God" is strong. Hip Hoppers, like theologians throughout time, wrestle with these notions and in turn the offspring of some of these tensions is nihilism. The former Snoop Dogg (Now Snoop Lion) has been noted as 'rap's atheist' in his prose and response to the absent and apathetic God. Yet, Snoop, in 2011, had a "spiritual awakening" and converted to Rastafarianism and made it a point to discuss his spiritual journey. At the heart of conversions such as Mase's and Rev. Run's (Run DMC) to Christianity, is a hope and belief that God would eventually "redeem" the negative experiences and that a hope in something supernatural was better than no hope.

a Hip Hop manner. In his song, "Vice Versa," Troy grapples with the evil that has been done, the lies that have been told from hegemonic structures, and conjoins them in a religious tone by asking what if God was the devil and the devil was God? In other words, Troy is posing a very relative and hermeneutical question:[19] if these structures have lied to "us" (meaning Blacks and/or urban youth) before in regards to education, the economy, politics, and law, what makes "us" think that they have not lied to us about religion and God? What if what we call sacred, morally upright, and "just" is actually a devil in disguise? What if the very construct upon which faiths have built meaning is actually the pursuits of evil? In the midst of oppression and displacement within society, the search for meaning continues; in this case the "oppressed" seek knowledge from sources and spaces that the oppressor has deemed evil (Freire 2000).

Thus, Troy is walking the line outside the normalized space of theological inquiry and making the Hip Hop community think deeper on what we label as 'good' and 'evil.'[20] In the song, he opens with:

> Yeah, yeah, yeah, yeah
> What if Heaven was Hell and vice versa
> If I told you go to Hell, would you tell I cursed ya?
> I reimbursed ya with the truth so you know my fate
> And pray I die, I'm that nigga that they love to hate
> I wanna make you use yo mind, God has sent a sign
> And when you listen to these rhymes, nigga take your time
> Again I ask, Heaven was hell and vice versa
> Would you start doin' evil in order to nurture—the spirit man?
> Do you understand that there's a war?
> It's ragin' on and the devil got some ammo too
> Don't get me wrong, but I put my trust off in the Lord
> It's too corrupt, know that God gon' help me blow 'em up I give a fuck,
> Heaven was hell and vice versa, I have no fear

---

19   As one observes theomusicology, the profane is an area that, some argue, is also a space in which God and theology are worked out. In the Christian Bible, David was "a man after God's own heart" but he was also sexually licentious; the same is true of Paul, Peter, and in some spaces Judas. It stands to reason that Hip Hoppers would seek God in spaces and arenas that are not always "approved" forms of search. They also seek to find God in spaces that are in fact foreign to theological pursuits. Pastor Troy is doing just that.

20   This is also a meaningful line of theological inquiry that Kelly Hayes found in her study with women in Brazil. If God is all good, then only the devil can combat evil and if you are going to combat evil, then you need to make it a "fair fight" and use evil (2011, 176–179).

VIOLENCE, DEATH, & SUFFERING IN HIP HOP CONTEXT   133

> I done witnessed too much Hell right here, lend me your ear Recall the beer we had to po'
> For all our niggaz hit the Devil with the .44.
>   TROY 2001

One might contend after viewing this verse that Troy is attempting to construct a theological inquiry for the oppressed and those who have suffered under White Supremacy.[21] Troy begins to distort the lines of morality and force the listener to think critically about heaven and hell. Troy continues with an even clearer picture in the second verse:

> Payback nigga
> My liquor keep my from tryin' to enter, battle alone
> And to deal with all this wickedness, I smoke a zone
> Know I'm grown, but I'm still a baby
> It's vica versa so I guess I'll beg Satan to save me
> God I'm confused, the fuse of all these motherfuckers, makin' me sick
> (*Virgin Mary never fucked nobody, but she suck dick*)
> With a clique of nasty concubines, and vice-a versa
> So she'll probably do the whole nine, that nasty ho
> I don't know where I'm a go this Christmas, it's Satan's birth
> I'm a try to smoke a pound of weed, and ease the Earth
> While Jesus equipped with angels, the Devil's equipped with fire
> For God so love the world that he blessed the thug with rocks
> Won't stop until they feel me
> Protect me Devil, think the Lord is tryin' to kill me
> It's vica versa.
>   TROY 2001

In addition to introducing this switch in deity, Troy offers a hermeneutic of the profane by associating the birth of Satan with the birth of Christ, an offense

---

21 It is interesting to note that underground rap artist Paris has stated, on numerous occasions, that the worse thing to happen to Black folks was Jesus. In this line of challenge, Paris is making the connections between the use of Jesus by Whites to support slavery, segregation, Ku Klux Klan events, and the oppression of Blacks by Whites with Christianity as its ally. Some in the urban context that I interviewed feel as though Christianity has runs its course and a more contextual and relevant religious discourse is needed. Is it Hip Hop? That still remains a question and something we will examine more closely in Chapter 6.

worthy of the auto-da-fé of the Spanish Inquisition. Yet, it is an offense that Troy must take in order to begin a necessary dialog with contextualized theological analysis for the Hip Hop community.

Troy is merely attempting to access something that has been controlled by the dominant society. Troy is willing to make amends with what society has labeled as "bad." While this line of inquiry is not openly accepted throughout Hip Hop, the tension of following "God" but still remaining critical enough to not adopt the "White man's religion" continues to exist. Still, as Ebony Utley has noted, "...the tempter opposes God. Whereas God allows trials and tribulations to help humans become their best selves, the devil offers an easy way out" (2012, 79). So is Troy just skirting too close to the devil in this sense? Or are his attempts a genuine attempt to make access to God a contextualized approach in a manner that makes sense for him and his people?

Further, this type of transmediated discussion of good and evil that Troy is performing is important for Hip Hoppers attempting to carve out a space of their own theological meme in relation to the often extreme forms of violence and oppression coming their way. Troy, as a rapper, continually has theological imagery in his album cover art and has been recorded as wanting to construct a relative theology for the 'hood.[22] Pastor Troy considers himself a type of "pastor" for the 'hood and recognizes his role as a theological interpreter who can "help" his listeners "find God."[23]

Geto Boys, conversely, are a group who work out their pain and suffering in their music. Coming from Houston Texas, the 9th Ward was known as "Hell's Gate" and was characteristically associated with nefarious violent behaviors and a litany of post traumatic individuals who were left there since the end of the Vietnam war. The sex trade existed in this part of the city long before it was popularized as a national "problem" and often times the victims of this trade were found dead in heinous ways in the Gulf Of Mexico. The Geto Boys were forged in this environment and rapped about their experiences as a group.

In a very brief interview with one of the group's rappers, Scarface (Brad Terrance Jordan), he revealed that the group was attempting to work out the extreme violence and living conditions in which they found themselves. He states:

> For us, shit, it was like working out our problems like in mutha fucking therapy G. Them politician mutha fuckers didn't understand that. And shit, look at what they be doing; killing mutha fucking babies and shit out

---

[22] Two interviewees stated this. Further, Troy's theological work, however, is still largely rooted in Judeo Christian constructs and philosophies.

[23] Taken from two backstage interviews with Pastor Troy.

in countries like Iraq and Afghanistan. But that shit is cool cuzz somehow them niggas over there are terrorists.

Scarface continued to talk about the power of socio-political rhetoric and how the Geto Boys' raps were manifestations of their environment and context.

They wanted to ban our shit back in the day. But for what? You got the same shit going on, even worse, on TV, in movies, and places like that where women be getting raped and people think that shit is entertainment.

What Scarface is referring to is the 1990 blockage by Geffen Records to distribute their album because the lyrics of one song which detailed necrophilia and murder proved to be too much for the record company and its associates. Their debut album was later picked up by Rick Rubin, who released the album on his label Def American. For Scarface, the double standard is a bit overwhelming. If the 'rule' was for everyone (e.g. censorship of violent lyrics), then it would be okay, but the 'rule' was not for everyone and movies with that much more violence (e.g. Terminator, Die Hard) do not receive nearly as much criticism in regards to their "violent" images. Scarface and The Geto Boys detailed and narrated these living conditions, and as he and other rappers with "controversial lyrics" have stated, movies, commercials, and media in general are all much more violent. Hip Hop should not be the scapegoat of such 'pushback' from the public and politicians.

The era between 1987 and 1995 was a time when politicians such as Dan Quale, George Bush Sr., Delores C. Tucker, Jesse Jackson, and Bill Clinton openly condemned rappers for their "violent lyrics." Yet, they did not object to films such as *Reservoir Dogs* (1992) which detailed the torture and death of a police officer; *The Terminator* (1984) and *Terminator II* (1991) in which the actor and former governor of California Arnold Schwarzenegger plays a cyborg assassin who hunts down "Sarah Conner" in cold blood and murders police officers; *Goodfellas* (1990) which follows the life of mobsters who among other victims kill a teenager and grandmother; *Boxing Helena* (1993) that shows a surgeon obsessed with a woman he had an affair with and who has now moved on, amputates her limbs and keeps her body alive in a box in order to have sex with her; *Man Bites God* (1992) where a film crew follows a serial killer then ends up helping him out; *Romper Stomper* (1992) where a group of skin heads become alarmed at the number of minorities moving into their community and begin killing them; *Natural Born Killers* (1994)[24] where two serial killers run about

---

24 This film did receive national attention with its amount of violence, but in comparison to rappers such as Ice T, Geto Boys, 2 Live Crew, and Ice Cube, it was short lived and the film

the country brutally killing people on a whim; *Frisk* (1995) which is about a gay serial killer and the details of those killings; *Cannibal Holocaust* (1980)[25] which depicts horrific scenes of rape, murders, and the gang rape of a young woman who is later impaled on a stake. While this list is not exhaustive, it does give creed to the claim that Scarface and many other Hip Hoppers make that the double standard as to "who" can transmediate[26] violence is problematic. Moreover, films that connect with the dominant meta-narrative of conquest and supremacy such as any World War II film, are often glossed over for their violence (for example, *Saving Private Ryan* (1998) which aired on prime time television unedited).

For the Hip Hop community, this is simply not a good enough response. The Geto Boys—along with rappers like them—also desire to "keep it real" and tell a story that is "true to their history" as well. As Scarface argued,

> So what do you want? You want me to actually do the things I talk about in my music? Or is it better that I work out my thoughts and emotions in my music? Hmm? You tell me that.

Scarface and the Geto Boys are a reflection of the violence living in a subset of the city that has, as we have seen in Chapter 1, been forgotten by many politicians and society. Therefore, songs such as "Chucky," "Declaration of War," "Bring It On," and "Mind Playin' Tricks" are reflections of the violence and pain endured by those living within those vehement enclaves.

In the song "Mind Playing Tricks," Scarface narrates the effects of this violence and pain. He elucidates clearly what is happening to him and for so many other individuals in this context:

Verse One: Scarface
At night I can't sleep, I toss and turn
Candle sticks in the dark, visions of bodies bein burned
Four walls just starin at a nigga
I'm paranoid, sleepin with my finger on the trigger

---

was never pulled or banned nationally. Further, there were never congressional hearings on the film to determine its "moral" status.

25   This film was banned in the U.K. and its director Ruggero Deodata was arrested in Italy and charged with making a snuff film; it was still aired in the U.S.

26   This is the process of taking aspects and parts of a story, event, or issue and placing them into electronic and/or digital mediums; in this process, the story can then be edited, truncated, and reformatted for whatever space it is being published or viewed in.

> My mother's always stressin I ain't livin right
> But I ain't going out without a fight
> See, everytime my eyes close
> I start sweatin, and blood starts comin out my nose
> It's somebody watchin the AK'
> But I don't know who it is, so I'm watchin my back
> I can see him when I'm deep in the covers
> When I awake I don't see the motherfucker
> He owns a black hat like I own
> A black suit and a cane like my own
> Some might say, "Take a chill, B"
> But fuck that shit! There's a nigga trying to kill me
> I'm poppin in the clip when the wind blows
> Every twenty seconds got me peepin out my window
> Investigatin the joint for traps
> Checkin my telephone for taps
> I'm starin at the woman on the corner
> It's fucked up when your mind is playin tricks on ya
> BOYS 1991

This song, listed as one of the best songs from Geto Boys, is one that gives insight into the post traumatic stressors which take place after living a life in a context of violence. It is also part of what Henry A. Giroux describes as a language in critical educational pedagogies that do not reduce the issues of power—in this case, the power of violence and the need to bring some resolution to it. Giroux goes on to argue that critical pedagogies need to learn from new forms of knowledge in postmodern settings. Here, there is an attempt to do just that in Hip Hop form (1996, 691–692).

Throughout music and art, in various eras, the more persecuted and oppressed people become, by and large, the more the group leans toward religious and spiritual understanding in order to make sense of the suffering and oppression. As I have stated earlier, some withdraw and come to the realization that there is no God, or take a nihilistic approach to both religion and life. However, for the Hip Hop community, with its roots in Abrahamic faiths, religious and spiritual quests are crucial to the survival of the group. Hip Hop legend and noted "godfather" of rap Afrikaa Baambatta, was quoted as saying that the reason Hip Hop found itself in exile and spiritual decay is because it had abandoned its tenth foundational element, spirituality.[27] It is possible

---

27   Told to me in an email exchange in 2009.

that on the underground scene, spiritual quests to find meaning in a time of suffering is a continuing practice. Regardless of the theological tradition (Zulu, Islam, Christianity, Jewish), the pursuit remains the same: find some sense of peace within the violence and suffering. Scarface continues in the song with this spiritual pursuit:

> Day by day it's more impossible to cope
> I feel like I'm the one that's doing dope
> Can't keep a steady hand because I'm nervous
> Every Sunday mornin I'm in service
> Prayin for forgiveness
> And tryin to find an exit out the business
> I know the Lord is lookin at me
> But yet and still it's hard for me to feel happy
> I often drift while I drive
> Havin fatal thoughts of suicide
> BANG and get it over with
> And then I'm worry-free, but that's bullshit
> I got a little boy to look after
> And if I died then my child would be a bastard
> I had a woman down with me
> But to me it seemed like she was down to get me
> She helped me out in this shit
> But to me she was just another bitch
> Now she's back with her mother
> Now I'm realizing that I love her
> Now I'm feelin lonely
> My mind is playin tricks on me
>   BOYS 1991

In this sense, Scarface stated that he was attempting to find some sort of "cure" in the pain and suffering of it all. He felt as though God was his only answer to "hope" and "peace." The song was merely an attempt to "work out" his pain in context. Monica Miller reminds us, using Wu-Tang's RZA as an example, that tactics and strategies are important during times of duress:

> RZA's unique combo of Eastern philosophy, chess, and kung fu movies have all, in some way, contributed towards constructing "war" (tactics, positionalities, strategies, etc.) as a heuristic by which to navigate the

hills and valleys of his tumultuous life. The many "taos" that become a part of RZA's life represent, among other things, a strategic pragmatic application and mapping of various ideologies from which to make use of or rethink various positionalities in his life. He makes use of *hybrid* steams of thought at various moments; however, these thought structures don't become totalizing, in a determined sense, in RZA's life. RZA represents and embodies a quintessential postmodernist subject—*poaching* what he can and when he can as a life strategy, never being fully *faithful* nor *unfaithful* to one or the other, yet making use of the category of "experience" as a contestable way to call into question the very foundation of the thought structures themselves. His philosophies are fluid and open ended, always morphing, changing, according to the "training" of life and struggle. And yet, while he represents a postmodern way of being and doing in the world, there are hints of universalizing tendencies in his philosophy. The "tao" becomes one for the many—the textual representative of all ways of life represented in and through one path of life. If RZA is selling anything here, it is nothing more and nothing less than the ideation of "wisdom" itself (2013b, 64).

I would argue that Scarface and The Geto Boys are keeping true to what religion is supposed to be: a working out of the principles of life in real time and seeking out the supernatural and the 'beyond' for assistance. Anthony Pinn continues with:

> From this sense of connectedness to a scene much larger than oneself, comes the inspiration for transformation. That is, the proper working of a religion must involve collective efforts to identify the sources of oppression and the store housing (and sharing) of vital, self-affirming cultural information. Only a religiosity that participates in and affirms the cultural life of the community and speaks plainly to pressing issues without paying tribute to unproven theological assertions—no new wine in old skins—is in keeping with the meaning of religion (1995, 134).

Scarface in fact attempts to keep with the true meaning of religion in his work, along with artists such as Mos Def, Kanye, Wu-Tang Klan, X-Clan, Mobb Deep, Brand Nubian, Beastie Boys, MC Lyte, Lauryn Hill, Bone Thugs-N- Harmony, and Tupac. For them, keeping with the meaning of religion means reconciling God with the conditions of the community, society, and even the hegemonic structures. "Trusting God" is not good enough if that God cannot relate or is only in support of the oppressors' ways. Thus, this process of dealing with violence and seeing a God who can "be there" is a stronger theodicy and one that is more applicable.

Ice T, in similar fashion, faced political, social, and national resistance to his lyrics and messages. During the early 1990s his short lived rap-metal group Body Count recorded an album with a song titled "Cop Killer." This drew national outrage and political fury as pundits accused Ice T of instigating violence toward police. The group opened to thousands of cheering fans while on tour with Metallica and Guns & Roses, most of whom were White, working class, blue-collar males. Black and Latino Hip Hop artists also responded favorably to Body Count. Once again, the message and intent of what Ice T meant went unheard and unnoticed. In 1992, Ice T gave an interview with Rolling Stone Magazine and divulged his intent: corrupt cops and officers who take the law into their hands and beat young Black and Brown males. The song was designed as a warning for those types of police officers and as a way of exacting some sort of retribution (much like a retaliatory strike against a nation who attacked us) for those who bore the brunt of police brutality in the urban environment. The song details what the group would do to these cops—kill them in the same manner they killed innocent youth—and that they would have very little remorse for their mourning family members—similar to rhetoric used by George Bush during the war in Iraq:[28]

> They're led by a brutal terrorist named Zarqawi, Al Qaida's chief of operations in Iraq, who has pledged his allegiance to Osama bin Laden.
>
> Their objective is to drive the United States and coalition forces out of Iraq and to use the vacuum that would be created by an American retreat to gain control of the country.
>
> They would then use Iraq as a base from which to launch attacks against America and overthrow moderate governments in the Middle East and try to establish a totalitarian Islamic empire that reaches from Indonesia to Spain.
>
> That's their stated objective. That's what their leadership has said.
>
> These terrorists have nothing to offer the Iraqi people.
>
> BUSH: All they have is the capacity and the willingness to kill the innocent and create chaos for the cameras.
>
> They're trying to shake our will to achieve their stated objectives. They will fail.
>
> America's will is strong. And they will fail because the will to power is no match for the universal desire to live in liberty.

---

28 Taken from the transcript of George W. Bush's presidential speech: FDCH/ e-Media.

(APPLAUSE)

The terrorists in Iraq share the same ideology as the terrorists who struck the United States on September the 11th. Those terrorists share the same ideology with those who blew up commuters in London and Madrid, murdered tourists in Bali, workers in Riyadh and guests at a wedding in Amman, Jordan. Just last week they massacred Iraqi children and their parents at a toy giveaway outside an Iraqi hospital.

This is an enemy without conscience, and they cannot be appeased. If we're not fighting and destroying this enemy in Iraq, they would not be idle. They would be plotting and killing Americans across the world and within our own borders. By fighting these terrorists in Iraq, Americans in uniform are defeating a direct threat to the American people.

Against this adversary there is only one effective response: we will never back down, we will never give in, and we will never accept anything less than complete victory.

(APPLAUSE)

BUSH 2005

If one is to take out the distinguishable demarcation of "terrorism" and input "police," "urban terrorism,"[29] or "White Supremacist police," then the rhetoric might be almost parallel in fervor. Ice T and his group Body Count would have argued the same type of discourse of violent response towards police officers who kill Black lives mercilessly and brutally. In the Hip Hop community whose post-soul prose requires it to call out social hypocrisies, this type of discourse, which Bush used, is exactly how they would respond to hegemonic oppression and attacks on their community. Therefore, once again, whose avenging takes precedence?[30]

Next, we will explore the groundwork for this type of transmediated violence as being a contextual manifestation for the urban and Black poor. And within the framework and setting of this violence, a type of justice arises to the point where God is able to redeem both them and the violence in a contextualized manner.

---

29 This is a term that is frequently used in post 9/11 America by scholars, activists, and Hip Hoppers alike to define the brutality, violence, and occupation of police departments in urban communities across the U.S. Some interviewees even told me that they could relate to someone from Palestine because they experience a similar kind of police occupation. This was strengthened when Palestinian activists took to social media to support those in the uprisings in both Ferguson and Baltimore, giving them not only verbal support, but tactics on avoiding the effects of tear gas.

30 Take for example rap artist and Hip Hop political activist, Paris. His album *Sonic Jihad* (2003) begins to answer this question.

Transmediated Violence & A "Just God"

The Vietnam War was the first transmediated war in history. Displays of sheer brutality, death, horrific suffering, and a U.S. military force that, for the first time publicly, was receiving a beating from a much smaller yet militarily robust country, took the nation by surprise. War was seen as it truly was: evil, disreputable, odious, and awful, not the manufactured images and messages of a "just war" being shown to the U.S. public during World Wars I and II. Further, the Vietnam War was the first war to broadcast images of death on both sides which lit a fuse for many around the world for objection, rebuttal, and protest against it. However, as Tupac had argued, if it were not for those images being shown to the public about the graphic nature of war and the actual "justness" of it, the war might have continued on for much longer. The public, once privy to the actual ethos of war, wanted nothing to do with it and made it known in many facets. It is in that same manner and spirit, that artists like Tupac, KRS-One, Too $hort, Spice 1, Ice T, Ice Cube, Yo-Yo, and Dr Dre wanted to bring attention to the horrifying living conditions of the ghetto and, in their minds, bring an end to the anguish, violence, oppression, and suffering in the 'hood.[31] The answer was: we will put it in our videos and in our music. KRS-One stated:

> We put it in our music. We put it in graffiti. We put it on walls. We put it in our videos. It was our way of saying, 'hey, its messed up here, come help!'[32]

Tupac also attempted to make the transmediated violence known as well:

> It's like you've got the Vietnam War, right? And just because the reporters show us pictures at home of the Vietnam War, that's what made the Vietnam War end when it did, or the shit probably would have lasted longer. If no one knew exactly what was going on, we just thought they were just dying valiantly, in some beautiful way. But because we saw the horror, that's what made us stop the Vietnam War. I thought, 'That's what I'll do as an artist, as a rapper. I'm gonna show the graphic details

---

[31]   This is similar to what Johanna Sumiala reports as macro mediatized rituals. She states, "The mediatization of mourning rituals includes the power of the media to frame the meaning of different ritual activities and to manage public emotions and key actors related to these rituals" (2013, 100). These rituals become national and part of that transmediated message, but only for the dominant culture, and rarely for others outside of that.

[32]   Taken from an interview in Thomas Gibson's *Letter To The President* (2005).

of what I see in my community, and hopefully they'll stop it, and the violence will end[33]

Chuck D's now infamous saying of "Hip Hop is the Black CNN," was much more than just a prompt to make Hip Hop a news casting magnate; it was also a manner in which rappers like him desired to make an attempt to end the violence by showing the horrors of it, in transmediated stylings within rap music and rap videos. Chuck D also meant it as a way in which the current media—who seemed to transmediate other countries' perils and violence—could not do and/or would not do for the Black and urban community. Thus, Hip Hop had to take up that space and do its own "reporting."

Therefore, videos that showed rape, incest, molestation, drug sales, Black on Black crime, and the litany of social scourges, were what the Hip Hop community wanted to display in order to bring about some type of change and betterment. Transmediated violence in videos was one method that Hip Hoppers used. Of course there was the music too—which I have shown in previous chapters—and when the music combined with the moving pictures, it made for a strong point and message.

This was at the heart of Hip Hop's Golden Era: to show the world that not everyone in America was living under "equality" and "justice for all." Hip Hoppers desired to use the power of media to promote their message of inequality and oppressive living conditions, in order to bring about change.[34] Rappers such as Public Enemy gave the community a socio-political message in which racism, corruption, redlining, neighborhood zoning, racial profiling, and White Supremacy, were all openly challenged, criticized, and deconstructed. Public Enemy—who were known by many in the Hip Hop community to have been on the F.B.I. federal 'watch list'[35] because of their lyrics and affiliations with

---

33 Taken from an interview with Tupac at age 19; video is archived from my 2005 research on Tupac.

34 Not every rapper then or present has had this intent. Tricia Rose (2008) has argued that the commercialization of Hip Hop and rap has made it money- and self-hungry and left it morally inept to see the bigger cause. Moreover, even rappers during the Golden Era of Hip Hop were in it to "get paid" and nothing else. Once the 'hood was seen as a profit making machine, it became a commodity just like shoes, automobiles, and food. Further, once White executives were able to capitalize on the suffering within the 'hood (Charnas 2010), it became a commodified and transmediated story only to make more money, such that the actual care for the people in those communities is typically lost (Tate 2003; Watkins 2005).

35 It has long been argued that there is a division of the government that has been designated to watch and patrol certain Hip Hop groups and artists; they have been called the 'Hip

certain Nation Of Islam members—was in pursuit of finding the justification for crack being peddled in the Black and urban community for the benefit of a "war"—the C.I.A sold weapons to the Iranians to help fund the Contras in Nicaragua to overthrow the Sandinistas (Webb 1998, 21–38).[36] Public Enemy, whose name was a reflection of the way they believe the rest of America felt toward Blacks, had the aim of helping to bring awareness through the transmediation of violence in videos like "Fight The Power," "Fear Of A Black Planet," and "Brothers Gonna Work it Out" to help create that structure of awareness. However, far too often this was met with resistance and a social stigma that saw Public Enemy as hate mongers, racist, immoral, violent, and rebel rousers. Their message was often lost and fell prey to the political rhetoric that said rap should be banned.[37] Public Enemy, while remaining entirely socio-political, rarely intertwined with religion, and while Chuck D was a believer in God, Terminator X and Professor Griff were open about their connections with The Nation Of Islam and the Zulu Nation. In press interviews with Professor Griff, he openly talked about the challenges of a White Jesus, that Blacks needed a better image of deity, and that this was the "oppressors' God" not intended for Black people.[38]

Within all of this transmediation is an attempt to reconcile God with the violence. Once again, how can a 'just God' allow such mayhem and violence? Public Enemy was a prolific rap group for Hip Hop, and Chuck D continues to be a voice and advocate for social, political, racial, and sexual equality. His social awareness has not stopped with the heterosexual, hyper-masculine, Christian,

---

Hop Police.' Members from the Naughty By Nature group, Snoop Lion, Ice Cube, KRS-One, Mobb Deep, Common, Mos Def, and MC Lyte have all testified to having been wire tapped and stalked by mysterious 'agent' looking individuals.

36 Some Hip Hoppers such as Tupac, Kanye, Kendrick, Missy Elliott, and Mos Def among many others, contend that the reasoning behind extreme pockets of poverty located in the urban area, the continual ignoring of violence in Black communities is a result of the 'crack era' and the explosion crack created in the inner cities of the U.S. during the 1980s.

37 Between 1991 and 1995, there was a push in congress to ban all rap music because of its "gangster appeal" and the fear that it would cause "good kids to do bad things." Public Enemy and KRS-One wrote songs that touched on letters to the president, the banning on Capitol Hill, and the murdering of Black males by the police. The politicians later ceased pursuit of such a measure, but later albums from Public Enemy addressed their audience to rise up and to vote out certain congress members.

38 This was heard in off-camera phone interviews that were given to me for the purpose of this research and not made public. Professor Griff and I were on a radio show together and he was vehement about his negative feelings toward Christianity and the oppression it has caused, particularly in the Black community.

Black male, which, in many regards is refreshing, as he is a person who claims to be a follower of God. Chuck D is married to Gaye Theresa Johnson who is a Sunni Muslim and a professor in the department of Black Studies at UCSB (University of California, Santa Barbara). Chuck D's attempt for social justice comes from a personal space and a deep-seated desire to find some sort of peace here on Earth while we can and while we are all alive.[39]

Rap videos which transmediate violence are often misunderstood and seen as a modus for the said violence. Often they are labeled as being instigators of violence and malice, and the public (including Blacks, Latinos, and Asians) tend to see rap music as being just that: violent and callous. In turn, rappers must reconcile God within this, for they will not receive much resolution or sympathy outside the Hip Hop community. They reconcile this 'just God' in five different domains as it pertains to the violence

1. God has not forgotten "us" in this space
2. God is a God that comforts in times of pain and will send that comfort in different methods (including forms of discouraged drugs such as marijuana)
3. God must have a heaven for "us"
4. Death is a resting place and, at times, a desired one to leave this "unjust world"
5. God redeems us and allows our blood to speak for justice

Within these five domains, Hip Hoppers take on a Psalmist approach in lament, anger, avengement, and hope. This ontology toward peace and hope is a Hip Hopper's way of reconciling the deep pain they are in and, moreover, the continued cross examination they will receive and have received from outsiders (e.g. pathologies of resisting arrest, boot-strap processes, forgive and forget). They need to understand that a God, out there, has not forgotten them, down here. And that 'one day' God will return to redeem this 'mess' in the city. However, in the end, for some, death is a resting place, given that year after year in urban environments such as South Central Los Angeles, the South Side of Chicago, and The Bronx, many young people (particularly males) see death as a place of peace—some have even gone as far to pre-pay for their funeral arrangements at the early age of fourteen. This stigma of death is nothing new. Many Hip Hoppers have rapped about death being a 'better place than here'

---

39 This is my conclusion based on over 12 interviews and one with KRS-One in which he discussed social issues and the concern towards equality for all.

and that death is a time of peace and resting in the 'other world.'[40] While the mystery of death still confounds some in the Hip Hop community, the promise of death being a 'final resting place' is one of great promise and the hope is that God will give them that rest, regardless of their religious pursuits (e.g. Zulu, Christian, Jewish, Nation of Islam, Five Percenters).

Often the controversial drug marijuana is at the center of debate when rappers are shown utilizing its powers in videos and films. Yet, as many of my interviewees stated, the weed is what gave them a release. It was the weed that gave them a transcendental experience much like that of Native Americans in their use of peyote. As Richard told me,

> I'm like Pac [Tupac] man…I smoke weed to take the pain out, cuzz if I wasn't high I'd blow my brains out! That's real homie; straight up. Shit, you mean to tell me God gonna trip if a nigga smoke a lil' weed? C'mon now. Fuck, if He up there trippin' then…I don't know if I really wanna serve that God… you feel me tho?

In a lot of ways, weed is a mystical aid in the presence of pain, violence and suffering. It is a way to escape the terrors from external and internal sources. Quite often, the users find a God who is in their presence and cares 'for them,' and as Richard pointed out, who wants a God who cannot handle him? In other words, if God is that perfect and dogmatic, then maybe 'he' really is the oppressor's God and not one worthy of following in any regard. If God really can handle my pain, then surely a little weed will not mar God's view of 'me.' These are worldviews that, in many regards, help the persons escape, even though momentarily, from the space in which they find themselves. When conjoined with the music of Hip Hop, it becomes a numinous force and coping tool for survival in violent contexts; it is comparatively much like Black slave protest music. Jon Michael Spencer notes that, "Black song was an irreplaceable survival tool for the oppressed. It equipped those raised in black communities with a system of core beliefs regarding the providence of God" (1990, 92).[41]

---

40   This was a theme that arose in many of the artists and groups studied. It was more prevalent in groups on the West Coast during the mid-1990s, but also a theme with contemporary artist such as Pastor Troy.

41   See also Henry H. Mitchell and Nicholas Cooper-Lewter, "Soul Theology: The Heart of American Black Culture," (1986), pp. 2–4 for a robust discussion of Black slave music and its place for survival amidst oppression. Singing songs is part of this experience and crucial to the Black community for survival. Crucial too is this 'singing,' in this case rapping, for survival and hope.

Similarly, weed is a tool to help cope with the violence in their particular social context.[42]

These five domains are reflective of the way a community processes and copes with violence. The loss of hope and a vision for oneself is not a popular worldview in the Hip Hop community. Conversely, the notion of a White Jesus who appears as the oppressor is also not a viable idea for the Hip Hop community in processing violence and pain. These five domains are a constructed means by which the individual is able to make an attempt at making some sense of the life in which they find themselves. This process is no different than any other constructed form of theological discourse in that regard; simply because one has the numbers and popularity toward being 'right' does not necessarily make that line of thought 'right' or the 'right one.'[43]

Chapter Summary

Chapter 4 has explored problems surrounding violence, pain, and non-standard responses to disenfranchisement. This chapter provided a look into how the Hip Hop community theologically wrestles with issues of violence. Chapter 4 argued that violence, at times, is relative and when the dominant culture is threatened, attacked, or challenged, violence can be 'morally' right and publically accepted. Violence, when done in response to what a state or government defines as a "just cause" can not only be accepted but deemed "holy" and "moral." More importantly, as I have demonstrated, once the public, and/or society, has deemed war and violence 'acceptable' in the name of "justice," the line connected to God becomes easily visible.

Violence, suffering, and pain are something all humans have to visit at some point in the life cycle. The Hip Hop community however has argued for decades now that their pain and violent contexts have been vastly ignored and

---

42 Scott Macdonald and Michael Viega argue that music therapy and songwriting are crucial in the therapeutic healing process for those who have experienced PTSD. Using rap music and elements of Hip Hop culture, the two demonstrate the power of Hip Hop in context within a professional therapeutic session (MacDonald and Viega 2013, 154–170).

43 In terms of actually attaining a practical resolution to this pain, suffering, and life within violent contexts, Edgar Tyson has discussed the power of using Hip Hop elements in a professional therapeutic session with a young Black male and Tyson clearly shows the power of Hip Hop in a therapeutic session. While religion is not necessarily a component within this setting, the power of the culture remains. Further, Tyson argues that the growing science around the many uses of Hip Hop are signs that it is more than just a musical genre, but in fact a space to create 'new life' (Tyson 2013, 293–296).

overlooked by the dominant society, so, artists such as Public Enemy, KRS-One, Tupac, and Ice T, have taken it upon themselves to transmediate this violence in order, in hope, to bring an end to the violence. This, often enough, is misinterpreted and seen as Hip Hoppers promoting more violence and crime and allowing 'immoral lifestyles' to prevail. Thus, Hip Hoppers have to create a space to reconcile God with the violence and pain they incur.

Chapter 5 will now continue this theme of deity exploration and consider a key messianic figure: Jesus. But not just any 'Jesus'—a Black and Hip Hop Jesuz, with the 'Z' added to signify a particular cultural context. A Jesuz that smokes weed, 'kicks ass,' curses out the unjust, and 'beats down' anyone who would dare 'trip on a nigga.'[44] Chapter 5 will keep violence, pain, suffering, and the issue of transmediation in mind as we look specifically at how a Hip Hop Jesuz is constructed. More importantly, the racial and ethnic opus of Jesuz will be considered as race continues to be a relevant topic in the theological and religious domains within Hip Hop.

---

44   These are phrases that interviewees reflected back when asked what they considered to be a "Hip Hop Jesus."

CHAPTER 5

No Jesus in the Wild: Race, & The Jesuz Figure

Why is it that Christianity seems impotent to deal radically, and therefore effectively, with the issues of discrimination and injustice on the basis of race, religion and national origin?

HOWARD THURMAN

•••

I charge the white man with being the greatest swine-eater on this earth. The greatest drunkard on this earth! He can't deny the charges! You can't deny the charges! We're the living proof *of* those charges! You and I are the proof. You're not an American, you are the victim of America. You didn't have a choice coming over here. He didn't say, "Black man, black woman, come on over and help me build America." He said, 'Nigger, get down in the bottom of that boat and I'm taking you over there to help me build America.' Being born here does not make you an American. I am not an American, you are not an American. You are one of the 22 million black people who are the *victims* of America. You and I, we've never see any democracy. We didn't see any... democracy on the cotton fields of Georgia, wasn't no democracy down there. We didn't see any democracy. We didn't see any democracy on the streets of Harlem or on the streets of Brooklyn or on the streets of Detroit or Chicago. Ain't no democracy down there. No, we've never seen democracy! All we've seen is hypocrisy.

MALCOLM X

•••

Is there any help to be found in the religion of Jesus that can be of value here?

HOWARD THURMAN

∴

Racial relations in the U.S. have been a muddied and turbulent road since the creation of the country. White culture has been upheld as the dominant culture and racial group in the U.S. and has created intricate systems and institutions to reinforce its supremacy—deity, religion, and faith being one of those (Battle 2006; Belton 2010; Bennett 1993; Cone 1990; Jay and Forman 1971; Wells-Barnett 1969). The Euro-Western captivation of the Christian church has manipulated pious symbols, such as the image of Jesus into a blonde, White, blue-eyed, deity, that is irrelevant outside of those White contexts and makes the religion of Christianity a problematic one for anyone attempting to find a deity who is racially and ethnically appropriate (Hempton 2008; Rah 2009). In this sense, for some, religion cannot be redeemed because of the centuries of racism. The past is too historically skewed toward whiteness, and any attempt to reach 'reconciliation' will result in the oppressed becoming more oppressed and disenfranchised (Jones 1973). Further, with a White image of Jesus, one is never able to appreciate fully the message of Jesus, because it will always be tainted with racialized imagery which, for some scholars, distorts the Christology and 'gospel message' within (Cone 1997a, b; Jay and Forman 1971; Jones 1973; Rah 2009). For scholars like William Jones, a 'divine racism' takes place when an 'in-group' and 'out-group' is created. Those who are outside of 'God's grace' are hostile towards God and in return, God is hostile towards them. In other words, God does not value all persons equally. Further, the out-group suffers more than the in-group and God becomes indifferent toward that suffering of the 'out-group' as they are outside God's 'will' and they will be made to suffer. The racial and ethnic categorization is also crucial under 'divine racism' as it divides those who are 'blessed' from those who are not. Constructs of a racial deity are conflated under discourses of sin, immorality, and debauchery, and a pathology is created for those who are labeled as sinners, immoral, and debauched (Jones 1973, 3–6).

To see this more closely, Traci West writes compellingly that "for Christians of African descent in the United States, certain teachings about Jesus can advance their acceptance of white-supremacist ideas about their own black humanity" (2012, 114). In other words, the mere notion of having a "White Jesus" clouds, disrupts, and corrupts the theological pursuits by not only Blacks, but all ethnic minorities. West (2012, 15) continues with a set of powerful questions:

> When missionaries who converted enslaved blacks in the Americas or colonized blacks in Africa taught a Christology informed by white dominance—black inferiority mythology, their evangelism confused truth with lies. How did such Christology rooted in confusion teach anti-black devaluation of embodied, human worth? Currently, what kinds of theo-ethical understandings of Jesus as Christ might assist Christians in disrupting racialized (and kindred heteropatriarichal) paradigms of

human subjugation that continue to exist within Christian-dominated societies? In a contemporary liberationist Christian ethics that foments such anti-racist intervention, the varied permutations of anti-black racism interwoven for centuries into the Christology initially introduced to black converts would need to have been discarded—right?

Centuries of seminary training, theological teaching, missions, and a colossal breadth of Sunday (and Saturday) morning sermons have created a Christology which places whiteness at the top and Blacks near the bottom.[1] What is even more problematic and troubling is that Blacks and other ethnic minority religious leaders continue the traditions of a White supremacist Jesus simply because it is "truth" to them and tradition and culture are far more convenient than a search for contextualized Christologies. Howard Thurman (1976, 7) argues that

> The significance of the religion of Jesus to the people who stand with their backs against the wall has always seemed to me to be crucial. It is one emphasis which has been lacking—except where it has been a part of a very unfortunate corruption of the missionary impulse, which is, in a sense, the very heartbeat of the Christian religion.

Thurman is establishing parallels between the life of Jesus and the experiences of African Americans, or, for that matter, all oppressed peoples who seek out a contextual image of Jesus. William Hart tells us that "as a Jew, Jesus was shaped by his ethnicity, as were Black Americans; furthermore, he was poor and a member of a despised minority group dominated by a great imperial power" (2012, 158). Jesus' back was, using Thurman's metaphor, "against the wall" and in the context of Jesus' time, was oppressed and disenfranchised.

Tim Wise, noted anti-racist and opponent of White privilege, recalls the first time he brought up the issue of Jesus' ethnicity to an all-White Catholic college. The audience was quick to insist that Jesus' ethnicity was irrelevant, yet could not entertain the notion that Jesus could have been Black (Hart 2012, 156–157). Their resistance gave in to the myth that Jesus' race is insignificant and their

---

[1] For example, Immanuel Kant writes that, "…humanity is at its greatest perfection in the race of the Whites" (Kant 1997, 64). Kantian ethics is taught in numerous classrooms including some Christian churches. This type of White supremacist worldview is in the social, cultural, and pedagogical DNA and creates a Euro-tribal theos which is, above all else, perfection and THE form of study; different pursuits are treated as 'others' and marginalized the same (Rah 2009, 78–79).

failure of imagination and ensuing outright resistance to imagine a Black Jesus reveals just how deeply racial ideology has affected the Christian imagination (Wise 2008, 54–56). Jennifer Harvey, in "What Would Zacchaeus Do?" states that, "Traditional Christianity has committed this sin [dis-acknowledgment and dis-embracing of a Black Jesus] in its invention of the white Jesus" (2012, 90). Those mythological notions that Jesus was White, the downplaying of his ethnic background, the impression that he was Euro-centric, and his inability to cope with minority groups, have become not only problematical for the Hip Hop community but also created a strong sense of contempt among Hip Hoppers toward most things "Christian."[2]

Therefore, it stands to reason that James Cone argues that there must be continuity between the historical Jesus and the kerygmatic Christ, defined as the modern movement for a theology that seeks to orient scientific theology to Christian life and apostolates, and thereby to bring about an interaction of theology, social, and apostolic action (Malone 2003, 158). If not, then any community (especially those in power) might interpret "the kerygmatic according to its own existential situation" (Cone 1990, 113), and craft a Jesus in their own image. Cone continues to assert that Black Liberation Theology is the appropriate ontological symbol for the divine because the "white American inability to recognize humanity in persons of color...blackness, then, stands for all victims of oppression who realize that the survival of their humanity is bound up with liberation from whiteness" (Cone 1990, 7). If Blacks and ethnic minorities alike must seek a Christology from Whites, then the theological inquiry is already skewed and White models of perfection, morality, values, and living "pure" are already set in from the initial setting (Cone 1990; Pinn 2003b; Thurman 1976).

To complicate this further, Christian biblical interpretations of ethnicity have been hazy and obtuse at best. Africans brought over in the Trans-Atlantic Slave Trade were "baptized" as "Christians" under the idea that a Eurocentric religion was "better for those savages" (Walls 2002). Paul's letters in the New Testament were interpreted as an endorsement for slavery when Paul writes "Slaves obey your masters" (Colossians 3:22) in his letter to Philemon in which

---

2 A note of interest is that even though this distrust exists for Christianity, artists, as noted in this book, have continued to reference Jesus as a central piece of their faith expressions. Rap artists such as Kanye West, Nikki Minaj, Tupac, Lauryn Hill, Jay Z, Big Syke, King T, DMX, and Geto Boys still keep close connections with Jesus, yet, as we will see later in this chapter, see Jesus as the suffering, Black, disenfranchised image they can relate to and that is most similar to their own living conditions and upbringing.

he encourages a slave is to return home to his master.[3] These erroneous biblical interpretations continued, and a sense of shame, guilt, and inferiority was developed by Africans which continues, in many ways, to this current era (Pineda-Madrid 2001; Pinkney 2000; Pinn 2002; Wilder 1999). Cheryl Townsend Gilkes gives a richer picture of this:

> When using the Bible as a tool for racial domination, white people in Europe, the United States, and South Africa assume that Jesus and the ancient Israelites are white. These readers have chosen and expanded upon selected portions of the Bible. Those selections sometimes refer to people of African descent, noted in English translations as Ethiopians or Cushites. The curse of Ham is actually non-existent. In Genesis 11, Noah's curse is placed upon Canaan, Ham's son. The other sons of Ham, who are the eponymous ancestors of Cush and Mizraim, are excluded from Noah's utterance. In order to argue that black people are cursed, white people have engaged in a massive misreading that reaches back to Ham in order to include Africans under that curse. Since the presumption of whiteness applies to everybody else in the Bible, whiteness is never specifically identified in biblical racial ideology—once again whiteness is silent. There is a problem with failing to acknowledge and identify whiteness in the Bible. Whenever white skin is specifically mentioned there is usually a terrible problem. Those biblical stories that could not be construed to be about whiteness are about leprosy, usually a curse from God (2012, 71).

Whiteness and the White gaze toward Blacks is constructed theologically within domains such as the Christian Bible. What Gilkes argues here is profound because she illustrates the significance of interpretations, translation, and ultimately the construct of subservience, shame, guilt, and inferiority within religious and theological domains. Conflate these under centuries of teachings, and the image of Jesus is sullied under the guise of Whiteness.

Soong-Chan Rah also suggests that racism is at work within theological pursuits outside of Western White mantras. Rah asserts:

> Because theology emerging from a Western, white context is considered normative, it places non-Western theology in an inferior position and

---

[3] In turn, many Africans despised the New Testament and focused largely on the message, life, and theology of Jesus Christ. While Moses and the Children of Israel were an important part of early African American Christianity, Jesus and his message of liberation was what many Black slaves focused on (Paris 1985; Walls 1996, 2002).

elevates Western theology as the standard by which all other theological frameworks and points of view are measured. This bias stifles the theological dialogue between various cultures (2009, 78).

As Rah suggests, race plays a central role when it pertains to matters of *the* theological inquiry and *the* standard of life.[4] The image of Jesus, therefore, becomes that of a White male and one who is indifferent at best to those who do not fit within the scope of that Whiteness. This Western mantra of singularized salvation, autonomous faith (e.g. personal savior), problematized secular societies, defined pathways to "sin," and a "savior" who is represented as a White male is contentious for the Hip Hop community.[5] Rah continues with an examination of racism within Christian theology and links much of the racism to consumerism and materialism. In other words, the desire for more "stuff" and "safe" geographical locations crosses with the idealization that "nice" and "safety" is associated with Whiteness or docile and/or "domesticated" ethnic minorities (Rah 2009, 46–63).

A type of sense of "the other" is created when cultures such as Hip Hop create a Jesus figure in their likeness. Black theology, liberation theology, third eye theology, Zulu Nation theologies, and Five Percenter theology are all categorized as "the other" in comparison to White, Western Christianity.[6] Rah says regarding the historical context of otherness:

---

[4] Alexis de Tocqueville notes that standardization, especially for politics and religion, is a dangerous brew. For him, it set up the White (or as he describes the Anglo-American) as the "right" and "moral" one creating a system that benefits them through systems, policy, law, and ultimately religious belief structures. One can then conclude that a "savior" such as Jesus, would in turn "favor" the White race (Tocqueville 1998, 121–128).

[5] Tied to this is Christian Identity which, according to Michael Barkun, has extreme White supremacist ties such as the Klu Klux Klan, Nazis, and Skin Head movements. With such hate associated with a religion, messages of inferiority, social outcasts, and weakness in ethnic groups outside of Eurocentric ones can be easily slipped into the pedagogical ethos and a "savior" who is White is all but certain for groups like this (Barkun 1997, 4–14).

[6] What makes this potent is that not only White evangelicals believe and embrace this thought, but Blacks, Latinos, Asians, and the rising Christian populations in south and central Africa do as well. This Western belief is intertwined with a typology of being right, moral, and correct. Andrew Walls, a noted African missiologist and Christian historian, has argued that in contexts such as Ghana, Sierra Leone, Brazil, Argentina, and Kenya, even their "own" theologians are overlooked, de-valued, and marginalized for the place of White, Euro-tribal theologians continuing to promote a White Western agenda in settings that are far from that (Walls 1996, 2002).

> Creating 'the other' allowed Western culture to express its power over non-Western cultures. Inferiority is inferred when a culture or people are categorized as 'the other.' In the same way that Western culture diminishes non-Western culture through the creation of an 'otherness,' Western Christianity diminishes non-Western expressions of Christian theology and ecclesiology with the creation of 'otherness' (2009, 78–79).

To this, Edward Said—whose reflections on otherness in connection to Arabic and Middle-Eastern cultures is similar—adds that, "European culture gained strength and identity by setting itself off against the Orient as a sort of surrogate and even an underground self" (2003, 3). So, when Hip Hop is defined as completely secular, non-religious, and/or profane, this type of otherness is created which gives precedence to zealots such as G. Craig Lewis (who is Black himself), to call "all of Hip Hop satanic" and "worldly."[7] This is just another example of this noxious process in creating the other established by Western Christianity.

Even with these atrocious aspects of a racialized Jesus, the Jesus figure, while racially controversial, remains a central piece in Hip Hop culture. Kanye West, for instance, on a 2006 cover of *Rolling Stone* magazine, adorned himself with a crown of thorns, a beard, and bloody scars crisscrossing his face. His burlap cloth and the subtitle, "The Passion of Kanye West," immediately signals a Christ appropriation by the rapper. The title of the article was in reference to Mel Gibson's 2004 film *The Passion of Christ*, which graphically reenacted the crucifixion of Jesus. West takes on the persona of Jesus by asserting he is "crucified in the media" and "...my misery is your pleasure" (Ogunnaike 2006). West clearly feels as though he is a martyr of some genus while appropriating the image of Jesus to placate his own media persona.

---

7 G. Craig Lewis' DVD series "The Truth About Hip Hop" places Hip Hop as an agent of the devil and continues to inform his audience, who are a majority Black, that demonic forces are at work within Hip Hop. When I approached his ministry organization—Ex Ministries, named after being a former person of the world—for a panel discussion or interview, Lewis' staff refused, and told me "Minister Lewis does not debate. His word is from the mouth of God and that cannot be debated." Further, Lewis has continually ignored any type of confrontation even from Christian rappers and other Christian pastors. He preaches his message solely to Black, religiously conservative audiences whose age averages between 45–54 years of age, and who have largely become indoctrinated in a Western theos of otherness—in this case Hip Hop. What better way to dehumanize someone than by labeling them "evil," "satanic," or "demonic?"

The cross is representative of suffering, pain, disenfranchisement, and political oppression; it is a crucial element of and for the Hip Hop community. The cross represents these key aspects for the Hip Hop community:

- A savior
- Victory over "death"
- Redemption through suffering and pain and of that suffering and pain
- The "devil" or evil presence, defeated
- Victory over "sin"
- Resurrection to a new life
- Resurrection as a way of life
- Pain for peace

These representations of Jesus in the Hip Hop community are critical and Jesus, in turn, becomes a central figure for a culture and people who already feel as though they are in similar situations. As Michael Eric Dyson notes, Hip Hoppers see a contextual 'Black Jesus' as "the God who literally got beat down and hung up, the God who died a painful, shameful death, subject to capital punishment under political authority and attack, but who came back, and keeps coming back, in the form and flesh we least expect" (2003, 286). To this, Ebony Utley adds, "The cross represents Jesus' victory over death. Cheating death makes Jesus the gangsta's hero. The cross as a symbol of death visually resurrects memories of unjust persecution form Jesus to ancestors who hung from lynching trees" (2013, 57–58). Therefore, Jesus is much larger than just a persona. Jesus is representative for so many who suffer under oppression of hope and aspirations to "a better life" and "brighter tomorrow" as Kelly, one of the interviewees, states. Despite the racial connotations that Jesus carries, he is still powerful for rappers—especially Black rappers—for the struggles and psychological violence enacted to perpetuate slavery and the continued modern slavery through the prison industrial complex. Thus, West is evoking this historical imagery and connecting his life to that lineage.[8]

Conversely, Remy Ma, one of the only female rappers to connect to Jesus in both a visual and lyrical way, created an album cover with her body being crucified on a cross. With an apocalyptic background using negative space and

---

8 To further understand West's theological construct, one must look at the Christian Bible in John 1:1–14. Here, Jesus introduces the Word who became flesh. West utilizes this, not as a blasphemous or heretical pursuit, but to reference both his connection to Jesus, and also his own personal suffering alongside Jesus. The cover of the magazine is representative of this and illustrates West's connection to this "flesh" from the secular context (Utley 2013, 59–60).

vibrant oranges, reds, and yellows to represent fire, destruction, and a halo type light above the top of the cross, Remy Ma is shown with bloody hands and a slender loin cloth covering her. Remy Ma's long hair covers the very tip of her nipples while the sides of her breasts are exposed. Her body is clearly shown and is curvaceous, while her arms have blood on them. A cemetery is in the background, a skull over her head, and a black crow off to her right. The caption on the cover in the upper left hand corner reads "Queen of NY/The BX Savior" which is a symbolic representation of a savior and a source of hope for a specific geographical space. On the bottom of the cover it reads "Y'all bitches working on y'all albums go back to the studio immediately" to signify that her album is in fact, stronger and more valid, especially since she is taking on a savior persona. Remy Ma is connecting to a Jesus that not only suffers, but also offers a type of redemption through lyrics.[9]

Remy Ma feminizes Jesus on her mixtape *Shesus Khryst* (2007) and, in turn, begins a treatise of feminization of the Jesus image through her imagery. Though still rooted in heteronormative ideologies, her video for "Shesus Khryst" shows Remy Ma predominantly on a cross, a head adorned with a crown of thorns, and negative space surrounding her eyes which give a supernatural eerie feel to the video while she stays barely covered with a sack-cloth material covering her breasts and loins. The camera pans up her body to her face where she references Jay Z as "Jay Hova" and Nas as "God's son" in the lyrics. While most of the video has her on the cross peering up to the camera, there are several shots with her looking out onto the wilderness and symbolically pondering the moment—much like Jesus in the wilderness and on the Mount of Transfiguration in the Gospels of the Christian Bible.[10]

Further, Laura and Alison from the interviews contend that Remy Ma is " a brave ass bitch for doing what she do" (Laura), and that "...she's representing the feminine side of Jesus and God" (Alison). These images are powerful because female representation in Hip Hop is limited and sparse. What Remy Ma does in some regards is to create a space and discourse for womanist

---

9   Ebony Utley adds that while the Jesus persona is the "gangstas Jesus," gangstas are typically not feeding the hungry, clothing the poor or loving women and children. Crucified Jesus is the prototype for visual depictions of death as well as life after death for rappers "crucified" by media and malcontent competitors (2013, 57–58). Remy Ma is also doing similar things in her music and visualizations.

10 Even still, I will argue, much like Ebony Utley (2012) might assert, that Remy Ma is using the production of Christian symbolism for her own gain and record sales. Religious marketplace constructs are not relegated to churches; rappers like Remy Ma can also utilize this for the use of economic gains. This is an area of research in Hip Hop studies that needs further examination.

theological constructs to emerge and be re-imagined outside a White, Western, paternalistic modality and inside of a Hip Hop context.

Aaron McGruder's web series *Black Jesus*, while not directly related to rap artists, gives a contextualized non-Western approach to the sacred in a profane manner. McGruder, producer of the series *The Boondocks*, created a series of film shorts on the topic of Black Jesus. This Jesus is not the Jesus of White ancestry and Westernized tones, but is the Jesus of the 'hood. His mannerisms, his bravado, his "swag" are all those of Hip Hop urban males and he enjoys a marijuana smoke with; they are his "homies" (disciples). The video spends the opening minute illustrating the multi-facets of Black Jesus. A Black male, played by Gerald 'Slink' Johnson, with a goatee, crown of thorns, and cloth like garb, walks around the city attempting to "make things right." Dealing with issues of lust, greed, envy, lying, and thievery, the series—while holding true to Christian doctrine—uses street rhetoric to exemplify those points. Using phrases like "ungrateful ass niggas" or "y'all muthafuckas don't be listening to Jesus" or "you need to open up your heart my nigga" or "did a nigga not lay his life down for you," *Black Jesus* is about social awareness and bringing about self-consciousness at the street level. The audience he preaches to seems to be uninterested or unengaged with what Black Jesus is talking about and challenging them to do, indicating that the message falls on "deaf ears." In one episode, Black Jesus argues with two young men who tell Black Jesus that his crucifixion and death is "getting old." They tell Black Jesus "Fuck, nigga, the shit is getting old." Black Jesus continues to argue back, mentioning the blessings he has given them but they roll up their window. Black Jesus does not take a passive posture but replies, "Man, Fuck you homie. Fuck you!" The humorous reply is still undergirded by the truth of Jesus' message for "his people" of that of love, respite, peace, and compassion. The setting locates Black Jesus in an irreligious space while still attempting a sacred approach to the community's problems.

This original series took shape and gained momentum on the Comedy Network. The television series, also named *Black Jesus*, follows the same character around South Central Los Angeles and while still profane, maintains a supernatural state for healings and miracles. Black Jesus is on a mission to "help the 'hood" and in doing so creates community within that profane place. While the television series needs further examination, the YouTube version of this, which was much more surly in nature, was a popular draw for many in the Hip Hop community. The television series, which took to the air in the fall of 2014, was highly publicized and also protested against by Christian groups who deemed it "blasphemous" and "evil." Christian organizations such as Focus On The Family called for the show's termination. A boycott and national petition against the series was initiated, but much like other "Christian protests," it fell on deaf ears and the show has not been cancelled. This illustrates, once again, the disconnect between a soulist/modern perspective on theology and the post-soul attempt to find God in non-traditional, secular, and profane localities.

McGruder presents post-soulist themes in a satirical format which still has a strong undergirding message of hope. *Black Jesus* is done in a way that Hip Hoppers will understand. What is troubling, however, is that *Black Jesus* still references women as "bitches" and "hoes." Heteronormative standards continues to be an issue in many spaces within Hip Hop.

Trap Jesus, contrariwise, is a Jesus that is a drug dealing, pimp that instills fear within his followers. From the mind of Lil Wayne, *Trap Jesus* represents the more violent and hyper masculine symbol of Jesus that many urban males—principally Black males—find themselves in. Found on Spike Televisions Adult Swim network, Trap Jesus lives a lavish lifestyle and yet, is compassionate when The Sweet Tea Mobsters arrive (who are consequently arguing and bickering) and offers them empathy and guidance. Trap Jesus, while rugged and questionable regarding his own lifestyle, still sits atop and gives The Sweet Tea Mobsters actual help. *Trap Jesus* is understanding and compassionate toward the issues that Black males face and exemplifies a "brighter way" while still living in the reality of the 'hood. Ebony Utley states on this point:

> If nothing else, Trap Jesus understands him [Black males] better because they are living the same life as black men facing obstacles while on their daily grind. His confinement is not a hindrance as much as it is a reality that black men can help each other overcome. Trap Jesus is trapped in the prison system because he was caught trapping (selling drugs) in the trap (hood). Both "traps" represent a cycle of impoverishment and imprisonment. Because Trap Jesus embodies this predicament, he is an accessible companion who looks and acts like his followers (2012, 55).

Thus, *Trap Jesus* becomes the secular articulation of a ghetto-appropriated Christ, who, as the author of the Hebrew passage suggests "sympathizes with our weakness..." and one who was "...tempted in all things as we are..." (Chapter 4, verse 15).

Henceforth, Hip Hoppers produce an ontological discourse and pious treatise to gain a formidable understanding of the cosmos, afterlife, death, pain, suffering, and relative social conditions no different than a Karl Barth, Martin Luther, Henri Nouwen, or Jürgen Moltmann do for the Western Eurocentric Jesus.[11] As Chapter 3 demonstrated, Hip Hop artists such as Tupac create a space for theological meaning to happen in a contextualized manner and

---

11   For an in depth study into these racial pedagogies in theological settings, see (Carter 2008) which engages this phenomena further.

for their audience to grapple with the social, cultural, and societal conditions within the urban and city geographic locations. We will now examine Hip Hop communities' intersections of the Jesus figure and how they interrelate with Jesus outside of the White symbolic imagery most have received.

The Hip Hop Community & The Jesus Figure

The Jesus symbol is a crucial part of the socio-religious sensibilities within Hip Hop communities. Hip Hop embraces various Christological paradigms which fit in the Hip Hop setting. In one sense, you have a view of Jesus as liberator, embracing the social justice aspects of a messiah. On the other hand, you have a Karl-Barth-like Jesus that sees Christ in the trinity, having an ambiguous nature, being a mediator, being both elected by God and being an elected man. Still, in other circles you have a Rudolf-Bultmann-style Christ which sees Jesus through the lens of mythology which breeds a wider, postmodern if you will, understanding of Jesus in the form of a mythological hero. For artists like Nas, Common, Lauryn Hill, and Erykah Badu, Jesus is Paul Tillich's Christ which engages the intellect, stirs the mind, and embraces a deep theological study. From Tillich's perspective, Christ is no different from humankind in substance, just in "degree," hence the term "Degree Christology" (1959, 150). I will now examine the variations of Jesus in the Hip Hop community which connects with aspects of the Zulu Nation and Five Percenter theology.

So, the likenesses of a Hip Hop Jesus[12] are vast and complex. Let us look at five likenesses a Hip Hop Jesus is assigned (c.f. Heyward 1999, 122–123):[13]

---

12 The Hip Hop Jesus is one that is a relational and contextual image of Jesus. For some Hip Hoppers, even the name "Jesus" should be changed from *Jesus* to *Jesuz*. Note the letter "s" has been dropped to demonstrate the contextualization of the Christ figure for the 'hood. And the letter "z" at the end of Jesus' name was added to give a portrait of a Jesus that could sympathize and connect with a people that were downtrodden and broken. The letter "z" is consistent with Hip Hop's vernacular to change words and phrases to fit the context and enunciate words for a Hip Hop community. The "z" also represented a Jesus that was not only "above" in theological discussions, but also "below" in reachable form. The "z" gives new dimensions to the portrait of Christ and validates the struggles, life, narrative, and spirituality for many Hip Hoppers. Tupac and The Outlawz use "Jesuz" to give a more contextual application for their audience. Thus, when "Jesuz" is used, they are referring to the aforementioned definition (Hodge 2010, 2013a).

13 These are very similar to KRS-One's theological premise for Hip Hop as well. While he does not name "Jesus" outright as the deity, these likenesses are present throughout his discussion (One 2009).

1. Abandons moralism and the authoritarian model of relationships. Not that Jesus complete allows for anything and or does not hold a standard, quite the opposite, yet the Hip Hop Jesus allows the community to grow in their faults, errors, and sins.
2. Acts redemptively to bring the spiritual power of love and cohesion to the present moment while being aware of what it cost Him and what it will cause us and the community of Hip Hop.
3. Accepts the true nature of people and intellectually, narratively, communally, and spiritually encourages the person to change and continue the journey for consciousness and healing.
4. Seeks to reject standardized and absolute messages of salvation, church, and religion while establishing new worldviews of each of these paradigms.
5. Challenges the status-quo and argues for equal rights, justice, and cultural change in systems which oppress His people, while still allowing for the people in these oppressive social structures/systems to change and follow Him.

These five likenesses of a Hip Hop Jesus create paradigmatic pedagogies, which Hip Hoppers can come together on, regardless of faith background:[14]

- Liberating oppressed people and creatures
- Healing personal wounds: ours, others, and those of the community
- Liberating the community of Hip Hop from fear, greed, lack of confidence, and low self-esteem
- Healing peoples, nations, tribes, and earth of their ailments, sorrows, pain, and disorders
- Love for others
- Peace & harmony amidst the community is valued

These all go together with a Hip Hop Jesus that focuses more on love and encourages the community of Hip Hop.[15]

---

14   These are very similar to the fifteen universal beliefs of the Zulu nation which present a broader, more accepting aspect of Jesus that moved outside of Judeo Christian circles (Nation 2010).
15   KRS-One, in his Gospel of Hip Hop volume, has similar tenets and focuses largely on the peace, love, and respect aspect of the Gospel, which are also similar to this component of a Hip Hop Jesus.

For those in the Hip Hop community, however, who tend to not subscribe to this 'love and peace' message as a result of their environment, another likeness of a Hip Hop Jesus is present, much like that of Trap Jesus. A view of Hip Hop Jesus that is rough, tough, hyper-masculine, rugged, and authoritative is particularly attractive to urban males[16] whose postures are comparable to that. A Hip Hop Jesus that elicits a masculine posture does not necessarily mean that this Jesus is completely unaware of his female followers, but it does mean that this type of Hip Hop Jesus at least prefers a heteronormative posture much like that of Trap Jesus. This likeness of Jesus has the following dimensions to him:

- Fundamental attitudes regarding church, Jesus, and scripture.
- Supports male dominance and "man of the house" ideologies.
- "Beats down" those who are in his way.
- Instills fear as a form of control and power.
- The devil is not only an entity, but a system and institution.
- Weakness will not be tolerated.
- Jesus is in control and powerful.
- The profane and secular parts of life are embraced and valued as sacred.

Therefore, this likeness of a Hip Hop Jesus is more apt for a ghetto context and one that can bring value and context to difficult geographic spaces in which a 'loving' stylized Jesus cannot. Rap artists like Big Syke, King T, Geto Boys, Ice Cube, Mobb Deep, and even Ice Cube would prefer a Hip Hop Jesus like this. As we have seen with Trap Jesus, he is compassionate, but with a street edge and wisdom. He will help, but will need to check you out by having his disciples hold you up at gun point to see if you are "for real." He will be generous, but will also tell you to "not fuck around, cuzz he watchin'" just to make sure you will still follow "his ways." This likeness of a Hip Hop Jesus is much more "street" and "ghetto" yet possesses elements of a messianic figure.

---

16   While males tend to be attracted to this image, and there is a group of females who have adopted and indoctrinated themselves to hyper masculine and heterosymbolic perspectives. Female rappers like Lil' Kim and Foxy Brown take on male personas in the music and worldview and because there is a lack of female MCs in Hip Hop culture who can mentor these women in a female context, masculine traits become a norm for these women (Morgan 1999; Sharpley-Whiting 2007).

Where these two likenesses of Jesus intersect (the loving and peace based vs. the heteronormative) are:

- True community: community that not only embraces each individual, but also makes room for the community to learn from each other.
- Open answers: the historical Jesus did not move when people challenged him, questioned him, or tried to anger him. The historical Jesus was bold enough to handle doubt, questions, ambiguity, and mystery—key aspects to Hip Hop's post-soul theological constructs. Thus, a Hip Hop Jesus would be the same.
- Embracing Uniqueness: a Hip Hop Jesus is not afraid of dealing with people who do not look right, talk right, smell right, and "believe right." He embraces a uniqueness in which everyone is created. He refuses to accept a person in their current state and looks beyond the obvious faults to what they could become—another aspect of Hip Hop cultures' beliefs.
- Rejection of the Institutionalized Church: the historical Jesus had his strongest words for "church-folk" and religious officials. In fact, some of his most pointed, charged, direct, and heated words were towards people claiming to be religious. When Jesus did address "sinners," he did so in a manner that was both respectful and enlightening to the person, pointing them to a consciousness not condemning them to 'hell.' A Hip Hop Jesus is about community that grows intellectually, spiritually, and theologically in a variety of modes and faith practices. A Hip Hop Jesus rejects the institutionalizing of dogmatic churches and aggressively advocates for unity and community in "church like" settings.
- Truth is a quest not something to be conquered: the argument over "truth" has disabled contemporary denominations and paralyzed many religious people. A Hip Hop Jesus knows that truth is relative to the context, time period, and people seeking it. Moreover, a Hip Hop Jesus realizes that interpretation of a sacred word will be open to just that: interpretation. So, a Hip Hop Jesus will be one in search of truths in a variety of places—another post-soul idea. A Hip Hop Jesus knows that truth is a quest, not a mission with an end.

A Hip Hop Jesus is a relatable Jesus with whom Hip Hoppers are able not only to identify with, but also to embrace and love well beyond the traditional, White, Western Jesus. A Hip Hop Jesus is not concerned with church attendance numbers, tithes and offering totals, and/or which church has the biggest choir. A Hip Hop Jesus cares about the people and their quality of life.

These elements of the Hip Hop Jesus[17] constitute the *figura*[18] of Christ in the Hip Hoppers' experience. This all has roots in African American Christology. This image of the figura of Christ is part of the African American Jesus experience (Evans 1992). Jesus is seen as the liberator and mediator for Blacks. What Hip Hop has done, in essence, is that it has taken that image of Jesus, contextualized it for themselves, and then remixed it for different ethnicities. The same basic principles apply and are all rooted in Black theology (Cone 1997a), but for different ethnicities and contexts. This concept can be applied to a Hip Hop Jesus. In the Black Christology tradition James Evans tells us that:

> Jesus Christ was a figura in the sense that he was a cosmic reflection of Adam, the firstborn, the image of God, as well as the historical reflection of Joshua, who led the Israelites into the Promised Land. Jesus Christ was also a figura in the sense that he was a cosmic projection of 'the new Adam,' the image of God restored to its original state, as well as the historical projection of liberated humanity, evident in the mystical/concrete notions of the church as the 'body of Christ' and 'the people of God' (1992, 787).

The key element for many Hip Hoppers in understanding Christ is the difference between a traditional Western perception of Jesus and the likenesses listed here. As I and other scholars have argued, theological pedagogy over the last millennia is rooted in a Euro-tribal mantra and will be difficult to deconstruct and/or argue against. This is one of the reasons why Tupac is so powerful; he embodies elements of the Jesus figura in not just his music, but also his life. It is also why rappers/singers like Erykah Badu, Paris, Mace, and Kendrick Lamar continue to have such a prominent effect on young audiences across the

---

17 The figura of Jesus for Hip Hoppers better connects them with the messianic narrative. As I have observed, it is within that narrative that Hip Hoppers would be able to grow spiritually and theologically. That narrative comes in many forms: the artists themselves, concerts and performances, the music, spoken poetry, silent times outside urban centers, and community gatherings. A lot of the spiritual growth and development I observed took place in much smaller venues with fewer than two hundred people and with close knit friends. Underground communities provide that space and place for the growth, and, as I noted throughout the interviews, the aspects and qualities of a Hip Hop Jesus emerged in those spaces and places.

18 The figura of Christ is not a new concept. It is borrowed from Black Christology which borrowed it from Greek and Roman thought to express "…an idea of something that both reflects something that already exists as well as projects something yet to be." (Kärkkäinen 2003, 206). The idea here is the cultural appropriation for contextualizing a deity figure in the Hip Hop context.

Globe—they are, in many ways, the embodiment and external articulation of a Hip Hop Jesus. It is this figura of a Hip Hop Jesus that Veli-Matti Kärkkäinen further observes, "The Messiah was vested with the authority to usher in a new age in which the power structures of this world would be overturned and freedom would prevail" (2003, 207). A liberationist perspective is a strong characteristic of a Hip Hop Jesus (Gutiérrez 1987). "Freedom" for a Hip Hop Jesus would be freedom from economic, social, political, educational, emotional, spiritual, theological, and familial oppression—expressly those oppressive conditions emanating from hegemonic institutions.

A Hip Hop Jesus, in this sense then, becomes a type of messianic figure that brings voice, shelter, identity, hope, dreams, love, and passion for a community seeking a higher consciousness. He is a messianic figure that does not singularize pathways to them. Rather, they are open to various pathways so long as the end result is a higher personal and social consciousness. Evans gives us an example of this in Black Christian contexts; he states:

> The Messiah embodies the nationalistic hopes and dreams of an oppressed people...It is noteworthy that continued oppression and travail did not destroy the messianic dream but intensified it. Indeed, the more evil abounded, the more powerful the idea of the Messiah became. As the actual historical liberation of Israel seemed to recede into the remote provinces of probability, the Messiah became one capable not only of transforming the historical situation of the people, but of transforming history itself (1992, 79).

Broadly, A Hip Hop Jesus becomes someone who lifts up people and gives them a new hope. A Hip Hop Jesus then establishes a relevant theological framework that is contextual for that community. This pushes past a Western Eurocentric image of Jesus, and moves out of kerygmatic creeds keeping this figure locked in one religious affiliation.

Given that the discourse of Jesus tends to be associated with Christianity and assumes the stereotypes of mainstream conservative Christians (homophobic, dogmatic, Western, judgmental), some in the Hip Hop community who religiously affiliate closer to Zulu, Nation Of Islam, Five Percenter, and Muslim spiritual practices might not be that closely tied with a "Jesus figura." Ice Cube's 2006 song "Go To Church" scorns images of Jesus and marks him as weak, feeble, and incapable of being able to handle the reality of 'hood life.[19] This type of Jesus, largely rooted in Western constructs, is not one that many in

---

19 While these are stereotypes that are within Hip Hop culture, I will add that those stereotypes are still rooted in Western models of Jesus—a Jesus who is impotent to the reality

the Hip Hop community can take for very long. Still, the aforementioned qualities of a Hip Hop Jesus—peace, love, joy, and happiness—are aspects that most spiritual guides and religions promote. The name might be problematic for some, but the qualities are nonetheless important and valuable.

The figura of a Hip Hop Jesus is not a Jesus that is easily digestible. It is a hostile form of Jesus for those who only see him in singularities and in constrained theological proportions according to what they have interpreted and learned. This type of Jesus will be filled with a multitude of problems, heresy, and blasphemy for them. Yet, I argue that these types of likenesses of Jesus are what Hip Hoppers are seeking and what they desire to connect with as a "messianic" persona. A Hip Hop Jesus could, in fact, be that 'hostile' part of the gospel because he would be hostile to the traditions, teachings, training, and spirituality which have created spiritual prisons for so many. A Hip Hop Jesus would come to "set them free" from those types of religious bondage.

Now, let us look closely at a specific song and how the song and artists trudge on in this spiritual journey.

The Outlawz & Black Jesuz

As seen, Hip Hop pushes past a socially constructed traditionalized White, blonde, blue eyed, construct of Jesus[20] and asks for a Jesus that smokes like we smoke, drinks like we drink, and acts like we act. A Jesus that "we can relate to in the 'hood." This type of Jesus also questions authority, seeks to increase social consciousness, validates and acknowledges the social isolation as valid and real to all in the 'hood, and every now and then "puts a foot in someone's ass to tell a muthafucka he real" (Hodge 2009, Interview). Continuing the analysis using Jon Michael Spencer's framework of theomusicology, I will analyze Tupac Shakur's song "Black Jesuz"[21] to argue that sensationalized images of Jesus are the missing pieces which mediate the growing gulf between traditional Christianity and Hip Hop culture, and that Hip Hop produces a more relevant and applicable theological mantra for Christianity.

---

of life and a Jesus who is still White and un-relatable. That is the main image that rappers like Ice-Cube are rebelling against.

20   The traditional image of "Jesus" has been that of a bearded, White, long haired, blue-eyed person (Cone 1997b; Edwards 1975; Pinn 2002). The societal reinforcement of this image from White dominant culture has been problematic for many in the Hip Hop community, therefore the push to have a form of Christ more contextual and relevant for the context in which Hip Hoppers find themselves (e.g. the ghetto and oppressive conditions from hegemonic systems).

21   This song, above all the others, was mentioned in the interviews as being instrumental in having the ability to see a Jesus beyond a Western lens and White hegemonic structures.

NO JESUS IN THE WILD: RACE & THE JESUZ FIGURE

As has been argued, the dominant narrative of Jesus as a White, perfected image of deity has proven to be both problematic and offensive to rappers and the Hip Hop community (Cone 1997b; Miller 2013b; Pinn 1995; Utley 2012). Thus, the need for a contextual, relevant, and appropriate Christ was—and still is—needed to interpret deity and spirituality for the 'hood. In the song "Black Jesuz" by Tupac and The Outlawz (Outlawz) there is an attempt to make a god, which appeared too perfect, too nice, and too White on a social level, more accessible to the 'hood.

Within the song "Black Jesuz," an attempt to make life in the 'hood more understandable from a theological perspective is under way. It is a song making an attempt to create a space for the thug, the nigga, and the pimp to find God. It is a space for some sort of reconciliation to the hegemonic image of a White Jesus and the hope of a Jesus that is not only Black, but also Hip Hop. The intersection of Spencer's (1991b) trinary construct is at work—where the sacred and the profane both reveal themselves in secular contexts, in this case, Hip Hop artists. Tupac and the Outlawz reverse the hermeneutical flow (Kreitzer 1993, 1994) and use culture, in this case Hip Hop, to interpret God in a context which is hostile.

The song is in three parts: (1) the Doxology: giving respect & acknowledgement; (2) the Lament: how is life and love done in this ghetto hell; and (3) the Benediction to Black Jesuz: we are searching for a Jesus *for* us. Tupac opens the song with a call out to a Jesus who can relate—the Doxology:

> Searching for Black Jesus Oh yeah, sportin jewels and shit, yaknahmean? (Black Jesus; you can be Christian Baptist, Jehovah Witness)
> A God whose religious affiliation does not matter:
> (Black Jesus; you can be Christian Baptist, Jehovah Witness) Straight tatted up, no doubt, no doubt (Islamic, won't matter to me I'm a thug; thugs, we praise Black Jesus, all day) Young Kadafi in this bitch, set it off nigga. What?

Once again, Christina Zanfagna (Zanfagna 2006, 5) reminds us that "Hip-hop wrestles with the ways in which the hedonistic body and the seeking soul can be fed and elevated in dynamic tension. This wrestling is often expressed through a dialectic of pleasure and pain or recreation and suffering." The "thug Jesus" is someone to be praised and a deity figure needed from the Outlawz stance. Here, the search is clear; a Jesus who is "blinging," without a denominational affiliation and one who can relate to the suffering, pain, disenfranchisement, and historical oppression that those in 'hood enclaves are experiencing.

Kadafi from the Outlawz exegetes his environment with laments to Jesus: (1) it is a nightmare, (2) times are desperate, (3) the form of religion does not relate, and (4) questions whether God can relate.

> Stuck in a nightmare, hopin' he might care. Though times is hard, up against all odds, I play my cards like I'm jailin,' shots hittin' up my spot like midnight rains hailin' Got me bailin' to stacks more green.
> OUTLAWZ 1999

The visibility of pain and suffering is evident while the assertion to "survive" and make money is also evident. Can a God who "loves" everyone conjure up a resolution within a "nightmare" situation? The ageless theological inquiry of doubt begins to manifest itself:

> Gods ain't tryin' to be trapped on no block slangin' no rocks like bean pies. Brainstorm on the beginnin.' Wonder how shit like the Qu'ran and the Bible was written. What is religion? Gods words all cursed like crack Shai-tan's way of getting' us back, or just another one of my Black Jesus traps

Storm follows and presents the following three questions:

1. Who has the guts to stand beside him in hell?
2. Can we meet at the intersection of the profane and sacred?
3. Is heaven a possibility or even a reality?

> Who's got the heart to stand beside me? I feel my enemies creepin' up in silence. Dark prayer, scream violence—demons all around me Can't even bend my knees just a lost cloud; Black Jesus give me a reason to survive, in this earthly hell. Cause I swear, they tryin' to break my well I'm on the edge lookin' down at this volatile pit. Will it matter if I cease to exist? Black Jesus.

Tupac, allowing members of the Outlawz to go first, then enters and creates a relatable Jesus, one who can affirm the social isolation and disinherited:

> In times of war we need somebody raw, rally the troops like a saint that we can trust to help to carry us through. Black Jesus, hahahahaha. He's like a Saint that we can trust to help to carry us through Black Jesus

Tupac reminds Storm that surroundings in the 'hood are similar to war-like conditions but that there is a saint which can carry "us through."

Young Noble begins the Benediction—the fourth verse—affirming that race, culture, and religion are different in the 'hood.

> Outlawz we got our own race, culture, religion
> Rebellin against the system

Noble keeps the lament tension intact while still begging Black Jesus to "please watch over my brother." This delicate treading between the sacred and the profane is similar to what Spencer refers to as "unreligious people's quest for the sacred" (1991b, 16–17). Spencer argues that this is a way to understand the nature of irreligious music and the community therein which produces it (1991b, 161–162).

Thus, Young Noble, in an irreligious way, is in search of a God who does not flinch in the setting of blasphemy, the heretical, and the sacrilegious.[22] He is engaging in a conversation with Black Jesuz to which the answers of his pain are still yet to be revealed. This is similar to David's prayers in the Psalms: "Keep me safe, O God, for I have come to you for refuge" (Psalm 16:1 NLT), "My God, my God! Why have you forsaken me? Why do you remain so distant? Why do you ignore my cries for help? Every day I call to you, my God, but you do not answer. Every night you hear my voice, but I find no relief" Psalm 22:1–2 NLT); these passages are similar to Noble's own apprehension which he is laying before Black Jesuz:

> The President ain't even listenin' to the pain of the youth. We make music for eternity, forever the truth. Political prisoner, the two choices that they givin' us. Ride or die, for life they sentence us, oh Black Jesus, please watch over my brother Shawn. Soon as the sky get bright, it's just another storm. Brothers gone, now labeled a statistic. Ain't no love for us ghetto kids, they call us nigglets. History repeats itself, nuttin' new. In school I knew, e'rything I read wasn't true, Black Jesus

In the fifth verse, Tupac discusses the ill effects of a life within nefarious conditions:

---

22 Monica Miller also argues that within these ostensibly profane areas, religious meaning is still constructed (Miller 2013b).

> To this click I'm dedicated, criminal orientated. An Outlaw initiated, blazed and faded. Made for terror, major league niggaz pray together. Bitches in they grave while my real niggaz play together. We die clutchin' glasses, filled with liquor bomblastic cremated, last wishes nigga smoke my ashes. High sigh why die wishin,' hopin' for possibilities I'll mob on, why they copy me sloppily Cops patrol projects, hatin' the people livin' in them I was born an inmate, waitin' to escape the prison

In this verse, he exegetes the life of the thug, the pimp, and the pusher. Moreover, he asserts what those types of lifestyles produce: drug abuse, hate, and distrust of systems. Church as an institution, for Tupac and the Outlawz, is no different. In their estimation, if the cops beat you, schools lie to you, and systems fail you, why would the "church" be any different? Tupac ends the verse with:

> Went to church but don't understand it, they underhanded God gave me these commandments, the world is scandalous blast til they holy high; baptize they evil minds. Wise, no longer blinded, watch me shine trick which one of y'all wanna feel the degrees? Bitches freeze facin,' Black Jesus

Michael Eric Dyson asserts that "Tupac was the secular external articulation of an ongoing religious debate about the possibility of identifying with a God who became what we are" (Peters 2001, DVD Interview). In other words, Tupac surmises that within the fallout of failed systems, promises, and theologies, there is a need for a Black Jesuz; one in which "bitches freeze"[23] when standing in his manifestation.

Kastro finishes the last verse with a declaration to Jesus: we are hurting, please help. Kastro shows a Jesus who "walks through the valley." Once again, a Jesus who can identify with hunger; a Jesus who realizes that this is not the intended mode of life for humans; a Jesus who, as Ebony Utley asserts, was gangsta, hung out with thieves, prostitutes, beat down some fools, used foul language to cast off religious pastors and rejected the religiosity of his day:

> Jesus is the transitional God figure because, according to the Bible, God 'out there' sent Jesus 'down here' to sacrifice himself via death, burial, and resurrection to redeem humanity. The physical experience of walking the

---

23 In other words, individuals who are weak morally, ethically, spiritually, and pursue oppressive paths are not able to withstand in the presence of a God who is for justice, reconciliation, ending oppression, and creating spaces in which people are valued over things (Watkins 2011, Chapter 6).

> earth anchors Jesus to the human experience...only a God who walked among humans could truly redeem them. This perspective is not lost on gangstas who connect with Jesus' experience with haters (persecutors), murder (crucifixion), and resurrection (redemption). Jesus is familiar with suffering because he suffered. Jesus is familiar with victory because his resurrection conquered death.
> UTLEY 2012, 8

Kastro wants to see something better than the life he has now and has experienced thus far.

> And it ain't hard to tell, we dwell in hell. Trapped, black, scarred and barred. Searching for truth, where it's hard to find God I play the Pied Piper, and to this Thug Life, I'm a lifer proceed, to turn up the speed, just for stripes. My Black Jesus, walk through this valley with me. Where we, so used to hard times and casualties. Indeed, it hurt me deep to have to sleep on the streets. And haven't eaten' in weeks, so save a prayer for me, and all the young thugs, raised on drugs and guns Blazed out and numb, slaves to this slums. This ain't livin... Jesus

Kastro wants a deity that is "down here" and can redeem the mounting negative experiences within the 'hood.

Lastly, Tupac, in the last call of the song, exhorts to us that they are in search of a Jesus that hurts like we hurt, smokes like we smoke, drinks like we drink, and understands where we are coming from—a basic ontological hermeneutic for us all:

> Searchin' for Black Jesus. It's hard, it's hard! We need help out here! So we searchin' for Black Jesus! It's like a Saint, that we pray to in the ghetto, to get us through. Somebody that understand our pain, you know, maybe not too perfect, you know, somebody that hurt like we hurt, somebody that smoke like we smoke, drink like we drink; that understand where we coming from That's who we pray to We need help y'all

Dyson tells us,

> Black Jesus for Tupac meant for him that figure that identities with the hurt, the downtrodden, and the downfallen. The Black Jesus is a new figure; both literally within the literary traditions of black response to suffering, but also religious responses to suffering. If this is the Black Jesus of history, it is the Jesus that has never been talked about and

most people who talk about Jesus would never recognize (Peters, DVD Interview).

Tupac not only knew this, but also embodied this within his body of work, which is one of the many reasons he argued in so many songs for the contextualization of the Gospel for the 'hood. Tupac blurred the lines between the sacred and the profane. Tupac entered into blasphemous zones and waded into deep heretical waters while searching for this Black Jesuz who could not only create a space for the thug and the nigga to find deity, but to redeem his context (the 'hood and inner city spaces) of being what most of society has labeled a "bad place" and undesirable location. "Black Jesuz" is a song made in an attempt to bring a type of 'hood redemption to non-traditional church members living within the post-industrial urban enclave called the ghetto.

Toward Sensationalized Images of the Hip Hop Jesus

Jesus was, and still is in many ways, a controversial persona. He was not one to mince words nor miss an opportunity to connect with the disinherited. Utley observes that

> Jesus fraternized with sexually licentious women, cavorted with sinners, worked on the Sabbath, had a temper, used profane language with religious people, praised faithfulness over stilted forms of religious piety, and honored God more than the government. Gangstas respect Jesus because they see the parallels between his life and theirs. (2012, 49)

However, most of the critical, radical, and post-soul images of Jesus have been lost and too often domesticated for either political or racial reasons. In other words, the critical, radical, and post-soul image of Jesus with which many Hip Hoppers could readily identify are often marred by a Jesus symbol that is quiet, turn-the-other-cheek, meek, and mild mannered. Hip Hoppers in rough and rugged situations need a deity that can connect better with the rough and rugged.

Is it possible that seemingly blasphemous images of the sacred Christ create spiritual awareness? Theologian Tom Beaudoin has told us that "offensive images or practices may indicate a familiarity with deep religious truths" (Beaudoin 1998, 123). One must understand the authority of "official" sacraments to de-valorize them forcefully. Likewise, it takes a true believer in the power of worship to turn curses into praise, the word "nigga" into a nomination of the highest respect. The point here is not to allow degrading terms, but to acknowledge that such rhetorical devices are making a serious theological attempt at grasping a practice of inequality that is *very* real (c.f. Cupitt 1998).

Tupac and The Outlawz present a Jesus that is not only relatable, but one who is able to connect with the inequalities of life. While most of the song questions whether Jesus can connect to the inequalities of life, the subtext of the song is about a Jesus who can relieve the burden of ghetto life. In the Psalmist's terms, Jesus is a shepherd and causes those in dire straits to lie down in green pastures. In a contemporary context, Jesus is able to blow through the blunt smoking persona and redeem those who hurt.

These sensationalized images of Jesus are needed as they push beyond the traditionalized symbols of Jesus and offer not only a contextual appropriation but one that is contemporary for younger audiences.[24] More importantly, they are needed in the discourse of Christian theology as many of these personas of Jesus get lost within the dominant, Western, Eurocentric, American evangelical model of Christianity (c.f. George 2004; Taylor 2007; West 1993; Yinger 1957; Zizek 2008). Suffering in context is nothing new. The search for meaning within that suffering is also nothing new.

Sensationalized images of Jesus such as Aaron McGruder's Black Jesus, Lil Wayne's *Trap Jesus*, and Tupac's Black Jesuz represent a fundamental attempt to make the deity, the divine, and the sacred more accessible to those who typically do not grace the sanctuaries of Christian churches. They represent the fusing of the sacred and profane—a space that Spencer argues is vastly misunderstood. They use culture to help interpret the sacred scriptures and to break away some of the seriousness characteristically associated with Jesus.

Finally, they are more relevant and applicable to those seeking Jesus from the post-soul, Hip Hop, and urban generation. This generation is not interested in a God that sits in multi-million dollar churches. They reject pastors who net more than their congregations make in a year combined. They despise the double standards of a Church that limits the spiritual possibilities of person by telling them that "this" is the "right way." Finally, they do not want a Jesus that is "too perfect." What Tupac and The Outlawz do well is present a Jesus in human form for this current time and generation.

---

24 This is no different to what Jürgen Moltmann or Henry Nouwen argue when they discuss contextual Christologies which relate and connect with current geographic spaces (Nouwen 1989; Moltmann 1990).

Chapter Summary

This chapter has been concerned with illuminating the racial dimensions, likenesses, and aspects of the person and image of Jesus. Race continues to be a significant issue for those living in the U.S. and Hip Hop is all too aware of the issues surrounding racial ideologies and religion. Hip Hoppers have been presented, too often, with a White, Americanized version[25] of Jesus with whom most ethnic minorities cannot relate or aspire towards. Sensationalized images of Jesus such as the one in Aaron McGruder's web series *Black Jesus* and Lil Wayne's *Trap Jesus* provide an insight into a side of Jesus rarely, if ever, seen. These sensationalized images actually provide stronger socio-religious connections for the Hip Hop community and move past Western, messianic constructs of Jesus. A Hip Hop Jesus is, therefore, created in the vacuum and given dimensions like love, peace, community, truth seeking, non-absolute facets, and a passion for community and personal growth. These likenesses, while still using the name of Jesus, are more appealing for the Hip Hop community and provide a more relevant image of Jesus. Tupac and The Outlawz demonstrated this in the song "Black Jesuz," and we were able to see a Hip Hop Jesus engaged by rappers.

This chapter has argued for a contextual and relevant image of Jesus. It challenges the notion that the only Jesus figure is a White one and places a more relevant one, a Hip Hop one, at the theological and religious table. A Hip Hop Jesus is a 'hostile' one if, in one sense, one sees Jesus in a singular form and being solely of the Christian religion. What this chapter has argued in essence is that a Hip Hop Jesus is much more universal, holistic, and pantheistic in manner. Thus, this Jesus embodies a 'hostility' toward religions that desire to claim him as 'their own.' For a Hip Hopper seeking out their own religious ideology, a Hip Hop Jesus is the image they would most likely be attracted to, and one that could be much broader in approach than a Western one.

In the next chapter, I will look broadly at theological conceptual frameworks within Hip Hop contexts and expand further on the five central typologies of Hip Hop sensibilities mentioned in the Introduction. Chapter 6 will conclude this study and argue that Hip Hop has post-soul religious features to it. The book's progression from Chapter 1 to the present chapter has built up the various characteristics of Hip Hop's socio-religious workings: context, geographical location, the cypher, Tupac's sainthood, violence, suffering, and a Hip Hop Jesus. All have arisen out of this exploratory study and now we will turn to my conclusions from this data.

---

25   Also depicted as pro-war, patriotic, and against social programs.

CHAPTER 6

Conclusions: What is Theology & Spirituality in Hip Hop?

> And to all future generations of Hip Hop, know this; it is this Love that has delivered this gospel to OUR PEOPLE for OUR correction and survival. This gospel comes to us as the physical manifestation of God's grace and love for Hip Hop.
>
> KRS-One

∴

> Often we view religion and science as having a zero-sum relationship. But for many sociologists, religion and science are both narratives that explain social reality—the former based on traditional authority and faith and the later on scientific methodology.
>
> TOM KERSEN

∴

> If religion was a thing money could buy, the rich would live, and the poor would die.
>
> JAMES BALDWIN

∴

So, as posed in the introduction, does a Hip Hop 'theology' even fit? Is there an actual motif which Hip Hoppers are espousing within the supernatural realm? Is there an actual religious discourse within Hip Hop or is it a manufacturing of artists for more profit? I began this project with an open mind, intending to explore the socio-theological within a culture that, in full transparency, is close and dear to me. However, within the process, the initial methodology of lyrical analysis yielded only a small sample of songs which had a theological slant in them. This was most troubling, as the culture I had come to study in my previous works was alive with a theological, hermeneutical, and spiritual journey. Theomusicology was a much better fit because it allowed for Hip Hop's true 'voice' to be heard in the context of the sacred, profane, and secular. This project set out to give a critical approach to Hip Hop, its people, its culture, and the environment in which it is formed.

This book has been concerned with exploring the spiritual and theological dimensions, aspects, sensibilities, and features of Hip Hop culture. While the field of theological and religious studies is rich with history, social awareness, gender, and racial sub-fields, Hip Hop Studies is a relatively newer study and one that has emerged over the last decade.[1] This book has explored the context and environment in which Hip Hop was formed. It has argued that Hip Hop is a post-soul theological construction and a space in which those with 'alternate identities' are able to find a space in which to explore God, deity, spirituality, and the issues surrounding the supernatural (e.g. death, the afterlife). This book has also observed the cypher within Hip Hop and the artists which construct a socio-spiritual discourse within their music, life, and poetry. The cypher is central to Hip Hop culture and offers the engine to the actual narrative within Hip Hop. This gave way to probing one of Hip Hop's greatest cypherologists, Tupac Amaru Shakur. This examination gave insight into one of Hip Hop's touted 'ghetto saints' and observed the theological contours of rapper and artist Tupac Shakur. Chapter 1 through Chapter 3 was a way of exploring the various aspects of Hip Hop's spiritual and theological tenet. It gave a broad view of the culture's journey through and in theology, which then opened up to Chapter 4 which surveyed violence, pain, and suffering within the context of both Hip Hop and a God who is, at times, silent toward the suffering experienced in urban and Hip Hop communities. Then, we dealt with race and the messianic symbol in Jesus. Hip Hoppers, by and large, desire a 'messiah' that is relatable, smokes like they smoke, and drinks like they drink—a deity in human form, the Hip Hop Jesuz. This, in the end, is the ultimate pursuit of seeking a God symbol to which one can relate.

Hip Hop culture is not, however, a culture likely to be studied as an endeavor of religious research. With its infamous mug of minstrel caricatures, degradation of women, hypermasculinity, and a strong bend toward nihilism, one might overlook the subtle yet complex tones of religion within the actual culture. As with any group of people, numinous elements and divinity are there. The attempt to create an understanding of what 'life' is about and the meaning of that 'life' are also present. Hip Hop is no different.

---

1   There is also an emerging sub-field being established by Anthony Pinn and Monica Miller within Hip Hop Studies called religion and Hip Hop. While still in its early stages, it promises to delve more closely into this area of theology and faith in the context of Hip Hop.

CONCLUSIONS: WHAT IS THEOLOGY & SPIRITUALITY IN HIP HOP?

Still, Hip Hop, by its mere stance on social issues, advocacy for human rights, and its strong message against hegemonic systems often presents a problematic premise for those in religious settings, particularly those religious settings which adhere to the Abrahamic faith traditions. Hip Hop is not a "traditional" approach to religion and tends to give much more criticism than it does solutions to the problems. Moreover, Hip Hop is not a unified body of belief nor does it possess a 'majority rule' in its approach toward a religious premise, which is another post-soul tendency. Thus, within the research, it was difficult to arrive at a solid religious philosophy and theology as there are numerous ones which, at times, appear to be sections of a much smaller segment of Hip Hop. As Monica Miller states:

> ...the position that the category of what scholars have come to call "religion" is in fact a human doing, production, and manufacturing with a particular social and political history. Seen thus as an act of imagining and doing, religion eludes the theoretical and taxonomical category that has often privileged particular practices and experiences as 'religious' (2013b, 178).

As challenging as Miller's thoughts are here, I still found five theological generalities which do emerge, which give insight and responses to these questions which we will examine first, prior to inspecting the five reoccurring typologies:[2]

1. *The Hip Hop community crafts its own space for meaning and understanding of the mystery of God:* KRS-One, known as the "God-father of Hip Hop" because of his instrumental music, philosophy, and commitment to the culture, discusses the significance of Hip Hop's unique space to experience 'life' and all the love, pain, and suffering that it has to offer. As has been shown in this book, Hip Hop is a community that is able to produce a space and locality in which people are able to find themselves and seek the mystery of who God is in their time, their speed, and without an overarching judgmental dogma that some religions tend to have (e.g. sin).
2. *Doubt is fundamental:* if one thing is clear within all of the research, doubt is an essential element to Hip Hop's spiritual dimensions. The ability to struggle and hold in tension a God who is 'out there' and may or may not be able to 'save' is critical for the Hip Hop community. While

---

[2] These were formed from a culmination of the research and the interviews with various artists.

Zulu, Christian, Jewish, and Islamic faiths tend to have a more established route to 'faith' and 'assurance,' Hip Hoppers push against this 'assurance' (as a result of living in communities being in such dis-assurance and contempt) to provide a healthy tension of disbelief and doubt. Artists like Pastor Troy and Tupac intertwine a doubt that God even exists with a discourse of hope in a brighter tomorrow. Doubt produces a way of understanding for the Hip Hop community. For Hip Hoppers, those who are 'sure' and 'certain' are to be suspected and not trusted—for that 'assurance' typically brings with it dogmatic, rigorous, and judgmental theologies which can then produce hate, violence, and even war when those who do not fit into their scope of assurance make 'life' messy. Hence, the Hip Hop community remains in a state of doubt, which in many ways aids in the growth of the very 'faith' in which they are attempting to grow.[3]

3. *The suffering images of a God are preferred*: if there is one thing that the Hip Hop community understands, it is pain and suffering. Hip Hoppers desire a God who has suffered with them, a God who is able to connect with sources of pain. Therefore, the suffering and beaten image of Jesus and prophets alike is needed. Interviewee Shelly posed a question which arose in various forms during the research: how can one identify with a God who is too perfect, too clean, too neat, too nice, and too peaceful? In essence, Hip Hoppers desire a God who is as grimy, profane, and illicit as they are. They desire a deity which can ultimately relate to the context and disreputable conditions in which the community finds itself—a God who can walk with them through the pain and suffering because that God has experienced it.

4. *Toward a theology of suffering and chaos:* this leads to the next theological typology which is Hip Hoppers' ability to develop theological constructs

---

[3] It is noted that in the Islamic faith, the prophet Muhammad (born roughly around 570 CE) doubted that the words he received about the Qur'an's text actually came from God. Muhammad perceived it as a figment of his imagination and that he was making the whole thing up. He wondered if a God would even give him such a message and whether God even existed. He almost drove himself insane with doubt, until he hesitatingly began to put the canon into a document. While this narration is often overlooked and even ignored—conservative Islamic scholars argue that Muhammad was 'sure' and 'never doubted' the call of God—it is a crucial piece of the faith, that the prophet himself had major doubts in regards to God and the 'calling on his life.' This is a critical part of the history of Islam and of religion in general: doubt is the key ingredient of faith and of connection to a deity (Esposito 1999; Hazleton 2013b, a).

within the suffering and chaos. Throughout much of the Christian Bible, characters such as Isaiah, Ezekiel, David, Tamar, Ruth, Noah, Peter, and Judas had a profane nature to them. That is, there was an element to them that was, simply put, human: they used strong language; they abused friends; they lied; they sold out friends for 'booty'; they were sexually carnal; they were what Harvey Cox would describe as the *laos theou*—the people of God (1965, 125). Yet, among these 'people of God' was suffering, and at many levels, chaos and disorder—some were able to give off better personas of togetherness than others, but in the end, all were truly battling chaos. This is part of what Hip Hoppers wish to explore. How could a 'perfect' God put the message of 'truth' in people who are filled with such imperfection? Moreover, how does one deal, spiritually, with the chaotic conditions in which they find themselves without (a) killing themselves, (b) killing others, or (c) becoming a pessimistic cynic? These are theological pursuits that the Hip Hop community, by and large, is open to pursuing. Those in this community see a God who is able to journey with them and a God who will eventually begin to bring some type of redemptive quality to their situation. This, however, will require a God who is willing to be theologically 'messy'[4] which, in the end, Hip Hoppers, on the whole, are okay with because it is chaotic and it provides some solace to their suffering.

5. *Vengeance will fall upon the 'unjust':* in the end, most religions believe that the 'wicked' will, in some way, be punished. Whether it is returning to life in different forms until the true meaning of life is found or burning in an everlasting fire, the 'wicked' will receive their due 'justice.' For the Hip Hop community, it was found that even pimps, hustlers, and thieves believe this in some manner, and the 'injustice' they have received from society will in some way be recompensed in the supernatural realm for

---

4 Some conundrums and, by definition, non-answerable questions have no decisive resolution. For example, who sat in the room with God and the "heavenly hosts" in the book of Job? Why was Lot so willing to give up his daughters? Could there be a different God of the Old Testament who almost enjoyed killing those who did not agree with him, compared to the God of the New Testament who taught about peace, love, and against violence? Is not the story of Jesus pre-dated by Horus who had some of the same typologies within it (e.g. twelve disciples, one traitor, rose to save his people, died for humanity)? These are just some of the theological messes that the Hip Hop community desires a God to sit with, and yet trusting that God will eventually provide answers to 'life' at some later point—e.g. third eye consciousness.

their suffering.[5] In addition, the desire is that God will provide a retaliation, on some level, for those who are oppressed and a place for the 'unjust' to 'pay' for their ill manners and deeds. Interviewees Laura and Tali exclaimed that somewhere "up there" God had to be willing to deal with the evil doers "down here." Letty and MC Skillz also stated similar responses when asked "how do you, from a theological position, comprehend and deal with pain and suffering?" God was seen to be, ultimately, a 'just God' who will reward those who follow God's ways.[6]

These five typologies are representative of the broad theological paradigms derived from my research. I argue that a Hip Hop theology does fit and that there is substantial material in it to connect to a group of people performing what Charles Glock and Rodney Stark break up into a taxonomy of religious experience (1965, 43–62):

1. The Confirming Experience: the human actor simply notes (feels, sense, etc.) the existence or presence of the divine.[7]
2. The Responsive Experience: mutual presence is acknowledged, the divine actor is perceived as noting the presence of the human actor.[8]

---

5 The interviewees who were open enough to divulge their personal lives revealed that in the past, they were a variety of drug dealers, pimps, and street hustlers, but 'now' they had been converted and that their former lifestyle was not in line with what 'God' had intended life to be. This was also the case in my previous work with gang members in Los Angeles, CA. Almost all recounted to me that this lifestyle they lived was not one that they would choose, but was one that was thrust upon them by geographical location, social circumstances, and economic factors. Most desired to live a 'better life' and found some type of peace and hope in a God who would eventually give them rest either in death or heaven (Hodge 2009, 2010, 2013b). Dyson also noted that rappers sought after a more "Old Testament" style God as that God actually handled life the way the "streets did," an interesting observation (2001, 203–216).

6 Of course the notion and meaning behind "God's ways" is open to interpretation from a variety of positions. Here, most of the respondents in the interviews were referring to a life that was peaceful, loving, and one where they looked out for their sisters and brothers. While one might argue that you do not need a God or religion for this type of ideological construct. Nevertheless, the interviewees and research with the Hip Hop community points this toward a life 'with God.'

7 This takes place in or at concerts and spoken word venues (i.e. poetry readings).

8 This occurs when listening to certain artists or viewing particular videos which are transcendental for the person.

CONCLUSIONS: WHAT IS THEOLOGY & SPIRITUALITY IN HIP HOP? 181

3. The Ecstatic Experience: the awareness of mutual presence is replaced by an affective relationship akin to love or friendship.[9]
4. The Revelational Experience: the human actor perceives her or himself as a confidant of or a fellow participant in action with the divine actor.[10]

While Glock and Stark were referring to a general religious experience, from the research, the Hip Hop community is no different, and within this society, Hip Hoppers experience these four taxonomies in a variety of ways. These experiences are part of the larger spiritual experience within the culture which aids in creating meaning, context, and ultimately an ontological discourse for the person. As argued, Hip Hop may perhaps be an indigenous approach to deity and the supernatural by way of its core tenets and mantra. The fact that artists are able to work this out through a theological habitation either in their music, their concerts, or their personal life, is an example of the complexity and intricacy of a Hip Hop theology.[11]

However, it could also be argued that this is also a manufacturing of religious manifestations and used for maintaining the religious marketplace. This could certainly be the case in some cases where artists use religion as a selling point. For example, Mase's conversion to Christianity, then back to mainstream, then back to Christianity was a market value-driven move for his career. It caused him to sell albums and get his name in the headlines. We can also look at Snoop Dogg's conversion to Rastafarianism coming from an extreme position

---

9   For the Hip Hop community, this is when God reveals God's self in the poetry, music, or event which uplifts the person or community, such as the experience of social and/or economic equality.

10 This is the least common, but it occurs when the Hip Hopper (or community therein) actually feels God's presence and a sense of the divine. Artists such as Tupac, DMX, Lauryn Hill, Lupe Fiasco, KRS-One, and Lecrae have all reported this experience in and around their music and the power within a concert venue (typically smaller events). In this experience, Hip Hoppers often find a God who is compassionate, merciful, and able to embrace their 'sin' and 'shortcomings.' While uncommon, in a similar notion in his book (which is also shaped and colored in the form of an actual Bible), KRS-One argues that this is a crucial piece to spiritual growth and that Hip Hop could actually help in this experience (One 2009).

11 It could also be stated that Blues, Jazz, and R & B artists can do the same with their respective audiences in their respective contexts. Hip Hop could be this generation's Blues and Jazz culture, and, quite possibly, morph into a new genre and musical category over the next twenty years. But, nevertheless, Hip Hop is certainly not the first in music genres to wrestle with theological matters.

of Gnostic ideologies and the public announcement of his name change to Snoop Lion. In this same sense, the 2012 holographic use of Tupac's image at a concert in Coachella California by Dr. Dre and then Snoop Dogg drew much controversy about the sacredness of Tupac's life and message. Moreover, critics argued that Dr. Dre and Snoop used Tupac for promotional and financial promotions and that they were merely attempting to attain publicity in the public sphere—which, in the end, gave them a substantial amount of notoriety as the technology used to create such a lifelike image was groundbreaking. Further, with a sacred entity such as Tupac, the Hip Hop community was torn and the commercialism became, once again, a topic of tension.

Christian Hip Hop artists (also characterized as "holy Hip Hoppers") such as Lecrae, Shai Linne, Propaganda, and Sho Baraka offer a certain theological discourse rooted in a professed theological tradition—Christianity. They are not attempting to obscure their messages. They are clear and open about their faith, religious aspirations, and spiritual discourses (more on these artists momentarily). It could also be argued that, in essence, by labeling their music "Christian" or "holy Hip Hop" they are, by default, creating a marketplace for their art. After all, they are getting paid for their music and they charge for concert appearances. Would this not also be considered a construct within the religious marketplace? Also, with the growing sub-genre of "holy Hip Hop," the title of being "Christian" or "holy" carries with it a crowd of eager buyers for a version of Hip Hop that is "lighter" and without the 'fat.' These buyers and audiences tend to be suburban, upper middle class,[12] White, and evangelical. The artists can draw good sums of money and typically draw a crowd of individuals willing to pay for para-merchandise such as DVDs, t-shirts, books, and other paraphernalia. The Christian marketplace is vast and large. It also contains an economic factor which artists understand well, which is why that marketplace is engaged. Thus, what is the line between an authentic Christian message and a message for monetary profit?

The same is true, however, for commercial artists not given the label "Christian" or "holy Hip Hopper." There is money and notoriety to be had when an artist like Tupac, Nas, or Pastor Troy strongly criticizes the Black church and accuses it of thievery and licentious lifestyles. There is popularity to be gained

---

[12]   This notion of Hip Hop as being "lighter" is often a way for White, suburban, upper middle class adolescents to gain entry into Hip Hop culture. While artists such as Lil Wayne and Jay Z present too much of a threat to the parents, Christian Hip Hop artists offer a much "easier" entry and adaptation into Hip Hop culture. While these artists are not without controversy and criticisms, they still carry a "Christian" title which is better than a title of "secular" or "profane" associated with artists like Tupac, DMX, Remy Ma, and Nas.

CONCLUSIONS: WHAT IS THEOLOGY & SPIRITUALITY IN HIP HOP?

when Nas appears in the video on a cross with thorns on his head. People beyond the Hip Hop community consume this and pay good money at concerts to see these artists in action. Part of the argument here is that commercialism tears down any form of grass rooted symbolism and feeling, thus creating a space reserved solely for pecuniary profit and commercial success. This is not allocated just to Hip Hop. The organic food industry, which twenty-five years ago consisted of grass root farmers and "hippie like" groups, now maintains multi-million dollar contracts with entities such as Wal-Mart, Target, and Costco. Once those corporate entities come in, the 'heart' and 'soul' of the organization is lost, and profit is the sole purpose of existence. Thus, it is the same with Hip Hop and its corporate annexation during the late 1990s and early 2000s (Drane 2000; George and National Urban League. 1990; Neal 1997; Rose 2008; Tate 2003).

Yet, Hip Hoppers in such a genre as "holy Hip Hop" are, at times, continuing the market maintenance (Miller 2013b) of Christian proselytizing. Christian rap groups such as Gospel Gangstaz and Cross Movement both openly claim a Christian religion and in many of their tracks, name "sin" and "worldly" issues while offering a strong message to those who are "lost" to come back into the "fold" with Jesus. These records, as previously noted, sell and keep the Black religious marketplace alive by creating constructions of sin, morality, immorality, and a supernatural remuneration for "wrong deeds" within their music and messages. Artists like these, though unpopular among mainstream Hip Hop artists, create a space where dogmatic mantras are reinforced through the music of Hip Hop. And while it is at the core of Hip Hop culture, it resists dominant authority. Nevertheless, many Christian rap artists appear to capitulate to religious forms of hegemony. This troubling process would be true of Christian churches which do "outreach" to the "Hip Hop generation" but only use Hip Hop as a vehicle, when at the core, the same conservative, evangelical, right-wing based, dogmatic, and authoritative spirit is still present. This is problematic—especially for a culture such as Hip Hop which espouses to be non-judgmental in so many regards—because artists such as these posit themselves as moral authorities against "sin," "worldly possessions," and "secular attitudes," which in turn create a slender path to "salvation" and "morality." It is, as Monica Miller tells us, "When religion is positioned socially and intellectually as the 'sanitizer' of 'deviant' cultural production, this conflation produces (and maintains) dominant power" (2013b, 6).[13] For some Christian Hip

---

13   Miller further argues that within these processes, "...religion becomes understood as a hegemonic, dominant, and hierarchical agent of moral maintenance and deviance management" (2013b, 6). Within these types of maintenance and deviance management sessions,

Hoppers, this has been a troubling reality; they create a type of 'moral panic' in a particular audience (such as working class urban contexts) that is already simplistic and rigid in their religious pursuits (Glock and Rodney 1965; Stark and Glock 1968; Stark 1985). However, their core, even though clothed in the style and appropriations of Hip Hop culture, is essentially of a dominant power and continues a hegemonic socio-religious supremacy.[14]

Hip Hop does not stray too far from its Black Christian church traditions. In fact, even artists such as Tupac, who raved against and challenged Black Christian narratives as too traditional, dogmatic, and rigid, fell prey to these dominant forms of religion and Tupac was at times nihilistic in his approach towards the concept of 'hope.' We must not forget that KRS-One keeps a strong connection to the tradition of the Black Christian faith and much of the call and response comes from these faith traditions. Hip Hop is not immune to simplistic theodicies which creep into a lot of Black Christian churches. Hip Hop, at times, is the perpetrator of these theodicies. With pop-Hip Hoppers[15] such as Will Smith and The Black Eyed Peas, a theodicized message of "hope" is given and "the way" for that "hope" is often through God. Yet, no real solutions are given to the conditions of the 'hood, economic inequality,

---

theodicies such as "God is always good," "there is only ONE true God," and "Avoid secular music" are troped as reality and part of a "moral lifestyle." These become embedded into religious spaces such as the Black Christian church, some sects, and the Nation of Islam. They in turn create worldviews that create strong rules, norms, and theological mores which keep individuals within religious gates and sacred canopies.

14   One of the many commodifiable uses of Hip Hop is that of religious manufacturing. Shirts with the expression "Jesus Is My Homeboy" or "These Are My Church Clothes" are all products of a Hip Hop market that, by and large, is profitable on many levels. When one considers the profits being made by senior pastors in Black Megachurches (those over five thousand members), it would stand to reason that Hip Hop would be a commodifiable product of the Black Christian church as well as take the potential form of "evangelism" and "outreach." This is part of the complexity and problematic nature of religion in the marketplace.

15   It should be noted that within Hip Hop grassroots culture, a sentiment of resentment exists for artists perceived to have sold out and gone 'pop.' Legendary group EPMD rapped about this phenomena in becoming 'pop' and 'sold out' to 'R&B.' They, and others like them (Paris, Ice-T, Tupac, MC Lyte), were against the infiltration of commercialism and pop-style. Ice-T, in his VH-1 documentary *Planet Rock*, had this to say: "Rap was a counterculture that went against pop. But when you have Rihanna singin' on your records and you're doin' records with Katy Perry, that's no longer rap. It's pop music—that is, pop using rap delivery. When you hear Lil Wayne sayin' 'I got a chopper in the car,' you go, 'Yeah, right you do.'" The frustration is palatable.

social isolation, political demoralization, and disenfranchisement of the urban communities who are buying their music. Moreover, these areas are often overlooked, in order to preserve "peace" and maintain an "optimistic" outlook on life.[16] These are similar to the teachings and general messages of "hope" given by Black preachers and are often not too far away from the five-step process for "success" and prosperity gospel troupes which often give false hope to a group of people already struggling financially. So, it stands to reason that Black pastors such as Creflo Dollar appear in Nelly videos with the backdrop of Atlanta behind them.[17] "Name it and claim it" theologies along with prosperity based notions of God wanting a person to succeed financially are tangible with Hip Hoppers who have, in essence, already "made it." In other words, it is very easy to "give God the glory" when you have a million dollars in the bank. It is not difficult to claim that "God blessed me" when life appears to be moving in a successful way. Yet, for the people whose lives are not shaping up in this manner, it is as if a double standardized message is being received. Without critical thought and inquiry, one might actually believe they are "cursed" or, even worse, living in "sin" because their life is not "working out" like the ones they see in videos and on television. Compound this with a hyper-celebrity culture present in American society, and one begins to construct a theology that presents itself as a success driven, goal attaining, financially-based system in which God only rewards those who "follow his rules" in the moral manner "he desires." Money, God, heaven, and success are all conflated into a theological narrative which often leaves out the systems, policy, and historical contexts which created the inequality in which people in urban enclaves live. Therefore, it is easy to overlook the context and geographical history of a certain location like South Central Los Angeles—which was once a bright and vibrant middle class neighborhood before it was considered to be the 'hood—and place blame for those "evils" on the "devil" while telling those who believe otherwise, that a God will deliver them and that they should have "faith" through the tough times.

---

16   This is from an observation on the music of Will Smith, The Black Eyed Peas, MC Hammer, Beyoncé, Usher, Wiz Khalifa, Drake, and Chris Brown whose music, while very popular, tends to focus more on optimistic non-critical elements of life and society. Artists such as these are often criticized by members of the Hip Hop community for being too "soft" and/or "sell-outs" to the real problems of the urban context. It is interesting to note, still, that their music sells. In the end, someone is buying this and believing, even in some miniscule manner, that their message is one of "hope."

17   Atlanta is largely known as the Black Christian church "Mecca" and big name Black preachers such as T.D. Jakes reside there as well as in their Megachurches.

We now that turn to the five central typologies of Hip Hop's theological sensibilities where we will explore further these notions of God, commercialism, and sin.

Five Central Typologies of Hip Hop's Theological Sensibilities

The dearth of theological study in Hip Hop scholarship is, by and large, in need of organization of ideas and thought. Therefore, though growing and developing, these typologies seek to contribute a sense of organization for current and future Hip Hop scholars (particularly those investigating Hip Hop and theology/religion).

First, *Hip Hoppers create their own view of God, Jesus, and church in association with suffering, pain, and inequality*. Chapter 2 through Chapter 5 demonstrated these characteristics. Yet, for the Hip Hop community, the construct of God, Jesus, Allah, Mohammed, and other forms of deity still come into question. For example, take the construct of the Black Jesus. When Notorious B.I.G. adorned his now infamous Jesus Piece (a gold diamond encrusted medallion of the Jesus image), it was a White Jesus. The question becomes why was it not a Black Jesus, one that was more contextual and relevant? After all, Hip Hop is seeking the relevant and relatable. This might suggest that even though the Notorious B.I.G. was connected with a movement that questioned moral authority, he was still very much affected and influenced by the colonialist socio-religious worldviews that dominate the Western world (e.g. White Jesus, the Bible as 'moral authority,' salvation through one's savior). Just because a rapper is attempting new endeavors does not mean that they are immune to the worldviews and theologies which preceded that new endeavor.

This was most certainly the case for DMX, Tupac, and Lauryn Hill, all of whom celebrate, arguably, a Christian God. Yet, what is a Christian God? What did the centralizing of the Christian church in Rome create sociologically, psychologically, spiritually, and philosophically? In addition, how did a normalizing of Christianity into a Western, Greco-Roman culture, make other, more contextual forms of Christianity in Northern and Central Africa outcasts because they did not fit the normalized forms of "morality?" It has been noted that Western and Central African countries were practicing indigenous forms of Christianity, ones foreign to a Roman Catholic tradition. Yet, when brought over by slave traders during the sixteenth century, they were forced to submit to a Western Euro-tribal form of Christianity (Evans 1992; Franklin and Jr 2000; Frazier and Glazer 1966). Over centuries of colonizing through 'missionary work' and the politicizing of Christian morals, this created a religious worldview that is difficult to overcome. It is, as one might say, "in the water" and we now have innumerable generations of Black and Brown individuals who—even though in spirit they may be revolutionary and object to the dominant culture—in their religion still draw from the same hegemonic structure which has oppressed many for centuries. In other words, it is difficult to tell whether Tupac is indeed claiming a "new religion" or whether it will be one still rooted in Western tradition. That said, cultural transference from one generation to the next will always have some vestiges from the previous one.

So, while Hip Hoppers do in fact create a contextualized, relevant, and applicable God for their environment, one might dispute that this "god" is any different to the one proposed by, say, Billy Graham or Pat Roberts. The Hip Hop God is more ethnically and culturally appropriate yet it still possesses the typical evangelical tropes.

Nonetheless, there is something unique about the Zulu Nation, Nation of Islam, and the Five Percenters that may possibly usher in a more relevant form of deity. Rappers like Lupe Fiasco, a proclaimed Muslim, and Jasiri X, who has ties with both the Nation of Islam and Zulu, all have a renewed approach to deity and God within the contexts of suffering and pain. It is a God that moves well beyond the Western, Greco-Roman God which has adorned Western religion for a very long time. Additionally, with post-soul contexts existing within Hip Hop, a conglomeration of Christianity, Zulu, Nation of Islam, Five Percenter, and Judaism may be on the spiritual horizon for the next generation of Hip Hoppers.

Second, *the post-soul context helps to create a climate in which to question authority, rebel from current religious standards and worldviews, and to create a new path to God and church.* Due to the fact that the post-soul context is concerned with questioning hegemonic authority, deconstructing traditional values for examination, and is about communal experience over autonomous ones, Hip Hop is a candidate for this context because it too is concerned with the deconstruction of what is defined as "normality." From the inception of Hip Hop, the central mantra has been to challenge the forces that have created tradition, norms, and established modes of thought.[18] The post-soul is crucial for Hip Hop to survive and for it to have the ability to call out the evil in chaotic social climates such as the George Zimmerman acquittal, Hurricane Katrina in New Orleans, the Los Angeles uprisings in 1992, the overthrowing of the

---

18   With this in mind, it is now possible to argue that Hip Hop has, in the commercialized sense, created a hegemonic standard which needs to be challenged and deconstructed much like early Hip Hoppers did with disco, rock, and 80s pop-music.

government in Egypt, and the rise of a democratic voice in Iraq. All of these events have a Hip Hop spirit and ethos fueling its continual deconstruction of societal norms—no matter where the geographical location may be.

This is a crucial element that makes Hip Hop one of the few cultures and musical genres (rap) that can be taken in almost any context of oppression and still be relevant and innovative. For disenfranchised people around the globe, Hip Hop becomes not only a voice and musical escape, but a movement in seeking justice, equality, and impartiality.

Interviewees Cobra, Teek, and John all recounted the strength of Hip Hop and that it in fact "saved them" from death. This was a sub-theme within all of the interviews and in my previous work as well. Hip Hop is seen as a savior, without a deity or religious dogma. Hip Hop and the mere point that it allows one's voice to be heard, acknowledged, and affirmed, is a great space/place for those who are socially oppressed and overlooked. This may be why Hip Hop is so popular globally.

Third, *the felt need from the Hip Hop community aides in creating a spiritual avenue in order to make meaning of suffering, pain, and inequality.* For many Hip Hoppers, the concept of "sin" is less of a personal one and more of a systemic and institutional ideology that is in "everything, like the Matrix" as Huck and DJ Harper told me. Suffering, pain, and inequality, therefore, are looked upon not as a "sin" concept, but as sin created from the abuse, misconduct, corruption, and spiritual desolation of those who are leaders and who are allegedly 'in charge of' and/or against their communities.

It is similar to what Lynette stated:

> I think God has a special place for those who are either knowingly or even unknowingly doing harm to God's people. I didn't create sexism, but the men who created commercials that show women as servants and sex objects did. I didn't create the job losses that so many people are experiencing now, but the greedy bankers who run the banks did…those are sins that are huge and so large…you can't put that on the people who wanted to get a loan so they could own a home and get a piece of the 'American Dream' you just can't…they were doing right; they were playing by the rules; these other cats weren't…

For Hip Hoppers, Hip Hop and rap becomes a space in which these corporate sins can be acknowledged and deconstructed. The personalization of sin and evil upon which so much of Western Christianity has built its theological constructs are done away with, and the macro sin of JP Morgan Chase Bank, Wells Fargo, Fannie Mae, AIG, and Citi Corp are examined and confronted. Further, the very essence of whose suffering is important (as discussed in Chapter 4) and whose suffering gets attention are aspects Hip Hoppers continue to place at the table of leaders of societies.[19]

Within community, there is strength. In my previous work, I looked at the strength within the community spaces of Hip Hop and found that Hip Hoppers find transcendental meaning when they find others who are suffering just like they are. The problem itself may not be resolved, yet having someone who can relate to your current struggle is a comforting thought—even more so when that person is of the same ethnic, cultural, and social background as Hip Hoppers (Hodge 2010).

Fourth, *human action is directed toward problem solving. In this case, Hip Hoppers create a way to problem solve through their music, poetry, and lyrics.* Through the fog of sexism, braggadocio postures, male dominated messages, and commercialism, Hip Hop culture, is, by the very nature of its core community, about seeking solutions to the problems of life. Often overlooked and unseen from the media's eye is the daily grind of Hip Hop organizations such as the Save The Kids Foundation, Rap Sessions, Poetry Behind Walls, the Left Of Black web series, and the Hip Hop Congress, all working toward progressive solutions which not only aid people, but also aid the communities in which they serve.

Organizations such as these have popular rappers such as Chuck D, M-1, MC Lyte, Boots Riley, Talib Kweli, Common, Mos Def, Martha Diaz, and David Banner who not only speak out against macro social inequality, but also support local community activists solving local problems. Also, while this study has been concerned with the socio-theological nature of Hip Hop, issues such as date rape, incest, alcoholism, discrimination against LGBTQ people, drug abuse, systemic racism, the classroom to prison pipeline, economic disparities, political demoralization, the privatization of prisons, urban ecology, and

---

19 Even Black leaders such as Cornel West and Jesse Jackson have come under direct fire from the Hip Hop community. Cornel West, whose *Poverty Tour* is corporately underwritten by Wells Fargo and Wal-Mart, is a hypocrisy for most Hip Hoppers who not only call out, but also challenge the very message of West and Tavis Smiley. West's multi-million dollar penthouse in Manhattan and twenty thousand dollar plus honorariums are also part of that critique from the Hip Hop community. Jesse Jackson Jr.'s recent conviction also reveals Hip Hoppers claim that their own leaders have "lost touch" with the real issues. Jack told me "It's like these mutha-fuckers have lost all touch with reality and still think we in the Hip Hop community still got love for em. Nope! How the hell you gonna talk about Black issues and you don't have the damdest clue of what being broke really is in the 21st century? You tell me that? All them gotdamn leaders are a fucking joke."

environmental racism are large issues facing not just the Hip Hop community, but those living in urban centers and who are displaced from gentrification. Issues such as the ones listed have prompted organizations like these to put pressure on rappers such as Jay Z, Kanye West, Young Jeezy, Lil Wayne, and Nikki Minaj to speak on and address the issues facing communities in which they once lived.

However, the biggest service organizations like these do for the Hip Hop community is that they problem solve in communal settings. They use the core of who and what Hip Hop is to create a voice and use political, digital, and social avenues to distribute that message. As seen through the music, the culture, and the context of where Hip Hop is conceived, the Hip Hop community, by and large, seeks to find solutions to the problems facing their community.

And, fifth, *distrust of current systems, institutions, and social structures is a part of the worldview of Hip Hoppers within a Post-soul context*. This is the undergirding cosmological mantra for the Hip Hop community. Critique, critical engagement, distrust of traditions, distrust of power structures, and the questioning of authority is what made Hip Hop a culture to begin with. Rappers, a growing civil disruption, and the societal shift over the last forty years has seen a set of musical genres emerge, such as Grunge, Punk, and underground Metal, that also question and challenge the norms set before them. The Hip Hop community is merely one of a growing number of groups that call out the "powers that be" and bring into question the very facets of what society defines as 'reality.' I would argue that Hip Hop, however, is the loudest voice and gives social, cultural, and pedagogical fuel to other groups who also call for justice, equality, and egalitarian communities.

While we have examined artists such as Pastor Troy, Tribe Called Quest, Paris, Public Enemy, and Ice Cube, who all have a distrust for systems, let me return to and highlight religious and spiritual artists such as Propaganda, Jasiri X, and Shai Linne who profess a stated faith, but also distrust parts of those institutions in which they negotiate that faith. For example, in the song "Precious Puritans," artist Propaganda gives a critique on the centuries of colonialism, White racism, and Christianity dominated by White Evangelicals who, as Propaganda asserts, damage "churches of color." He posits that if White evangelicals do not acknowledge the "bones of their past," the racial gap between Whites and people of color will "never be bridged" (Thorn 2012).

In an interview, Propaganda states:

> The song was really designed to be a bait and switch. The indictment on the puritans is really a secondary point. They were not perfect in living out their theology. They had issues just like all of us. And I'm just as much guilty as them. The *real* point is the last line, "God uses crooked sticks to

make straight lines." God uses us despite our depravity. That's the main point…I'm guilty too!

Now about the secondary point. I think we as a culture tend to romanticize the past. We tend to treat people, preacher, politicians, etc. like comic book characters. Where the good guys are ALL good and the bad guys are ALL bad. And that's just not true. Real life is nuanced. I started noticing, as I traveled more and more, that we have the tendency to pedestal those preacher/theologians we agree with, and demonize those we don't. To me it seemed like we, the good Calvinists, spoke of the puritans almost like they weren't mere men with flaws. I, personally, can't hear someone speak of that time era in history and not think of slavery. We can't take people out of their cultural context. Point being 'there is not ONE group of believers that has figured out the marriage between proper doctrine and action.' We need to remember that as we pull from our past church leaders, they aren't inerrant. They are flawed men like you and me. They are "crooked sticks" that the Lord was pleased to use for his maximum glory.[20]

Propaganda, along with other prominent Black Christian rappers, have taken a stronger role as social critics, while embracing their Hip Hop roots, within their music. This refreshing stance—while a few decades overdue—is also part of the post-soul critique of dominant forms of religion. In this interview, Propaganda is almost made to defend what he raps about. While this is not uncommon for other rappers with controversial lyrics, within evangelical Protestant circles, critiques are often seen as deviant; especially from males of color, or to be more specific, Black males. So, the song received its line of criticism etched in socio-religious rhetoric from leading evangelical voices and bloggers: "spiritually divisive" (Duren 2012,); "dangerous" (Strachan 2012); giving Puritans a "bad rap" (Beeke 2012); and creating "bad theological" ideology (Leake 2012).

Shai Linne also criticized Black and White leading evangelicals in his song "False Teachers." This track specifically named individuals who, the rapper believes, have "falsely led the Children of God," focusing on money, fame, notoriety, and economic prominence. Shai Linne goes so far as to call them "evil" and "liars." This, as one could imagine, drew criticism not just from conservative Christian evangelicals, but also progressives and liberals. The song issues a strong critique of leading Christian leaders such as T.D. Jakes, Joel Osteen, and Paula White in a manner similar to that of N.W.A., Ice-T, Tupac, and

---

20   Taken from an interview Propaganda gave after the release of "Precious Puritans" in 2012.

Public Enemy in their critiques of the presidency and political leaders. Similar to Propaganda's critics, Linne's accusers were using socio-religious discourse that ranged from "wrong messages for young Christians" to "sinful." Linne, who received a large amount of tweets, Facebook posts, and emails, decided to respond to his critics, particularly to that of Paula White—a White, female evangelical that Linne specially names as a 'false teacher.' Interestingly enough, his critics were most outspoken about his challenge to a White, blonde, attractive, successful, and prominent woman. This is noteworthy since the continued significance of race lingers inside Christian evangelical circles; it would seem Linne hit a nerve. Linne's response to this was:

> I want to address a few of the false teachings themselves. I went straight to the Paula White Ministries website and your Youtube page so I could hear what you have released as representative of Paula White's teaching. There are many things I could speak on, but I'll highlight three here.
>
> Paula White did a series called 8 Promises of the Atonement, that at the time of my writing this, is currently featured on your ministry website. In it, she states that physical healing and financial abundance in this life are provided for in the atonement of Christ. See the following video at the 25:00 mark where Paula White teaches "salvation includes healing." She says it again at 28:30. But then she goes even further. If you keep listening, she talks about commanding her body not to be sick because of the blood of Christ. She ends this section by boldly declaring around 29:40:
>
> "You are not going to die of sickness. When you go, it's going to be because of your appointed time of old age and full of life"
>
> For Paula White to say this to a large crowd of people is both false and irresponsible. She has no idea how those people are going to die. The truth is that Christians do get sick. Many godly believers die at young ages from sickness and it is not due to their lack of faith or because they haven't embraced what's theirs through the atonement. It's because God is sovereign.
>
> As He says in Deut. 32:39, "See now that I, even I, am He, and there is no god beside me; I kill and I make alive; I wound and I heal; and there is none that can deliver out of my hand."
>
> Psalm 139:14 says "All the days ordained for me were written in your book before one of them came to be."
>
> God sovereignly (sic) determines when we live and when we die. And if He appoints or allows a sickness to take our lives, it is because His infinite wisdom determined that it be so.
>
> LINNE 2013

Note Linne's Biblical references, rebuttal, and theodicy at the end, something to which Christian rap artists fall prey all too often. His response goes on for about three thousand more words and offers very little response to the Black males he identified as 'false teachers.' Still, artists such as Linne and Propaganda are a shift from the elementary messages embedded within evangelical Christian/holy Hip Hop over the last twenty years and a reconnection with Hip Hop's more militant roots.

Jasiri X, who claims faith as a Muslim, receives much more support from his Muslim community and little to no push back from those within his religious tradition—granted his music and messages do not critique his faith or Muslim background—as he focuses much of his music and messages on social, economic, educational, and gender equality. He is very grassroots and involved in social justice events such as the Troy Davis execution, the Oscar Grant killing, and the Trayvon Martin trial. Jasiri conflates his message of social action with a sense of spirituality and personal consciousness. However, he does not proselytize in his music, nor does he "call those to God" as some Christian rappers do. Instead, while distrusting hegemonic powers, he strongly urges his listeners to take action. I mention Jasiri here in the conclusion because he is underground and does not make the top ten list of albums sold, unlike for example Lil Wayne or Jay Z. He deserves mention as he continues the core of what Hip Hop culture is about and questions authority, distrusts power structures, and challenges the systems in which he and his listeners live—not only in his music, but through his lifestyle as well.

We will now look at why Hip Hop is a post-soul tenet, and its post-soul centrality.

Hip Hop's Post-Soul Centrality

Slavoj Zizek asserts beautifully that for anyone wanting to discover a true sense of reality, they must first begin with and in the 'shit of life' and to go where 'the shit starts' (2008). Hip Hop does that. It begins with the 'shit' within life in which most of the community finds itself: the 'hood. It begins with a reality that is foreign to those living outside the ghetto context and offers the essentials of doubt, nihilism, uncertainty, reservation, and a pursuit of God that is laborious—a post-soul ideology indeed.

While religious zealots[21] would have one believe that Hip Hop is completely secular and profane, Hip Hop did not create the profane nor the secular. Those

---

21   One of the largest Christian zealots is G. Craig Lewis, a Black Christian minister, who claims that all aspects of Hip Hop culture are evil and "from the Devil." Lewis even claims

elements of life and society existed long before Hip Hop arrived into our culture. Hip Hop merely picked up where others left off and speaks to a lot of the truth with irreverence. Much of what rappers rap about did not originate with Hip Hop. From the use of Christianity to enforce slavery, to the Catholic Church's silence toward Hitler during WWII, to Muslim fanatics who blow themselves up "for Allah," evil and the profane have been a part of societal contexts for a very long time. So, to look at Hip Hop as being to blame is both erroneous and incorrect.[22]

The "Hoy Profane," as Teresa Reed puts it, is a deep part of the rich religious tradition in Black popular music. Reed (Reed 2003) states that, "The relationship between sacred and secular has been a source of controversy in both the African-American and the West-European musical traditions." This controversy has roots that go back into the early nineteenth century when Blacks were developing their musical genres. Most Whites considered "Black Gospel" an abomination in the eyes of God and did not see Black Gospel music as a valid form or source of spirituality (Hustad 1981; Southern 1983). Moreover, slaves concealed their narratives and music to avoid punishment by the slave-owners and to embrace their late-night worship (Reed 2003, 17–21). Fast forward into the twentieth century and there is the emergence of blues and jazz as musical forms to which people are gravitating. However, there is a distinct line in the sand that marks the differences between what is morally "right" and "wrong." Reed further asserts, "The emergence of the blues against the backdrop of the burgeoning black church at the end of the nineteenth century further ensured

---

that rap music labeled "Christian Hip Hop" is also "Satanic" and that true Christians avoid it. This type of worldview appeals to those who 1) despise Hip Hop to begin with, 2) misunderstand Hip Hop's theological complexity, and 3) appeal to a one-source-solution type of approach to problems, conflict, and suffering. Lewis is popular and has a five DVD collection documenting his "research" on how Hip Hop (and music labeled 'worldly') is both satanic, and evil. Ironically, though, in 2012, he released his own rap as a way to fund his ministry.

22 This particular study of profane music within Black traditions is nothing new. There are many scholars that discuss this issue at length. The parameters of this book limit the scope of this section to paragraphs, but that in no way diminishes the work that has gone before it. For an in depth study, I recommend Jon Michael Spencer, ed., 1992. *Sacred Music of the Secular City: From Blues to Rap*. Vol. 6. Durham, NC: Duke University Press; Cheryl L Keyes. 2002. *Rap Music and Street Consciousness*. Chicago IL: University of Illinois Press particularly Chapters 1–4; Eileen Southern. 1983. *The Music of Black Americans*. 2nd ed. New York: W.W. Norton & Company; Christa K Dixon 1976. *Negro Spirituals: From Bible to Folk Song*. Philadelphia: Fortress Press; Howard Thurman. 1975. *The Negro Spirituals Speak of Life and Death*. Richmond, VA: Friends United Press; & Jon Michael Spencer. 1993. *Blues in Evil*. Knoxville: University of Tennessee Press.

CONCLUSIONS: WHAT IS THEOLOGY & SPIRITUALITY IN HIP HOP?

the recognition of two distinct categories of music: one that was appropriate for church use and one that was not" (2003, 9). This type of anti-worldly and secular stance continued with other musical genres/cultures such as Jazz, Blues, Rock & Roll, and the hybrid Black Gospel/blues sound established in the late 1950s.

Hip Hop and the blues, for example, are connected, as noted previously in this book. The blues speaks to a style of "living" according to Anthony Pinn. The blues, like Hip Hop, speaks to that musical form of spiritual expression and moves the individual to ponder deeply the issues of life. Pinn further states:

> The blues, then, is a recognition of the value of African Americans through their ability to shape and control language and thus a world—a world full of sarcasm and tenacious black bodies. This has been a mature depiction of life that recognizes the often absurd nature of encounter in a way that avoids nihilism and calls into question the nature of social crisis. This music teaches that life can be harsh, but these crises are not always 'unto death,' and in some cases are quite laughable...it teaches that life is survivable and more. (2003b, 6–7)

This represents an attempt to enter into the tension at much deeper levels than a traditional theology would allow most individuals to do. As a result, what blues and jazz do, through Hip Hop, is continue the "...experimentation with black orality" which is "...the hallmark of rap, taking the themes and sensibilities housed in musical expression for centuries and giving them a postindustrial twist" (Pinn 2003a, 14). This, in turn, creates post-soul discourses in Hip Hop that help establish community, non-linear thinking, and collectivist values.

Still, for many in Black church traditions, this is all too "worldly," "secular," and "not of God" because it does not fit into the prescribed tradition of how a religious person's state should be. Yet, there are contradictions when Black Christian performers and gospel artists sample Hip Hop tracks and songs, place them in their own music, and call it "Christian music." The Hip Hop community sees this, and objects to the hypocritical condition. For instance, of Kirk Franklin,[23] a Black gospel artist who has on numerous occasions used Hip Hop samples and music, Christina Zanfagna states, "But in the face of current popular culture, where aesthetics often exist for their own sake, Franklin and other holy hip-hop artists are making noble attempts to align popular black

---

23 Franklin is among the many Black gospel artists such as CC Winans, Fred Hammond, Mary Mary, and Donnie McClurkin who use rap music and elements of Hip Hop culture in their music and fashion, yet would argue that Hip Hop is both "worldly" and "secular."

aesthetics with relevant spiritual messages" (2006, 4). Moreover, Dyson states a poignant statement which embellishes the elements within the Hip Hop's theology of the profane and that is, that "It is a central moral contention of Christianity that God may be disguised in the clothing—and maybe even the rap—of society's most despised members" (2001, 209). In this disguise, Hip Hop is able to produce a relevant post-soul message of hope, aspirations to social justice, and engage with the tension between the ideal (how it is 'supposed to be') and the reality of life conditions. Dyson points out the post-soul context in which and with which Hip Hoppers are willing to live. This brings us to the neo-secular aspect of Hip Hop's theological discourse that is part of the post-soul context.

The Neo-Secular Sacred within Hip Hop
Within the gray and blurred areas between the sacred and the profane lies what I call the neo-secular sacred within Hip Hop. This concept is directly derived from my doctoral research on Tupac's Gospel message and is a concept that has loosely and indirectly been discussed by scholars such as Craig Detweiler & Barry Taylor (2003), Tom Beaudoin (1998), David Dark (2002), and John Drane (2000). The concept of the neo-secular sacred comes directly out of the theology of the profane. It is the area in which the reality of life (e.g. white lies, sexuality, hate) all come together and still find theological connections with a God who can sit with the person in those tensions—not the idealized abstraction of good intentions (e.g. change this and that then God will 'bless you'), but the day-to-day nitty-gritty of life in hostile contexts. I would contend that God, from whatever faith tradition, is able to still love and comfort the individual in this state. God is not worried about dogmatic norms nor liturgical traditions, only the heart of the individual. In this sense, it is God's very *love* of the "sinful" nature of humanity that draws God close to the person. If there were no "sin," there would be no love. After all, who wants a perfect person? There are moments in Hip Hoppers' lives when they decide to engage and embrace the profane element to life and give up any sign of being pristine and "sacred." The neo-secular sacred is exactly that—the ability to be loved in that "mess" and "funk" and to accept life as it is, yet still approach God with an "as you are" ethos rather than an attempt to "get it right" prior to engaging God. The neo-secular sacred searches for deeper meaning to life and embraces the not-so-perfect aspects to life that often seem to come up when we least expect them to. The neo-secular sacred is that fine line which exists within most people which forms the quirks, idiosyncrasies, peculiarities, oddities, "bad sides," and rough nature to urban living. In other words, without sin, there is nothing to love; with sin, we are made to be loved by God.

Inside this theological paradigm, there is the opportunity finally to be human and be authentic with yourself and your God. The neo-secular sacred within Hip Hop has existed from its inception as both a culture and musical genre. Yet, it is better revealed as the post-soul takes shape, and in artists such as Tupac who possess contradictions in their life. Hip Hop, as we have seen, has its roots in the controversial holy profane, so it should be no surprise when Hip Hoppers embrace this element of God. For Hip Hop, the neo-secular sacred begins to answer some of the questions they have regarding pain and suffering, but, at the very least, give some hope in something beyond "this life." It also allows for certain contradictions that humans possess—to flourish while they "work out" the details with God. Christina Zanfagna, again, states that "Hip-hop's spirituality—its mystical allusions, contradictory images, and profaned exterior—can be 'tricky' and elusive to the average outsider not born or 'baptized' in the streets" (2006, 3).[24]

The neo-secular sacred within Hip Hop is, overall, about a transcendent experience and finding a transcendental force in the most obscure places of life—those obscure places just happening to be "profane." Therefore, the neo-secular sacred concept has three major elements to it that help it take shape within Hip Hop:

1. *It has a panentheism manner*: the term panentheism (not pantheism[25] which is a completely different concept) (Grk. *pan*, "all," *en*, "in," and *theos*, "God") was first coined by K.C.F. Krause (1781–1832) for the view that God is in all things. This particular element of the neo-secular sacred also sees the world and God as mutually dependent for their fulfillment. In other words, God needs imperfect humans to fulfill God's ultimate *Missio Dei* (The Mission of God)—which for Hip Hoppers is largely a message of hope and peace. This means that God acknowledges the "profane" within life, yet uses it to promote that same life—because that is what is real, and the nitty-gritty. This also means that God can use anything God so chooses to use in order to broaden the message of love and peace. So, if God is in all things, then it must include the secular—or that which

---

24 Zanfagna further states, "It follows that rap music embodies the pluralism of current religious energies as well as the spiritual touchstones of hip-hop's exalted predecessors, such as James Brown's wails for black power, the 'sexual healing' of Marvin Gaye, Stevie Wonder's prophetic preaching, the meditative bedroom lamentations of Al Green and Prince's lyrics of erotic deliverance"(2006, 3–4).

25 Pantheism views God as all and all as God and also refers to the belief that all religions have some aspect of the truth; God is too big to be enclosed in any one religion.

is supposedly "devoid" of God—even the things that are not so pretty. This fits nicely into an omnipresent theological paradigm and sees God as a part of everything, including that which most people care not to talk about. Panentheism, therefore, begins to find God in the oddest places of them all: the murk, the mire, and the sludge of life; this is a key element to the neo-secular sacred theological concept.

2. *It sees life as having both good and bad elements to it*: in this view, life is seen as both evil and good; both are always present. Now, whether we choose to (or the "Cosmos" does) is yet to be determined when it comes to how we engage with good and evil. The neo-secular sacred theological concept simply argues that both are present in our lives and that all of us are capable of ultimate good and ultimate evil. When one begins to deny the other—whether it be the good or the bad—one essentially denies the self. The secular—which the Oxford dictionary defines as "Of or pertaining to the world"—is a constant within all of us unless we choose to remove ourselves from contemporary society. The neo-secular sacred is this: embracing the two conflicting, at times opposing, forces within life that make us all "tick."

3. *Rejects religionism as the only form of reaching God*: Religionism is the belief and ritualistic practice of dogmatic, rigorous, religious traditions. Religionism believes that within those rituals God is found at a higher level. Religionism is "either/or," never in between or maybe; it either is or it is not. Religionism, when practiced, produces similar outcomes for many people and while there are instances in life when religionism may produce simplistic results (albeit non-realistic), the neo-secular concept rejects it as the only way of attaining a "direct line" with God. Religionism, for many Hip Hoppers, only covers up reality and ushers in inauthentic behaviors within people. For Hip Hop, religionism explains away life, problems, hurts, hopes, dreams, systematizes God and makes God into an idolistic icon which no one can reach. Within religionism, rational answers are preferred over the ambiguous and indefinite conclusions that the neo-secular sacred concept brings. For the Hip Hopper, when religion turns systematic, rigid, and impractical, it renders itself useless and results in a drone chasing the next spiritual high.

Hip Hop has the space to open up a complex spiritual life. To this, Paul Tillich comments on religion and both its glory and perils:

> Religion opens up the depth of man's spiritual life which is usually covered by the dust of our daily life and the noise of our secular work. It gives

us the experience of the Holy, of the something which is untouchable, awe-inspiring, an ultimate meaning, the source of ultimate courage. This is the glory of what we call religion. But beside the glory lies its shame. It makes itself the ultimate and despises the secular realm. It makes its myths and doctrines, its rites and laws into ultimates and persecutes those who do not subject themselves to it. It forgets that its own existence is a result of man's tragic estrangement from his true being. It forgets its own emergency character (1959, 9).

The neo-secular sacred ultimately remembers its "emergency character" while also making room for Tillich's glory of the Holy. These two worlds coexist within most humans, causing confusion for many, denial for others, and for the very few, acceptance of who we, as humans, truly are: both fallible yet capable of great deeds.

The neo-secular sacred within Hip Hop gives much more room for individuals to expand their knowledge about God and does not constrain them within narrow religious and doctrinal boundaries. In this manner, the neo-secular sacred could possibly be a better approach to spirituality using Hip Hop as merely one of its vehicles and allowing for the yin and yang of life to flow more naturally without guilt, shame, and rules which no one can live up to.

Further Research in Hip Hop & Spirituality

If we draw no other conclusion, Hip Hop is a complex culture. It presents a host of interdisciplinary studies that would yield great results. This book is a qualitative study, and while the narrative of voices reveals much, it leaves many questions unaddressed. Questions such as:

- What are the average number of White listeners who are spiritual or religious, that listen to Hip Hop?
- Building from the previous question, what correlations might there be between race and religion within Hip Hop culture? How might racism seep into sacred text and exegetical interpretations?
- What are the spiritual uses of rap music and Hip Hop Culture among those with PTSD?
- What is the number of Satanic Hip Hoppers and what are their socio-spiritual worldviews?
- How does Hip Hop deconstruct its problems with gender, sexual identity, and sexual orientation to better support LGBTQ groups and women?

Hip Hop studies is moving beyond lyrical analysis and into methods which include ethnomethodologies, film analysis, case studies, psychologically controlled studies, and quantitative surveys. Religion and Hip Hop needs this and the subfield is, at present, still an open door for exploration and further investigations into sexuality, race/ethnicity, class, education, and politics, all within a religious tone.

While this book has presented a theomusicological study, an ethnography would yield stronger analysis and require more time in the field with artists and Hip Hoppers alike. Further, longitudinal studies would also help the field of Hip Hop and religion. As the religious landscape of the U.S. changes, one might be interested in seeking to better understand how Hip Hop's own complexity affects that religious change and whether it offers any new insight to religion as it forms. In other words, is KRS-One's claim that Hip Hop is its own religion a valid one, or simply the idealistic thoughts of a Hip Hop legend? The study of Hip Hop and religion is in its initial stages, and the years ahead will have younger students asking stronger questions and posing new challenges.

Further, with rising Hip Hop communities in Iraq, Afghanistan, Morocco, Libya, Egypt, Saudi Arabia, Nigeria, Kenya, and South Africa, further research within these contexts will be needed. We have only just started to uncover the multi-facets of popular culture in Islamic nations and the power of Hip Hop in its discourse. Artists like Jasiri X are numerous in countries like the ones just listed, yet are rarely heard of in U.S. Hip Hop contexts. U.S. Hip Hop, while large, is taking a backseat to the grassroots communities located in countries like France and the United Kingdom. As more female Muslim activists arise, rap will be central to those movements and the study of those movements and rhetoric will be crucial to better understand the facets within them. There is also a growing number of scholars from Ghana, Nigeria, and Niger who are undertaking research regarding the commercialism and sexuality of Hip Hop within their context. These will be powerful studies from non-Western voices who can attest to the weaknesses and strengths of Hip Hop culture in localities around the world.

While this book had its delimitations of region, number of artists interviewed, time restraints, and budget, it still presents a study that is needed not only in the field of Hip Hop studies, but in the critical study of religion. While Hip Hop studies in general tends to be seen as jovial, non-academic, 'popular,' and without scholarly merit (although this view is changing as more work is published with academic merit), and is often overlooked and misjudged as being a passing fad, it still needs multiple voices to help shape its tone and academic weight. Much like the idea of film studies during the late 1970s and

CONCLUSIONS: WHAT IS THEOLOGY & SPIRITUALITY IN HIP HOP?

early 1980s as being a questionable field of study, Hip Hop studies is emerging as an academic contender and I would imagine that within the next decade, majors will be constructed around this field, as it presents a multidisciplinary approach to understanding and comprehending a host of issues. Hence, this book has added a much needed voice to this field.

Additionally, in the changing climate of Higher Education, Hip Hop studies presents not just a popular field to study, but one that is practical and feasible for students where they can receive project-based pedagogy while engaging with something to which they are already listening. The socio-religious aspect of Hip Hop will further one's educational pursuits by examining the various intricacies of the profane, sacred, and secular with Hip Hop as its lens. Further, emphasis on practical knowledge and the practical application of theoretical models is made easier through Hip Hop pedagogical models which includes areas of S.T.E.M. (Emdin 2007 2008, 2015; Hill 2013; Petchauer 2012). Hip Hop Studies also contributes to the field of business, with its wide array of entrepreneurialism.

My hope is that this volume will add a richness not only to the field of Hip Hop studies, but to the ever growing sub-field of Hip Hop and religion. Emerging scholars will need to push past lyrical analysis, in the same way that film and media scholars push past plot analysis, and give breadth to the ever changing religious and social landscape of Hip Hop. Once again, this study has concerned itself with just over 8,500 songs. Its timespan is between 1987–2011, and it contains interviews from those in the Hip Hop community. It uses Spencer's theomusicological methodology as a framework of analysis. Nevertheless, the field of Hip Hop and religion remains vast and complex, and future researchers could concern themselves with studying trends, themes, and cultural memes which are spiritually and theologically infused within the Hip Hop context. KRS-One's thesis—that Hip Hop is its own religion and spirituality—has the potential for inquiry and investigation to examine the validity of his claim. The commodification of deity and social manufacturing of religion in the Hip Hop marketplace also remains open to study, along with the connections to Black Christian religion and the ever growing prosperity Gospel. Rap artists such as Mase, DMX, DMC, and Curtis Blow (who have all claimed an aspect of Black Christianity) deserve their religious and spiritual inquiry as well. This book has briefly touched on the commodification and commercialism associated with Black Christianity, which has deep roots in Hip Hop culture. More importantly, Islamic, Zulu Nation, Five Percenter, and Gnostic spiritual belief systems are an open field of study within the field of Hip Hop and religion. Converge these studies with gender performativity and that offers a formidable and new direction for the research.

Hip Hop is more than a culture and form of music; it is a lifestyle. My other hope is that this volume will aid the broader academic community in seeing Hip Hop as much more than a music culture with loud, obnoxious, misogynic males who care for nothing more than their economic and sexual glorification. While those are most definitely aspects of the culture, Hip Hop is so much more, and the hope is that this volume has helped to distinguish the complexity that is the Hip Hop culture.

APPENDIX 1

The Source Magazine's Top 100 Rap Albums

- A Tribe Called Quest – Low End Theory
- A Tribe Called Quest – People's Instinctive Travels and the Paths of Rhythm
- A Tribe Called Quest – Midnight Marauders
- Above the Law – Livin' Like Hustlers
- Beastie Boys – License to Ill
- Beastie Boys – Paul's Boutique
- Big Daddy Kane – Long Live the Cane
- Big Daddy Kane – It's a Big Daddy Thing
- Biz Markie – Goin' Off
- Black Moon – Enta Da Stage
- Black Sheep – A Wolf in Sheep's Clothing
- Bone Thugs and Harmony – Creepin' On Ah Come Up (EP)
- Boogie Down Productions – Criminal Minded
- Boogie Down Productions – By All Means Necessary
- Brand Nubian – All For One
- Chill Rob G – Ride the Rythm
- Common Sense – Resurrection
- Cypress Hill – Cypress Hill
- Cypress Hill – Black Sunday
- Das EFX – Dead Serious
- De La Soul – Three Feet High and Rising
- De La Soul – De La Soul Is Dead
- Diamond D – Stunts, Blunts and Hip-Hop
- Digable Planets – Reachin'...
- Digital Underground – Sex Packets
- DJ Quick – Quick Is the Name
- D.O.C. – No One Can Do It Better
- Doug E. Fresh – World's Greatest Entertainer
- Dr. Dre – The Chronic
- Eazy E – Eazy Does It
- Eric B. and Rakim – Paid in Full
- Eric B. and Rakim – Follow the Leader
- Eric B. and Rakim – Let the Rythm Hit'Em
- EPMD – Strictly Business
- EPMD – Unfinished Business

- EPMD – Business as Usual
- Fugees – The Score
- Gang Starr – Step In The Arena
- Gang Starr – Daily Operation
- Genius/GZA – Liquid Swords
- Geto Boys – Grip It! On That Other Level
- Heavy D & The Boyz – Livin' Large
- Ice Cube – AmeriKKKa's Most Wanted
- Ice Cube – Death Certificate
- Ice T – Original Gangster
- Jazzy Jeff and the Fresh Prince – He's the DJ, I'm The Rapper
- Jay-Z – Reasonable Doubt
- Jungle Brothers – Straight Out The Jungle
- Jungle Brothers – Forces Of Nature
- Just Ice – Kool and Deadly
- Kool G Rap and DJ Polo – Road To Riches
- KRS One – Return Of the Boom Bap
- LL Cool J – Radio
- LL Cool J – Bigger and Deffer
- LL Cool J – Mama Said Knock You Out
- Lord Finesse – Funky Technician
- Main Source – Breakin' Atoms
- MC Lyte – Lyte as a Rock
- MC Shan – Down By Law
- Mobb Deep – The Infamous
- Naughty By Nature – Naughty By Nature
- Nas – Illmatic
- Nice and Smooth – Nice and Smooth
- Notorious B.I.G. – Ready to Die
- Notorious B.I.G. – Life After Death
- NWA – Straight Outta Compton
- Ol'Dirty Bastard – Return to the 36 Chambers
- Onyx – Bacdafucup
- Organized Confusion – Stress: the Extinction Agenda
- Outcast – ATLiens
- Pete Rock and CL Smooth – Mecca and the Soul Brother
- Pharcyde – Bizzare Ride…II Pharcyde
- Poor Righteous Teachers – Holly Intellect
- Public Enemy – Yo! Bum Rush the Show
- Public Enemy – It Takes A Nation Of Millions To Hold Us Back

- Public Enemy – Fear Of a Black Planet
- Queen Latifah – All Hail the Queen
- Raekwon – Only Built For Cuban Linx
- Redman – Whut Thee Album
- Roots – Do You Want More?
- Roots – Illadephalflife v.3
- Run DMC – Run DMC
- Run DMC – Raising Hell
- Salt N Pepa – Hot, Cool and Vicious
- Scarface – Mr. Scarface is Back
- Schooly D – Saturday Night: the Album
- Slick Rick – The Great Adventures Of Slick Rick
- Smif N Wessun – Da Shinin'
- Snoop Doggy Dogg – Doggystyle
- Souls Of Mischief – 93 Till' Infinity
- Special Ed – Youngest In Charge
- Spice 1 – Spice 1
- Stestasonic – On Fire
- 3rd Bass – Cactus Album
- Too Short – Born To Mack
- Tupac – Me Against The World
- Ultramagnetic MC's – Critical Beatdown
- Whodini – Escape
- Wu-Tang Clan – Enter the Wu-Tang
- X-Clan – To the East Backwards

APPENDIX 2

Top 25 List Generated from Interviewees of Hip Hop Theologically Influenced Artists

1. Tupac Amaru Shakur
2. Ice Cube
3. Nas
4. Snoop Lion (Formerly known as Snoop Dogg)
5. Kanye West
6. Kendrick Lamar
7. Macklemore
8. Eminem
9. Pastor Troy
10. Remy Ma
11. DMX
12. Rev Run
13. Jay Z
14. Lil Wayne
15. 50 Cent
16. Common
17. Mos Def
18. Talib Kweli
19. Lupe Fiasco
20. Lauryn Hill
21. Lecrae
22. Notorious B.I.G.
23. T.I.
24. Mase
25. Propaganda

Bibliography

1998. 100 Best Albums & Artists. *The Source Magazine: The Magazine of Hip Hop Music, Culture, & Politics*

Alim, H. Samy. 2006. *Roc the mic right: the language of hip hop culture*. New York, NY: Routledge.

Alper, Garth. 2000. "Making sense out of postmodern music?" *Popular Music and Society* no. 24 (4):1.

Althaus-Reid, Marcella. 2000. *Indecent Theology: Theological Perversions in Sex, Gender, and Politics*. New York, NY: Routledge.

Althaus-Reid, Marcella. 2004. *From feminist theology to indecent theology: readings on poverty, sexual identity and God*. London: SCM Press.

Arnal, William E. McCutcheon Russell T. 2013. *The sacred is the profane: the political nature of "religion."* New York, NY: Oxford University Press.

Barkun, Michael. 1997. *Religion and the racist right: the origins of the Christian Identity movement*. Rev. ed. Chapel Hill: University of North Carolina Press.

Battle, Michael. 2006. *The Black church in America: African American Christian spirituality, Religious life in America; Variation: Religious life in America*. Malden, MA: Blackwell.

Bauman, Zygmunt. 1998. "Postmodern Religion?" In *Religion, Modernity, and Postmodernity*, edited by Paul Heelas, 55–78. Oxford, UK; Malden, MA: Blackwell.

Beaudoin, Tom. 1998. *Virtual Faith: The Irreverent Spiritual Quest of Generation X*. San Francisco, CA: Jossey Bass.

Beeke, Joel. *Propaganda: Giving the Puritans a Bad Rap* [Website] 2012 [cited 7/10/2013]. Available from http://www.joelbeeke.org/2012/10/propaganda-giving-the-puritans-a-bad-rap/.

Belton, David. 2010. *God In America*. New York, NY: Corporation for Public Broadcasting (PBS).

Bennett, Lerone. 1993. *The Shaping of Black America*. New York NY: Penguin Books.

Best Steven, Douglas Kellner. 1991. *Postmodern Theory: Critical Interrogations*. New York NY: Guiliford Press.

Betts, Raymond. 2004a. *A History of Popular Culture: More of Everything, Faster, and Brighter*. New York NY: Routledge.

Betts, Raymond F. 2004b. *A history of popular culture: more of everything, faster, and brighter*. New York, NY: Routledge.

Block, Fred, Anna C Korteweg, Kerry Woodward, Zach Schiller, and Imrul Mazid. 2006. "The Compassion Gap in American Poverty Policy." *Contexts* no. 5 (2):14–20.

Boyd, Todd. 1997. *Am I Black Enough For You? Popular Culture from the 'Hood and Beyond.'* Bloomington & Indianapolis: Indiana University Press.

Boys, Scarface & The Geto. 1991. Mind Playin' Tricks on Me. In *We Can't Be Stopped*. New York, NY: Virgin Records.

Burgess, Omar. 2013. Yeezus Saves: Kanye West, Black Power & Consumerism. *Hip Hop DX*, http://www.hiphopdx.com/index/editorials/id.2126/title.yeezus-saves-kanye-west-black-power-consumerism.

Bush, George. 2005. Transcript: President Bush's Speech on the War on Terrorism. In *FDCH/e-Media*. Washington, D.C.: The Washington Post.

Bynoe, Yvonne. 2004. *Stand & Deliver: Political Activism, Leadership, and Hip Hop Culture*. Brooklyn, NY: Soft Skull Press.

Caramanica, Jon. *Behind Kanye's Mask* [Web newsprint]. The New York Times 2013 [cited July 9, 2013]. Available from http://www.nytimes.com/2013/06/16/arts/music/kanye-west-talks-about-his-career-and-album-yeezus.html?pagewanted=all&_r=0.

Carter, J. Kameron. 2008. *Race: A theological account*. New York, NY: Oxford University Press.

Chang, Jeff. 2006. *Total chaos: the art and aesthetics of hip-hop*. New York, NY: Basic-Civitas Books.

Charnas, Dan. 2010. *The Big Payback: The History of the Business of Hip-Hop*. New York, NY: New American Libriary.

Coe, Kevin, and David Domke. 2006. "Petitioners or Prophets? Presidential Discourse, God, and the Ascendancy of Religious Conservatives." *Journal of Communication* no. 56:309–330.

Cone, James. 1990. *A Black Theology of Liberation*. 20th ed. Maryknoll, NY: Orbis Books.

Cone, James. 1992. "The Blues: A Secular Spiritual." In *Sacred Music of the Secular City: From Blues to Rap*, edited by Jon Michael Spencer, 68–97. Durham, NC: Duke University Press.

Cone, James H. 1991. *The Spirituals and the Blues: An Interpretation*. Maryknoll, New York: Orbis Books.

Cone, James H. 1997a. *Black Theology and Black Power*. 5th ed. Maryknoll NY: Orbis Books.

Cone, James H. 1997b. *God of the Oppressed*. Maryknoll NY: Orbis Books.

Costen, Melva Wilson. 1991. "Protest and Praise: Sacred Music of Black Religion By Jon Michael Spencer Minneapolis, Fortress, 1990." *Theology Today* no. 48 (3):360–362. doi: 10.1177/004057369104800317.

Covert, Tawnya Adkins. 2003. "Consumption and Citizenship During the Second World War." *Journal of Consumer Culture* no. 3 (November 1, 2003):315–342.

Cox, Harvey. 1965. *The Secular City: A Celebration of its Liberties and an Invitation to its Discipline*. New York: The Macmillan Company.

Cox, Harvey. 1984. *Religion In The Secular City: Toward A Postmodern Theology*. New York: Simon & Schuster Inc.

Craig, Detweiler, and Barry Taylor. 2003. *A Matrix of Meanings: Finding God in Pop Culture*. Grand Rapids MI: Baker Academic.

Cube, Ice. 1994. My Skin in My Sin. In *Bootlegs & B-Sides*. Los Angeles, CA: Priority Records.

Cunningham, Lawrence S, and John Kelsay. 2010. *The Sacred Quest: An Invitation to the Study of Religion*. 5 ed. Upper Saddle River, NJ: Prentice Hall; Pearson.

Cupitt, Don. 1998. "Post-Christianity." In *Religion, Modernity, and Postmodernity*, edited by Paul Heelas, 218–232. Oxford, UK; Malden, MA: Blackwell.

Darity, William A., Jr. 2008. "Ethnomusicology." In *International Encyclopedia of the Social Sciences*, edited by William A. Darity, Jr., 19–20. Detroit: Macmillan Reference USA.

Dead Prez (Stic Man & M-1). 2000. They Schools. In *Let's Get Free*. New York, NY: Relativity Records.

Drane, John William. 2000. *The McDonaldization of the church: spirituality, creativity, and the future of the church*. London: Darton Longman & Todd.

Duren, Marty. 2013. *African-American Responses to Propaganda's 'Precious Puritans'* 2012 [cited 7/6/2013 2013]. Available from http://www.martyduren.com/2012/10/02/african-american-responses-to-propagandas-precious-puritans/.

Durkheim, Émile. 1965. *The elementary forms of the religious life. Uniform Title: Formes élémentaires de la vie religieuse. English, Free Press paperbacks;.* New York: Free Press.

Dyson, Michael Eric. 1996. *Between God and Gangsta Rap: Bearing Witness to Black Culture*. New York: Oxford University Press.

Dyson, Michael Eric. 2001. *Holler if you Hear Me: Searching for Tupac Shakur*. New York: Basic Civitas.

Dyson, Michael Eric. 2003. *Open Mike: Reflections on Philosophy, Race, Sex, Culture, and Religion*. New York, NY: Basic Civitas.

Dyson, Michael Eric. 2005a. *Is Bill Cosby right?: or has the Black middle class lost its mind?* New York, NY: Basic Civitas Books.

Dyson, Michael Eric. 2005b. *Is Bill Cosby Right? Or Has The Black Middle Class Lost Its Mind?* New York, NY: Basic Civitas Books.

Edwards, Herbert O. 1975. "Black theology: retrospect and prospect." *Journal of Religious Thought* (32):46–59.

Emdin, Christopher. 2007 "Exploring the contexts of Urban science Classrooms: Part 2—The role of rituals in communal practice." *Cultural Studies of Science Education* no. 2 (2):351–373.

Emdin, Christopher. 2008. "The Three C's for Urban Science Education." *Phi Delta Kappan* no. 89 (19):772–775.

Emdin, Christopher. 2015. "Affiliation and Alienation: Hip hop, rap and urban science education." *Journal of Curriculum Studies* no. In Press.

Epstein, Heidi. 2001. "Re-vamping the Cross: Diamanda Galas's Musical Mnemonic of Promiscuity." *Theology and Sexuality* no. 8 (15):45–65. doi:10.1177/135583580100801505.

Esposito, John L., ed. 1999. *The Oxford history of Islam*. New York, NY: Oxford University Press.

Evans, James E. 1992. *We Have Been Believers: An African American Systematic Theology*. Minneapolis: MN: Fortress Press.

Fanon, Frantz Farrington Constance. 1968. *The wretched of the earth, An Evergreeen black cat book*. New York: Grove Press.

Faulkner, Sandra L. 2007. "Concern With Craft: Using Ars Poetica as Criteria for Reading Research Poetry." *Qualitative Inquiry* no. 13 (2):218–234. doi:10.1177/1077800406295636.

Forman, Murray. 2002. *The 'Hood Comes First: Race, Space, and Place in Rap and Hip-Hop, Music/culture;*. Middletown, Conn.: Wesleyan University Press.

Franklin, John Hope, and Alfred A Moss Jr. 2000. *From Slavery to Freedom: A History of African Americans*. 8 ed. Boston, New York, San Francisco, St Louis: Mc Graw Hill.

Frazier, Franklin E, and Nathan Glazer. 1966. *The Negro Family in the United States*. Chicago, Ill: University of Chicago Press.

Freire, Paulo. 2000. *Pedagogy of the oppressed*. Translated by Myra Bergman Ramos. 30th anniversary ed. New York: Continuum.

Fuller, Jennifer. 2010. "Branding blackness on US cable television." *Media, Culture & Society* no. 32 (2):285–305. doi: 10.1177/0163443709355611.

George, Nelson. 1992. *Buppies, B-boys, Baps & Bohos: notes on post-soul Black culture*. 1st ed. New York: Harper Collins Publishers.

George, Nelson. 1998a. *Hip hop America*. New York: Viking.

George, Nelson. 1998b. *Hiphop America*. New York: Penguin Books.

George, Nelson. 2004. *Post-soul nation: the explosive, contradictory, triumphant, and tragic 1980s as experienced by African Americans (previously known as Blacks and before that Negroes)*. New York, NY: Viking.

George, Nelson, and National Urban League. 1990. *Stop the violence: overcoming self destruction*. New York: Pantheon Books.

Gilkes, Cheryl Townsend. 2012. "Jesus must needs go through Samaria: Disestablishing The Mountains of Race and The Hegenomy of Whiteness." In *Christology and Whiteness: What Would Jesus Do?*, edited by George Yancy, 59–74. New York, NY: Routledge.

Gilmour, Michael J. 2009. *Gods and guitars: seeking the sacred in post-1960s popular music*. Waco, TX: Baylor University Press.

Giroux, Henry A. 1996. "Towards a Postmodern Pedagogy." In *From Modernism to Postmodernism: An Anthology*, edited by Lawrence Cahoone, 687–697. Malden, MA: Blackwell Publishers.

Glock, Charles Y., and Stark Rodney. 1965. *Religion and society in tension, Rand McNally sociology series;*. Chicago, Ill: Rand McNally.

Gutiérrez, Gustavo. 1987. *On Job: God-talk and the suffering of the innocent/Uniform Title: Hablar de Dios desde el sufrimiento del inocente. English.* Maryknoll, N.Y.: Orbis Books.

Hall, Staurt. 1998. "What Is This 'Black' in Black Popular Culture?" In *Black Popular Culture*, edited by Michele Wallace and Gina Dent, 21–33. New York, NY: Dia Center for the Arts, The New Press.

Hart, William David. 2012. "Jesus, Whiteness, and the Disinherited" In *Christology and Whiteness: What Would Jesus Do?*, edited by George Yancy, 156–168. New York, NY: Routledge.

Harvey, Jennifer. 2012. "What Would Zacchaeus Do?" In *Christology and Whiteness: What Would Jesus Do?*, edited by George Yancy, 84–100. New York, NY: Routledge.

Hayes, Kelly E. 2011. *Holy Harlots: Femininity, Sexuality, & Black Magic in Brazil*. Berkeley, CA: University of California Press.

Hazleton, Lesley. 2013a. The Doubt Essential to Faith. In *TED Talks*. Edinburgh, Scotland.

Hazleton, Lesley. 2013b. *The first Muslim: the story of Muhammad*. New York: Riverhead Books.

Heelas, Paul, ed. 1998. *Religion, Modernity, and Postmodernity, Religion and Modernity*. Oxford, UK; Malden, MA: Blackwell.

Hempton, David. 2008. *Evangelical disenchantment: nine portraits of faith and doubt*. New Haven, CT: Yale University Press.

Heyward, Carter 1999. *Saving Jesus From Those who are Right: Rethinking what it Means to be a Christian*. Minneapolis: Fortress Press.

Hill, Marc Lamont. 2013. *Schooling Hip-Hop: expanding Hip-Hop based education across the curriculum*. New York: Teachers College, Columbia University.

Hine, Darlene Clark, William C Hine, and Stanley Harrold. 2010. *The African American Odyssey*. 4 ed. Vol. 1. New Jersey Prentice Hall.

Hodge, Daniel White. 2009. *Heaven Has A Ghetto: The Missiological Gospel & Theology of Tupac Amaru Shakur*. Saarbrucken, Germany: VDM Verlag Dr. Muller Academic.

Hodge, Daniel White. 2010. *The Soul Of Hip Hop: Rimbs, Timbs and a Cultural Theology*. Downers Grove, Ill.: Inner Varsity Press.

Hodge, Daniel White. 2013a. "No Church in The Wild: An Ontology of Hip Hop's Socio-Religious Discourse in Tupac's 'Black Jesuz.'" *Nomos* no. 10 (March 23, 2013):1–5.

Hodge, Daniel White. 2013b. "No Church in the Wild: Hip Hop Theology & Mission." *Missiology: An International Review* no. XL:4 (4):1–13.

Hodge, Daniel White. 2015. "Hip Hop's Prophetic: Exploring Tupac and Lauryn Hill using Ethnolifehistory." In *Religion in Hip Hop ('the volume')*, edited by Monica Miller, Bernard "Bun B" Freeman and Anthony B. Pinn. London, UK: Bloomsbury Academic.

Hughes, Richard T. 2003. *Myths Americans Live By*. Champaign, Il: University of Illinois.

Hurt, Byron. 2006. Hip Hop: Beyond Beats & Rhymes. USA: Media Education Foundation.

Hustad, Donald Paul. 1981. *Jubilate: Church Music in the Evangelical Tradition*. Carol Stream, Ill: Hope Publishing Company.

Iverem, Esther. 1997. "The Politics of 'Fuck It' and the Passion to be A Free Black." In *Tough Love: The Life and Death of Tupac Shakur*, edited by Michael Datcher and Kwame Alexander, 41–47. Alexandria, VA: Black Words Books.

Jay, David, and Crane Elaine Forman. 1971. *Living Black in white America*. New York: Morrow.

Jones, William R. 1973. *Is God a white racist? A preamble to Black theology*. [1st] ed, C. Eric Lincoln series on Black religion; Variation: C. Eric Lincoln series in Black religion. Garden City: N.Y., Anchor Press.

Jospeh, Jamal. 2006. *Tupac Shakur: Legacy*. New York, NY.: Atria Books.

Jr, Martin Luther King. April 15, 1960. Christian Theology for Today. In *King Collection*. Raleigh, NC: Crozer Theological Seminary.

Kain & Abel, & Master P. 1996. *Black Jesus*: The 7 Sins: Priority Records.

Kant, Immanuel. 1997. "Physical Geography." In *Race and Enlightenment: A Reader*, edited by Emmanuel Chukwudi Eze. Malden, MA: Blackwell.

Kärkkäinen, Veli-Matti. 2003. *Christology: a global introduction*. Grand Rapids, MI: Baker Academic.

Kelley, Robin D.G. 1994. *Race rebels: Culture, Politics, and the Black Working Class*. New York Free Press, Toronto.

Kirk-Duggan, Cheryl A. 2009. "The Theo-poetic Theological Ethics of Lauryn HIll and Tupac Shakur." In *Creating Ourselves: African Americans and Hispanic Americans on Popular Culture and Religious Expression*, edited by Anthony B. Pinn and Benjamín Valentín, 204–223. Durham, NC.: Duke University Press.

Kirk-Duggan, Cheryl, and Marlon Hall. 2011. *Wake Up! Hip Hop Christianity and The Black Church*. Nashville, TN: Abingdon Press.

Kirk, J. Andrew. 2000. "Following Modernity and Postmodernity: A Missiological Investigation." *Mission Studies* no. 17 (1):217–239.

Kitwana, Bakari. 2005. *Why White Kids Love Hip-Hop: Wankstas, Wiggers, Wannabes, and the New Reality of Race in America*. New York: Basic Civitas Books.

Kreitzer, L. Joseph. 1993. *The New Testament in Fiction and Film: On Reversing the hermeneutical Flow, Variation: The biblical seminar; 17*. Sheffield: JSOT Press.

Kreitzer, L. Joseph. 1994. *The Old Testament in Fiction and Film: On Reversing the Hermeneutical Flow, The Biblical seminar ;; 24;*. Sheffield: Sheffield Academic Press.

Lamar, Kendrick. 2010. The Heart Pt. 2. In *Overly Dedicated*. Los Angeles, CA: Top Dawg Entertainment.

Lash, Scott. 1990a. "Postmodernism as Humanism? Urban Space and Social Theory." In *Theories of Modernity and Postmodernity*, edited by Bryan S. Turner, 45–61. Thousand Oaks CA: Sage Publications.

Lash, Scott. 1990b. *Sociology of Posmodernism*. New York NY: Routledge.

Leake, Mike. *One Thing That Disturbs me about Propaganda's Song 'Precious Puritans'* [BLOG] 2012 [cited 7/15/2013]. Available from http://sbcvoices.com/one-thing-that-disturbs-me-about-propagandas-song-precious-puritans/.

Leeuw, Gerdardus Van der. 1963. *Religion in Essence and Manifestation*. 2 vols. Vol. 2. New York, NY: Harper and Row.

Leonard, Neil. 1987. *Jazz: myth and religion*. New York: Oxford University Press.

Lincoln, Eric C., and Lawrence H. Mamiya. 1990. *The Black Church in the African American Experience*. Durham & London: Duke University Press.

Linne, Shai. *Shai Linne Responds to Paula White Ministries' Open Letter* [Internet Radio] 2013 [cited 8/8/2013]. Available from http://wadeoradio.com/shai-linne-responds-to-paula-white-ministries-open-letter/.

Long, Charles H. 1987. Popular Religion. In *The Encyclopedia of Religion*, edited by Mircea Eliade. New York, NY: Macmillan.

Lynch, Gordon. 2005. *Understanding Theology and Popular Culture*. Malden, MA: Blackwell Publishing.

MacDonald, Scott, and Michael Viega. 2013. "Hear Our Voices: A Music Therapy Songwriting Program and the Message of the Little Saints through the Medium of Rap." In *Therapeutic Uses of Rap and Hip-Hop*, edited by Susan Hadley and George Yancy, 153–172. New York, NY: Routledge.

Malone, E.F. 2003. Kerygmatic Theology. In *New Catholic Encyclopedia*. Detroit: Gale.

Martin, C.F., Nas, and DJ Premier. 1994. N.Y. State of Mind. In *Illmatic*: Columbia Records.

Matusitz, Jonathan. 2013. *Terrorism & Communication: A Critical introduction*. Thousand Oaks, CA: Sage.

McRobbie, Angela. 1995. "Recent rhythms of sex and race in popular music." *Media, Culture & Society* no. 17 (2):323–331. doi: 10.1177/016344395017002011.

Miles, Jack. 2001. *Christ: A Crisis in the Life of God*. New York: Alfred A. Knopf.

Miller, Monica. *Commentary: It's Time to Be Honest with Lauryn Hill* [Op Ed]. BET Online 2013a. Available from http://www.bet.com/news/national/2013/05/21/commentary-it-s-time-to-be-honest-with-lauryn-hill.html.

Miller, Monica R. 2013b. *Religion and Hip Hop*. New York, NY: Routledge.

Miller, Monica, and Christopher Driscoll. 2013. *AAR Critical Approaches to Hip-Hop and Religion Group CFP* 2013 [cited June 12 2013]. Available from http://papers.aarweb.org/content/critical-approaches-hip-hop-and-religion-group.

Moltmann, Jürgen. 1990. *The way of Jesus Christ: Christology in messianic dimensions*. 1st Harper Collins ed. San Francisco, CA: Harper San Francisco.

Morgan, Joan. 1999. *When chickenheads come home to roost: my life as a hip-hop feminist*. New York: Simon & Schuster.

Moss, Otis. 2007. "Real Big: The Hip Hop Pastor as Postmodern Prophet." In *The Gospel Remix: Reaching The Hip Hop Generation*, edited by Ralph Watkins, 110–138. Valley Forge, Pa.: Judson Press.

Murray, Charles. 1984. *Losing Ground: American Social Policy, 1950–1980*. New York, NY: Basic Books.
Nas. 1994. The World Is Yours. In *The Illmatic*. New York, NY: Columbia Records.
Nation, Zulu. 2010. Zulu Nation Doctrines. In *Zulu Nation Pedagogy*. New York, NY.
Neal, Mark Anthony. 1997. "Sold out on soul: The corporate annexation of Black Popular Music." *Popular Music and Society* no. 21 (3):117.
Neal, Mark Anthony. 1999. *What the Music Said: Black Popular Music and Black Public Culture*. New York: Routledge.
Neal, Mark Anthony. 2002. *Soul Babies: Black Popular Culture and the Post-Soul Aesthetic*. New York: Routledge.
Neal, Mark Anthony. 2005. *New Black man*. New York, NY: Routledge.
Nelson, George. 2007. *Where Did Our Love Go? The Rise and Fall of the Motown Sound*. 2 ed, *Music in the American Life*. Chicago, Ill: University of Illinois Press.
Nouwen, Henri J.M. 1989. *In The Name of Jesus: Reflections on Christian Leadership*. New York, NY: The Crossroad Publishing Company.
Odum, Howard W. 1968. *The Negro And His Songs: A Study of Typical Negro Songs in the South*. 306 vols. Westport, Conn.: Negro Universities Press.
Ogunnaike, Lola. 2006. West World. *Rolling Stone*, February 9.
Oliver, William. 2006. "The Streets." *Journal of Black Studies* no. 36 (6):918–937. doi: 10.1177/0021934704273445.
One, KRS. 2003. *Ruminations*. New York: Welcome Rain Publishers.
One, K.R.S. 2009. *The gospel of hip hop: first instrument*. 1st ed. Brooklyn, NY: powerHouse Books: I Am Hip Hop.
Otto, Rudolph. 1950. *The Idea of the Holy*. 2nd ed. London, England: Oxford University Press.
Outlawz, Tupac and The. 1999. Black Jesuz. In *Still I Rise*. Los Angeles, CA: Interscope Records.
Paris, Peter J. 1985. *The Social Teaching of the Black Churches*. Philadelphia, PA: Fortress Press.
Petchauer, Emery. 2012. *Hip-hop culture in college students' lives: elements, embodiment, and higher edutainment*. London: Routledge.
Peters, Ken. 2001. Tupac Vs. DVD, USA: Dennon Entertainment.
Pineda-Madrid, Nancy. 2001. "In Search of a Theology of Suffering, Latinamente." In *The Ties That Bind: African American and Hispanic American/Latino/a Theologies in Dialogue*, edited by Anthony B Pinn and Benjamin Valentin, 187–199. New York, NY: Continuum.
Pinkney, Alphonso. 2000. *Black Americans*. 5 ed. Upper Saddle River, NJ: Prentice Hall.
Pinn, Anthony B. 1995. *Why Lord? Suffering and Evil in Black Theology* New York: Continuum.

Pinn, Anthony B. 2001. "Black Theology in Historical Perspective: Articulating the Quest for Subjectivity" In *The Ties That Bind: African American and Hispanic American/Latino/a Theologies in Dialogue*, edited by Anthony B Pinn and Benjamin Valentin, 23–35. New York, NY: Continuum.

Pinn, Anthony. 2002. *The Black Church in the Post-Civil Rights Era*. Maryknoll, NY: Orbis Books.

Pinn, Anthony, ed. 2003a. *Noise and Spirit: The Religious and Spiritual Sensibilites of Rap Music*. New York: New York University Press.

Pinn, Anthony B. 2003b. *Terror & Triumph: The Nature of Black Religion*. Minneapolis, MN: Fortress Press.

Pinn, Anthony. 2010. *Embodiment and the New Shape of Black Theology, Religion, Race, and Ethnicity*. New York, NY: New York University Press.

Pinn, Anthony B. 2012. *The end of God-talk: an African American humanist theology*. New York: Oxford University Press.

Planets, Digable. 1993. Rebirth of Slick [Cool Like Dat]. In *Reachin' (A New Refutation of Time and Space)*: Pendulum Records.

Potter, Russell A. 1995. *Spectacular Vernaculars: Hip-Hop and the Politics of Postmodernism*. New York: State University of New York Press/Sunny Series.

Powery, Luke A. 2009. *Spirit Speech: Lament and Celebration in Preaching*. Nashville, TN: Abington Press.

Quest, A Tribe Called. 1990. Youthful Expression. In *People's Instinctive Travels and the Paths of Rhythm*, New York, NY: Jive Records.

Quinn, Eithne. 2005. *Nuthin' but a "G" thang: The Culture and Commerce of Gangsta rap, Popular cultures, everyday lives;*. New York: Columbia University Press.

Rah, Soong-Chan. 2009. *The next evangelicalism: releasing the church from Western cultural captivity*. Downers Grove, Ill.: IVP Books.

Reed, Stephen A. 1991. "Exodus By Terence E. Fretheim Louisville, Westminster/John Knox Press, 1991." *Theology Today* no. 48 (3):362–366. doi: 10.1177/004057-369104800318.

Reed, Teresa L. 2003. *The Holy Profane: Religion in Black Popular Music*. Lexington, KY: The University Press of Kentucky.

Roof, Wade Clark. 2009. "American Presidential Rhetoric from Ronald Reagan to George W. Bush: Another Look at Civil Religion." *Social Compass* no. 56 (2):286–301. doi: 10.1177/0037768609103363.

Rose, Tricia. 1994. *Black Noise: Rap Music and Black Culture in Contemporary America*. Middletown CT.: Wesleyan University Press.

Rose, Tricia. 2008. *The hip hop wars: what we talk about when we talk about hip hop—and why it matters*. New York, NY: Basic Civitas.

Said, Edward W. 2003. *Orientalism*. 25th Anniversary ed. New York, NY: Vintage Books.

Seay, Davin Neely Mary. 1986. *Stairway to heaven: the spiritual roots of Rock 'n' roll, from the King and Little Richard to Prince and Amy Grant*. 1st ed. New York: Ballantine Books.

Sharpley-Whiting, T. Denean. 2007. *Pimps up, ho's down: hip hop's hold on young Black women*. New York, NY: New York University Press.

Shenk, Wilbert R. 2001. *Write The Vision: The Church Renewed, Christian Mission and Modern Culture*. Eugene, OR: Wipf and Stock Publishers.

Singleton, Micah. 2015. *To Pim a Butterfly: Kendrick Lamar's new album is perfect* [Hip Hop music Blog]. Vox Media 2015 [cited 5/28/2015 2015]. Available from http://www.theverge.com/2015/3/19/8257319/kendrick-lamar-album-review-to-pimp-a-butterfly.

Slobin, Mark, and Jeff Todd Titon. 1984. "The Music-Culture as a World of Music." In *Worlds Of Music: An Introduction to the Music of the World's Peoples*, edited by Jeff Todd Titon, James T Koetting, David P McAllester, David B Reck and Mark Slobin, 1–11. New York: Schirmer Books.

Smith, Rogers M. 2008. "Religious Rhetoric and the Ethics of Public Discourse." *Political Theory* no. 36 (2):272–300. doi: 10.1177/0090591707312447.

Song, Choan-Seng. 1979. *Third-Eye Theology: Theology in Formation in Asian Settings*. Maryknoll, NY: Orbis Books,.

Southern, Eileen. 1983. *The Music of Black Americans*. 2nd ed. New York: W.W. Norton & Company.

Spady, James G., Sammy Alim H., and Meghelli Samir. 2006. *Tha Global Cipha: Hip Hop Culture and Consciousness*. Philadelphia, PA: Black History Museum Press.

Spencer, Jon Michael. 1990. *Protest & praise: sacred music of Black religion*. Minneapolis: Fortress Press.

Spencer, Jon Michael, ed. 1991a. *The Emergency of Black and the Emergence of Rap*. Vol. 5, *Black Sacred Music: A Journal of Theomusicology*. Durham, NC: Duke University Press.

Spencer, Jon Michael. 1991b. *Theological Music: An Introduction to Theomusicology, Contributions to the Study of Music and Dance*. New York, NY: Greenwood Press.

Spencer, Jon Michael. 1992a. "Book Notes Rapsody in Black: Utopian Aspirations." *Theology Today* no. 49 (2):283–289. doi: 10.1177/004057369204900224, 10.1177/004057-369204800407.

Spencer, Jon Michael, ed. 1992b. *Sacred Music of the Secular City: From Blues to Rap*. Vol. 6. Durham, NC: Duke University Press.

Spencer, Jon Michael. 1995. *Sing a new song: liberating Black hymnody*. Minneapolis: Fortress Press.

Spencer, Jon Michael. 1997. *The new Negroes and their music: the success of the Harlem Renaissance*. 1st ed. Knoxville: University of Tennessee Press.

Stapert, Calvin. 2000. *My only comfort: death, deliverance, and discipleship in the music of Bach, Calvin Institute of Christian Worship liturgical studies series; Variation:*

Calvin Institute of Christian Worship liturgical studies series. Grand Rapids, Mich.: W.B. Eerdmans.

Stark, Rodney Bainbridge Sims. 1985. *The future of religion: secularization, revival and cult formation*. Bekerley, Los Angeles, London: University of california press.

Stark, Rodney, and Charles Y Glock. 1968. *American Piety*. Berkeley, CA: University of California Press.

Strachan, Owen. 2013. *Reflecting on Porpaganda's Fiery "Precious Puritans" Rap Song* [Blog] 2012 [cited 7/8/2013 2013]. Available from http://owenstrachan.com/2012/09/26/reflecting-on-propagandas-fiery-precious-puritans-rap-song/.

Sullivan, Lawrence Eugene. 1997. *Enchanting powers: music in the world's religions, Religions of the world; Variation: Religions of the world (Cambridge, Mass.)*. Cambridge, Mass.: Distributed by Harvard University Press for the Harvard University Center for the Study of World Religions.

Sumiala, Johanna. 2013. *Media and Ritual: Death, Community, and Everyday Life*. Edited by Stewart M Hoover, Jolyon Mitchell and David Morgan, *Media, Religion, and Culture*. New York, NY: Routledge.

Sylvan, Robin. 2002. *Traces of The Spirit: The Religious Dimensions of Popular Music*. New York, NY: New York University Press.

Tate, Greg. 2003. *Everything but the burden: what white people are taking from Black culture*. New York, NY: Broadway Books.

Taylor, Paul C. 2007. "Post-Black, Old Black." *African American Review* no. 41 (4):625–640.

Thorn, Joe. 2012. *Precious Puritans* 2012 [cited 8/5/2013 2012]. Available from http://www.joethorn.net/blog/2012/09/25/precious-puritans-pt-2.

Thugs-N-Harmony, Bone. 1995. Crossroads. In *E 1999 Eternal*. Los Angeles, CA: Ruthless Records.

Thurman, Howard. 1976. *Jesus and The Disinherited*. Boston, MA: Beacon Press.

Tilley, Terrence. 1984. "The Uses and Abuses of Theodicy." *Horizons* no. 11:304–319.

Tilley, Terrence. 1991. *The Evils of Theodicy*. Washington, DC: Georgetown University Press.

Tillich, Paul. 1959. *Theology of Culture*. New York: Oxford University Press.

Tocqueville, Alexis de. 1998. *Democracy In America*. Translated by Henry Reeve, Francis Bowen (Revision) and Patrick Renshaw (Introduction). Edited by Tom Griffith, *Wordsworth Classics of World Literature*. Ware, Hertfordshire: Wordsworth Editions Limited.

Townes, Emilie. 1993. *Womanist Justice, Womanist Hope*. Atlanta, GA: Scholars Press.

Troy, Pastor. 2001. Vice Versa. In *Face Off*. Atlanta, GA: Uptown, Unive Rsal Records.

Trulear, Harold Dean, and N. Lynne Westfield. 1994. "Theomusicology and Christian Education: Spirituality and The Ethics of Control in the Rap of MC Hammer." *Theomusicology: A Special Issue of Black Sacred Music: A Journal of Theomusicology* no. 8 (1):218–238.

Tuman, Joseph S. 2010. *Communicating Terror: The Rhetorical Dimensions of Terrorism*. 2 ed. Thousand Oaks, CA: Sage.

Tyson, Edgar H. 2013. "Hip-Hop Healing: Rap Music in Grief Therapy with and African American Adolescent Male." In *Therapeutic Uses of Rap and Hip-Hop*, edited by Susan Hadley and George Yancy, 293–306. New York, NY: Routledge.

Utley, Ebony A. 2012. *Rap and Religion: Understanding the Gangsta's God*. Santa Barbara, CA: Praeger.

Utley, Ebony. 2013. Kanye West's Yeezus May Be Sexist but is not Blasphemous. http://www.rapandreligion.com/yeezus/.

Valentín, Benjamín. 2009. "Tracings: Sketching The Cultural Geographies of Laino/a Theology." In *Creating Ourselves: African Americans and Hispanic Americans on Popular Culture and Religious Expression*, edited by Anthony B. Pinn and Benjamín Valentín, 38–61. Durham, NC.: Duke University Press.

Walls, Andrew F. 1996. *The missionary movement in Christian history: studies in the transmission of faith*. Maryknoll, N.Y.: Orbis Books: Edinburgh.

Walls, Andrew F. 2002. *The cross-cultural process in Christian history: studies in the transmission and appropriation of faith*. Maryknoll, N.Y.: Orbis Books.

Washington, James. 1986. *Frustrated Fellowship: The Black Baptist Quest for Social Power*. Macon, GA: Mercer University Press.

Watkins, S. Craig. 2005. *Hip hop matters: politics, pop culture, and the struggle for the soul of a movement*. Boston, MA: Beacon Press.

Watkins, Ralph Basui. 2011. *Hip-Hop Redemption: Finding God in the Rhythm and the Rhyme, Engaging Culture*. Grand Rapids, MI: Baker Academic.

Webb, Gary. 1998. *Dark alliance: the CIA, the Contras, and the crack cocaine explosion*. Seven Stories Press 1st ed. New York: Seven Stories Press.

Wells-Barnett, Ida B. 1969. *On lynchings: Southern horrors, A red record, Mob rule in New Orleans, The American Negro, his history and literature; Variation: American Negro, his history and literature*. New York: Arno Press.

Wells-Barnett, Ida B. DeCosta-Willis Miriam. 1995. *The Memphis diary of Ida B. Wells, Black women writers series; Variation: Black women writers series*. Boston: Beacon Press.

Wells-Barnett, Ida B. Alfreda Duster. 1970. *Crusade for justice: the autobiography of Ida B. Wells, Negro American biographies and autobiographies; Variation: Negro American biographies and autobiographies*. Chicago: University of Chicago Press.

West, Cornel. 1990. "The New Cultural Politics of Difference." In *Out There: Marginalization and Contemporary Culture*, edited by Russell Ferguson, 19–36. Cambridge MA: MIT Press.

West, Cornel. 1993. *Prophetic Thought in Postmodern Times: Beyond Eurocentrism and Multiculturalism*. Vol. 1. Monroe ME: Common Courage Press.

West, Kanye. 2004. Jesus Walks. In *The College Dropout* New York, NY: Roca Fella Records.

West, Traci C. 2012. "When A White Man-God is The Truth and The Way for Black Christians." In *Christology and Whiteness: What Would Jesus Do?*, edited by George Yancy, 114–127. New York, NY: Routledge

White, Russell Christopher. 2002. *Constructions of Identity and Community in Hip-Hop Nationalism with Specific Reference to Public Enemy and Wu-Tang Clan*. Ph.D. dissertation, University of Southampton (United Kingdom).

Wilder, Amos N. 1999. *Early Christian rhetoric: The language of the Gospel*. Peabody, MA: Hendrickson Publishers.

Wise, Tim J. 2008. *White Like Me: Reflections on Race From A Privileged Son*. Rev. and updated. ed. Brooklyn, NY Berkeley, Calif.: Soft Skull Press ; Distributed by Publishers Group West.

Wuthnow, Robert. 1988. *The restructuring of American religion: society and faith since World War II, Studies in church and state; Variation: Studies in church and state*. Princeton, N.J.: Princeton University Press.

Yinger, J. Milton. 1957. *Religion, society, and the individual; an introduction to the sociology of religion*. New York: Macmillan.

Zanfagna, Christina. 2006. "Under the Blasphemous W(RAP): Locating the 'Spirit' in Hip-Hop." *Pacific Review of Ethnomusicology* no. 12:1–12.

Zizek, Slavoj. 2008. *In defense of lost causes*. New York, NY: Verso.

Index

African American 9n14, 12n21, 15n27, 19n38, 20, 30, 32n1, 34n7, 36n13, 37n14, 38, 38n15, 40, 44n27, 97n7, 99n11, 101n16, 151, 153n3, 164, 194, 195
African American Humanism 19
Alim, Samy 56n6, 62, 130
Anger 2, 27, 39, 70, 81, 96, 97n7, 114, 128, 145, 163
A Tribe Called Quest 50, 57–62, 65, 67, 68, 71, 72n30, 190

Badu, Erykah 160, 164
Battle, Michael 36, 42, 150
Berry, Chuck 34
Blacks 2, 31, 60, 95, 117, 149, 182
Black Youth 11, 18n35, 36n11, 45, 76, 83, 127
Bone Thugs-N-Harmony 57, 73–77, 77n37, 139
Brand Nubian 50, 57, 139
Brooklyn 63, 149

Carter, J. Kameron 70n28, 159n11
Chang, Jeff 9, 32n1, 44, 45n29, 58n8
Chicago 32, 33, 35n8, 9, 145, 149, 194n22
Christian(s) 8, 31, 58, 100, 125, 150, 178
Christian Hip Hop 15n28, 182, 182n12, 194n21
Christianity 5, 14n24, 36, 40, 43, 60, 63, 70n28, 73, 74n35, 83n48, 110, 112, 112n48, 120, 131n18, 133n21, 138, 144n38, 149, 150, 152, 152n2, 153n3, 154, 155, 165, 166, 173, 181, 182, 186–188, 190, 194, 196, 201
Cipher 28, 55n4, 56
Common 2, 17, 22, 31, 34, 43, 58n9, 74n34, 81, 144n35, 160, 181n10, 189
Cone, James 4, 5n8, 17, 49n36, 102, 109, 110, 150, 152, 164, 166n20, 167
Cox, Harvey 49, 99, 179
The Cypher 52–94, 174, 176

Detweiler, Craig 49, 196
Devil 4n7, 23, 70, 73, 75, 76n37, 77, 77n37, 78, 83, 84, 84n49, 89, 95, 103, 127, 132–134, 132n20, 155n7, 156, 162, 185, 193n21
Digable Planets 57, 62–68, 68n21–23, 71, 72n30

DMX 16, 21, 128, 152n2, 181n10, 182n12, 186, 201
Dogg, Snoop 73, 131n18, 181, 182
Doubt 40, 51, 54, 90, 91, 91n62, 103, 107, 163, 167, 168, 177, 178, 178n3, 193
Dr. Dre 73, 87, 142, 182

Elements of Hip Hop 10, 28, 50–52, 87, 147n42, 195n23
Emdin, Christopher 201
Eschatology 27
Ethnicity 47, 62, 151, 152, 164, 200
Evangelical Christians 15, 64n19, 125, 191–193
Evans, James 36, 42, 164, 165, 186
Evil 4, 10, 11, 17, 18, 21, 25, 73, 74, 74n35, 77, 77n37, 87, 89, 95, 96n4, 99, 102, 103, 105, 113, 118, 120, 123n9, 131, 132, 132n20, 134, 142, 155n7, 156, 158, 165, 170, 180, 185, 187, 188, 191, 193n21, 194, 194n21, 198

Fanon, Frantz 5n8, 121n8
Five Percenter 12n21, 154, 160, 165, 187, 201
Franklin, Kirk 195

George, Nelson 2n2–4, 9, 26, 30, 32n1, 35, 35n8, 40, 44, 58, 99n13, 173, 183
Geto Boys 18, 50, 120, 131, 134–137, 135n24, 139, 152n2, 162
The Ghetto 5, 6, 6n10, 23, 24, 28, 29, 36n13, 39, 43, 44n24, 49, 51, 72n30, 76, 95, 96, 98, 101, 101n16, 103, 105n27, 107, 108, 110–114, 110n42, 112n48, 113n48, 127, 131, 142, 159, 162, 166n20, 167, 169, 171–173, 176, 193
Gilkes, Cheryl Townsend 153
Giroux, Henry 137
God 1, 31, 53–95, 116, 150, 175

Hegemonic 5, 6, 8, 11, 13, 21, 49, 51, 99, 117, 126, 127, 131, 132, 139, 141, 165, 166n20, 21, 167, 177, 183n13, 184, 187, 187n18, 193
Hegemony 43, 48, 183
Heyward, Carter 5n8, 24, 83n48, 160
Hill, Lauryn 2n5, 12, 31, 90–94, 120, 139, 152n2, 160, 181n10, 186, 201
Hill, Marc Lamont 201

INDEX

Hip Hop Community 2, 8, 15, 16, 23–30, 27n49, 54n2, 59, 61n14, 62, 66n20, 68, 69, 71n29, 72, 73, 76, 85, 90, 91, 94, 96, 107n33, 114, 116, 117, 120, 121, 128, 130–132, 134, 136, 137, 141, 143, 145–147, 152, 154, 156, 158, 160–172, 174, 177–179, 179n4, 180n6, 181–183, 181n9, 185n16, 186, 188, 189n19, 190, 195, 201
Hip Hop Culture 3, 6–14, 8n13, 16, 17n33, 20, 28, 30–53, 55, 56n6, 68, 69, 85, 94, 96, 97, 98n8, 117n4, 118, 121, 128, 147n42, 155, 162n16, 163, 165n19, 166, 176, 182n12, 183, 184, 189, 193, 193n21, 194, 195n23, 199–202
The Hip Hop Jesuz 51, 148, 176
Hip Hoppers 13, 14n23, 15, 16, 19, 20, 23, 25–28, 30, 37n13, 41, 45, 46, 49, 50, 52, 54, 55, 57–59, 62, 66, 66n20, 68, 69, 73n33, 75, 77, 78, 78n40, 81, 87, 89, 94, 95, 107n33, 112n48, 117, 119–121, 121n7, 127, 131, 13un18, 132n19, 134, 136, 141n29, 143, 144n36, 145, 148, 152, 156, 159, 160n12, 161, 163, 164, 164n17, 166, 166n20, 172, 174–176, 178, 179, 181–190, 181n10, 187n18, 189n19, 196–200
Hip Hop Studies 1n1, 9, 9n15, 13, 27n50, 29, 97n8, 157n10, 176, 176n1, 200, 201
Hip Hop Theology 8, 12n21, 14n22, 15, 15n28, 18, 19n38, 24, 175, 180, 181
Hodge, Daniel White 2n3, 2n4, 5, 12, 17, 37n14, 40–43, 46, 56n5, 58, 79, 96, 96n2, 98n8, 98n9, 99n13, 100, 102, 103n21, 107n33, 110, 111, 113n48, 49, 117n1, 130, 130n17, 160n12, 166, 180n5, 189
'Hood 5, 30, 32–41, 51, 59, 83, 85, 86n52, 88n56, 96–99, 103, 106–108, 106n33, 110, 112, 134, 142, 143n34, 158, 159, 160n12, 165–167, 169, 171, 172, 184, 185, 193
Hostility 22–27, 174

Ice Cube 10n18, 50, 57, 62n16, 82–86, 86n52, 87, 120, 121, 127, 135n24, 142, 144n35, 162, 165, 166n19, 190
Ice T 50, 62n16, 68, 121, 131, 135n24, 140–142, 148, 184n15, 191

Jakes, T.D. 103, 185n17, 191
Jasiri X 89n58, 187, 190, 193, 200
Jay Z 1, 14, 57, 59, 77, 77n38, 152n2, 157, 182n12, 190, 193
Jeezy, Young 190

Jesus 7, 49n36, 70, 97, 121, 149–174, 176
Jesuz 29, 51, 106, 113n48, 114, 148–174, 176
Johnson, Andre 12, 27n50

Kant, Immanuel 151n1
Kitwana, Bakari 2n3, 9, 14, 26, 32n1
KRS-One 1, 2n5, 7n11, 16, 26, 30, 31, 70n29, 142, 144n35, 144n37, 145n39, 148, 160n13, 161n15, 175, 177, 181n10, 184, 200, 201
Kweli, Talib 22–24, 189

Lamar, Kendrick 16, 57, 77n38, 86–90, 164
Lament 38, 109n40, 110, 111, 145, 167–169
Lecrae 181n10, 182
LGBTQ 1n1, 85, 85n51, 86n52, 93, 189, 199
Linne, Shai 182, 190–193
Los Angeles 32, 33, 35, 35n9, 37n14, 39, 43n24, 44, 54, 82, 82n45, 88, 118, 145, 158, 180n5, 185, 187

Master P 131
Miller, Monica 12, 13, 27n50, 56, 59n10, 87, 88, 93, 138, 167, 169, 169n22, 176n1, 177, 183, 183n13
Moralism 110, 161
Mos Def 1, 22, 58n9, 116, 121, 139, 144n35, 144n36, 189
Mythology 101, 123, 150, 160

Nas 53n1, 54, 54n2, 57, 68–73, 114, 157, 160, 182, 182n12, 183
Nation of Islam 10n18, 27, 55, 58, 62n15, 70n28, 83–85, 84n49, 50, 127, 144, 146, 165, 184n13, 187
Nation, Zulu 10n18, 14n25, 58, 60, 60n13, 62n15, 83, 144, 154, 160, 161n14, 187, 201
Neal, Mark Anthony 9, 9n14, 40, 41, 41n18, 43, 46, 51n38, 87, 89, 99n13, 183
Neo-secular sacred 21, 196–199
New Ecclesiology 27
New York 18n35, 32n1, 33, 35n8, 63, 79, 194n22
Nigga 24, 46, 50, 53, 58, 71, 82n43, 88, 98, 100, 104, 104n23, 105–107, 107n34, 109, 112, 119, 120, 127–130, 132, 133, 135–137, 146, 148, 158, 167, 170, 172, 173
N.W.A 2n5, 58n9, 73, 82, 82n43, 120, 191

Oakland 32, 35n9, 43n24
Osteen, Joel 191

The Outlawz 106, 106n28, 113n50, 129, 160n12, 166–174

Pain 2, 5–7, 10, 21, 26, 28, 56, 62n15, 69, 74, 83, 90, 91, 96, 97, 97n7, 98n10, 101, 104, 105, 105n26, 106, 108–111, 114, 115, 118–121, 121n8, 123, 126–131, 131n18, 134, 136, 138, 145–148, 147n42, 156, 159, 161, 167–169, 171, 176–178, 180, 186–188, 197
Pinn, Anthony 9–11, 15n27, 17, 19, 19n38, 20, 36n12, 42, 73, 96n4, 5, 99n13, 103, 105n26, 112n47, 119, 121, 139, 152, 153, 166n20, 167, 176n1, 195
Post modern 2, 2n4, 6, 10n16, 41n19, 43n22, 48, 49, 49n37, 50–52, 137, 139, 160
Postmodernism 2n4, 10n16, 32, 40, 47–52
Post-soul 2, 6, 26–28, 32, 40–47, 49, 50, 52, 85, 86, 89, 96, 96n4, 5, 97, 99–108, 110, 113–114, 141, 159, 163, 172–174, 176, 177, 187, 190, 191, 193–199
Post-soul centrality 193–199
Premier, D.J. 53n1, 57, 72n30
Propaganda 22, 182, 190–193, 191n20
Public Enemy 10, 31, 46n32, 50, 61n14, 143, 144, 144n37, 148, 190, 192

Race 3, 5n8, 10, 41, 46, 75, 79, 80, 85, 85n51, 86n52, 100n14, 105, 107n35, 121n7, 148–174, 176, 192, 199, 200
Rage 27, 96, 127
Rah, Soong-Chan 70n28, 150, 151n1, 153, 154
Rap lyrics 117, 118
Rap music 9, 11, 14, 15, 17, 21, 26–28, 32n1, 46n32, 48n33, 50, 51, 53, 55–57, 64n19, 82, 86, 89, 102, 127, 143, 144n37, 145, 147n42, 194n21, 22, 195n23, 197n24, 199
Restoration 36, 50
Rock, Pete 57, 69, 69n26, 27
Rose, Tricia 9, 32, 58, 87, 117, 127, 143n34, 183
RZA 57, 70n28, 121, 138, 139

Satan 76, 133
Scarface 18, 57, 69, 134–136, 138, 139
Self-awareness 16n32, 31, 44, 50, 58, 62, 63, 68, 85
Shakur, Tupac 2n5, 5, 11–12, 23, 28, 30, 57, 94–115, 166, 176
Sho Baraka 182
Smooth, C.L. 57

Snoop Lion 73, 87, 131n18, 144n35
Social conditions 10n17, 24, 28, 29, 31–40, 52, 59, 68, 94, 117, 121, 159
Spencer, Jon Michael 3, 10, 17n34, 18, 21, 25, 54n2, 81, 119n6, 146, 166, 167, 169, 173, 194n22
Suffering 5–7, 10, 11, 21, 23, 26–28, 49n36, 56, 56n5, 72, 73, 74n34, 76, 77, 78n40, 83, 101, 109, 115–148, 150, 152n2, 156, 156n8, 159, 167, 168, 171, 173, 174, 176–180, 186–189, 194n21, 197

Teleology 51
Theomusicological 12, 27, 28, 56n5, 94, 200, 201
Theomusicology 10, 21, 26, 54n3, 56, 62, 98, 132n19, 166, 175
Thurman, Howard 109, 112, 149, 151, 152, 194n22
Transmediated 72, 114, 134, 141–147
Tribe Called Quest 50, 57–62, 65, 67, 68, 71, 72n30, 190
Troy, Pastor 131–134, 132n19, 134n23, 146n40, 178, 182, 190
Tupac's Gospel 108–113, 196

Utley, Ebony 12–14, 27n50, 56, 58, 77, 79–81, 134, 156, 156n8, 157n9, 10, 159, 167, 170–172
Utopia 51

Wayne, Lil 31, 159, 173, 174, 182n12, 184n15, 190, 193
West, Cornel 9, 40, 47–49, 173, 189n19
Western Christianity 120, 154, 155, 188
West, Kanye 15, 69, 77–87, 152n2, 155
White
  Jesus 13, 84n50, 121n7, 144, 147, 150, 152, 167, 186
  people 43, 83, 96n6, 117, 153
World War II 32, 34–36, 41, 136

Young people 40, 42, 43, 60, 68n22, 145
Youth 3, 11, 14, 16, 18n35, 36n11, 40, 41, 44, 45, 51, 60, 61, 62n15, 63, 63n18, 65, 76, 83, 99n11, 117, 127, 132, 140, 169

Zanfagna, Christina 12, 17, 18, 27n50, 49, 55, 74n34, 79, 131, 167, 195, 197, 197n24

www.ingramcontent.com/pod-product-compliance
Lightning Source LLC
Chambersburg PA
CBHW070134080526
44586CB00015B/1681